THE HEART OF THE LOTUS SUTRA

The Heart of the Lotus Sutra

LECTURES ON THE "EXPEDIENT
MEANS" AND "LIFE SPAN" CHAPTERS

Daisaku Ikeda

World Tribune
Press

Published by World Tribune Press
606 Wilshire Blvd.
Santa Monica, CA 90401

Cover and interior design by Gopa & Ted2, Inc.

ISBN: 978-1-932911-88-6

LCCN: 2013949522

10 9 8 7 6 5

Contents

THE "LIFE SPAN" CHAPTER VERSE SECTION

Editor's Note

THE HEART OF THE LOTUS SUTRA brings together in one volume SGI President Ikeda's lectures on the "Expedient Means" and "Life Span" chapters. These lectures originally appeared in the *World Tribune* from May 19, 1995, through April 5, 1996, and were published those same years as a three-volume work titled *Lectures on the "Expedient Means" and "Life Span" Chapters of the Lotus Sutra.*

This work provides a line-by-line explanation of the key prose section of the "Expedient Means" chapter and the prose and verse sections of the "Life Span" chapter. Nichiren Daishonin taught that the Lotus Sutra's core teachings were contained in these sections, and he often urged his followers to recite them as a way to supplement their chanting of Nam-myoho-renge-kyo.

He never specified a format for such recitations, however, and the format evolved over the centuries. At the time these lectures were first published, the liturgy included all three sections: an excerpt from the "Expedient Means" chapter, the prose section of the "Life Span" chapter and the verse section of the "Life Span" chapter. SGI members recited these sections five times in the morning and three times in the evening.

In 2002, SGI adopted the current format for gongyo, which no longer includes the prose section of the "Life Span" chapter and reduced the number of recitations to once in the morning and once in the evening. The change was made for two main reasons: (1) to allow members to concentrate on their primary practice, chanting Nam-myoho-renge-kyo; and (2) to simplify the practice and make it more accessible to people all around the world.

Though SGI members no longer recite the prose section of the "Life Span" chapter, we have included in this volume all the original lectures because of their invaluable content. We also have left the original language that may refer to SGI members' recitation of the prose section, adding notes for clarity as necessary.

We have divided the book into three main sections: "Expedient Means" chapter, "Life Span" chapter prose section and "Life Span" chapter verse section. Each section begins with an introductory chapter and is followed by the pertinent sutra passages. We've numbered each passage for easy reference.

In the years since these lectures originally appeared, new translations of the Lotus Sutra and Nichiren's writings have been published. We've updated the text accordingly. For frequently cited works, we provide the following abbreviated citations in the text:

- GZ, page number(s)—refers to the *Gosho zenshu*, the Japanese-language compilation of letters, treatises, essays and oral teachings of Nichiren Daishonin.

- LSOC, page number(s)—refers to *The Lotus Sutra and Its Opening and Closing Sutras*, translated by Burton Watson (Tokyo: Soka Gakkai, 2009).

- OTT, page number(s)—refers to *The Record of the Orally Transmitted Teachings*, translated by Burton Watson (Tokyo: Soka Gakkai, 2004).

- WND, page number(s)—refers to *The Writings of Nichiren Daishonin*, vol. 1 (WND-1) (Tokyo: Soka Gakkai, 1999) and vol. 2 (WND-2) (Tokyo: Soka Gakkai, 2006).

Impressions of My Mentor's State of Life

To THIS DAY, memories of my mentor, Josei Toda, lecturing on the Lotus Sutra come vividly to mind, each like a scene in a great painting.

After World War II, the Soka Gakkai was in a state of ruin as a result of the campaign of suppression waged against it by the militarist government. At that time, Mr. Toda, later to become the second Soka Gakkai president, began efforts to reconstruct the organization by delivering lectures on the Lotus Sutra to a handful of members.

I was a participant in the seventh series of lectures he gave, which began on September 13, 1948. That was in the autumn of my twenty-first year. The venue was the old Soka Gakkai Headquarters in Nishi-Kanda, Tokyo.

"I see that everyone's arrived," he began. There were fifty to sixty people present. President Toda, his eyes sparkling behind his glasses, gazed around the meeting place, which consisted of two small rooms. Then he cleared his throat and began lecturing in a frank manner.

I was instantly awestruck, electrified by the profound ideas, the great and intense confidence, the compassionate cry of concern for the world and humankind that seemed to gush from his very being.

President Toda would never make things deliberately difficult or complex. His lectures were clear, straightforward and easy to understand. Yet they glowed with the light of extremely profound truth.

They conveyed philosophy rooted directly in life experience and in the Law that pervades the infinite universe. They were filled with breathtaking drama and joyous music. At one point, as I listened to him speak, the sun seemed to rise in my heart, and everything became brilliantly illuminated before my eyes.

That night, still filled with the thrill I felt during the lecture, I wrote a poem in the pages of my journal:

> *How I marvel at the greatness and profundity of the*
> *Lotus Sutra.*
> *Isn't it the path to salvation for all humankind?*
> *The teaching that enlightens one to the origin of life and the*
> *universe,*
> *The fundamental principle revealed to enable all people*
> *to acquire the loftiest character and happiness.*
>
> *I am twenty-one years old.*
> *Since setting out on my journey of life, what did I contemplate,*
> *what did I do, what did I make the wellspring*
> *of my happiness?*
> *From this day on, I will advance bravely.*
> *From this day on, I will live resolutely.*
> *I will live within the life of the Great Law, win over my*
> *sufferings.*
> *True sadness inspires one to lead a great life.*
> *I now see the true Great Path and perceive the true*
> *nature of life.*

Astonished at his profundity and breadth of knowledge, someone once asked President Toda, "When did you study these things?"

Smiling warmly, he replied: "While in prison during the persecution, I chanted Nam-myoho-renge-kyo sincerely and I studied. As a result, these things seem to have come back to me. The eighty thousand sutras, in fact, refer to my own life."

These lectures arose from the vast state of life of President Toda, who had awakened to the essence of Buddhism while in prison.[1]

The Lotus Sutra of the Former, Middle and Latter Days

Later, President Toda developed the format for his lectures on the Lotus Sutra. He instituted beginners' classes on the "Expedient Means" and "The Life Span of the Thus Come One" chapters specifically for those who had recently taken faith.

His lectures, so brilliant and full of conviction, planted the essence of Buddhism in the hearts of his listeners, without their even being aware of it. For these persons new to faith, many of whom thought of Buddhism only in terms of Shakyamuni, President Toda began each series of lectures by emphasizing that the Lotus Sutra is expressed differently according to the age—depending on whether it is the Former, Middle or Latter Day of the Law.

President Toda used to say:

> Everyone usually assumes that the Lotus Sutra indicates the twenty-eight-chapter text by that name. But there are in fact three kinds of Lotus Sutra.
>
> The first is the Lotus Sutra of Shakyamuni. This is the twenty-eight-chapter sutra of that name; this Lotus Sutra benefited people during Shakyamuni's lifetime and during the Former Day of the Law. Now, in the Latter Day, however, even if you should carry out the [Former Day] practices of reading and reciting this sutra and copying it out, you will gain no benefit thereby. Our use of the "Expedient Means" and "Life Span" chapters for morning and evening recitation, however, has a different significance.

The Lotus Sutra of the Middle Day of the Law is T'ien-t'ai's *Great Concentration and Insight*.

The Lotus Sutra for the Latter Day is Nam-myoho-renge-kyo, the seven-character Lotus Sutra hidden in the depths of the "Life Span" chapter. You need to understand that there are three kinds of Lotus Sutra and how they are related to one another.

In addition to these, there is another Lotus Sutra that was recognized alike by Nichiren Daishonin, Shakyamuni, T'ien-t'ai and Dengyo; this is the twenty-four-character Lotus Sutra taught by Bodhisattva Never Disparaging.

Shakyamuni of India taught the twenty-eight-chapter Lotus Sutra for those alive during his lifetime and in the Former Day. T'ien-t'ai of China expounded *Great Concentration and Insight* for human beings of the Middle Day of the Law. And Bodhisattva Never Disparaging taught the so-called twenty-four-character Lotus Sutra for the people of the Middle Day of the Buddha called Awesome Sound King.

President Toda explained that despite differences in the age and the form in which the teaching was expressed, these are all in fact the same Lotus Sutra. President Toda called the Lotus Sutra as thus conceived the "manifold Lotus Sutra."

The Lotus Sutra, therefore, is not simply the Lotus Sutra of Shakyamuni. It is also the Lotus Sutra of T'ien-t'ai and the Lotus Sutra of Bodhisattva Never Disparaging. This was a stunning perspective that only President Toda, who had become enlightened to the essence of the Lotus Sutra, could have revealed.

In listening to his broad-ranging lectures, his listeners, as a matter of course, could engrave in their lives the distinctions between the Lotus Sutra of Shakyamuni and the Lotus Sutra of Nichiren Daishonin.

Nam-myoho-renge-kyo Is the Lotus Sutra of the Latter Day

What do the different expressions of this manifold Lotus Sutra have in common? Ultimately, it is the teaching that everyone equally has the potential to attain Buddhahood. There are, however, great differences in the forms whereby Shakyamuni and Nichiren expressed this teaching.

Shakyamuni expressed it as the twenty-eight-chapter Lotus Sutra. Nichiren Daishonin revealed the ultimate truth of the Lotus Sutra as Nam-myoho-renge-kyo, enabling all human beings of the Latter Day to attain Buddhahood.

The Daishonin writes, "I, Nichiren, have abandoned both the approach that expands and that which condenses and favor the essence of the matter, which means the five characters of Myoho-renge-kyo that were transmitted to Bodhisattva Superior Practices" (WND-2, 489).

The five characters of Myoho-renge-kyo are the Lotus Sutra appropriate to this age of the Latter Day of the Law; they are the sutra's essence. President Toda therefore termed the Daishonin's teaching the Lotus Sutra of the Latter Day.

The Lineage of Votaries of the Lotus Sutra

One who expounds a teaching that can enable all people to attain Buddhahood is certain to encounter persecution. Even Shakyamuni underwent a succession of great persecutions.

Moreover, the Lotus Sutra itself states that whoever spreads it in the Latter Day of the Law is certain to encounter numerous persecutions even greater than those Shakyamuni faced. This is clearly shown in such phrases as: "Since hatred and jealousy toward this sutra abound even when the Thus Come One is in the world, how much more will this be so after his passing?" (LSOC, 203); "It [the Lotus Sutra] will face much hostility in the world and be difficult to believe" (LSOC, 246); the three powerful enemies (as described in the concluding verse section of "Encouraging Devotion," the thirteenth chapter; see LSOC, 232–34); and the six difficult and nine easy acts (as described in "Treasure Tower," the eleventh chapter; see LSOC, 218–19).

A votary who endures all these great persecutions and perseveres in spreading the teaching among the people embodies the heart of the Lotus Sutra. Enduring persecution to spread the teaching to others is, in fact, an expression of compassion.

The life of Nichiren Daishonin, who appeared in the Latter Day, was a succession of great persecutions, just as the sutra predicts. Nichiren notes that he had encountered persecutions matching in every respect those that the sutra predicts will befall its votary; and he declares himself to be the votary of the Lotus Sutra in the Latter Day, implying he is the Buddha of the Latter Day.

At the same time, Nichiren also designates Shakyamuni, T'ien-t'ai and Dengyo as votaries of the Lotus Sutra of their respective ages. They were all predecessors who expounded the Lotus Sutra out of their desire for the people's happiness and who were persecuted as a result.

In addition, in many writings, Nichiren praises and offers the greatest encouragement to his followers by calling them "votaries of the Lotus Sutra." One such follower was Shijo Kingo, who struggled to overcome great difficulties and persevered in faith without begrudging his life. One woman (the mother of Oto Gozen), who visited him in exile on Sado Island, brought her young daughter with her on the arduous journey. He goes so far as to say to the woman, "You are the foremost votary of the Lotus Sutra among the women of Japan" (WND-1, 325) and gives her the name Sage Nichimyo.

Buddhism Means Taking Action Among People and in Society

Nichiren also says, "Nevertheless, in the end, when the teachings of the Lotus Sutra have been widely propagated and made known, then they and all others alike throughout the world will become votaries of the Lotus Sutra" (OTT, 74–75). He thus indicates the principle that anyone in the world may become a votary of the Lotus Sutra.

"Votaries of the Lotus Sutra" refers to those who dedicate themselves to the mission of saving all people throughout the entire world and over the ten thousand years and more of the Latter Day of the Law. And "when the teachings of the Lotus Sutra have been widely propagated and made known" indicates a situation in which individuals, basing themselves on the Mystic Law, contribute to others and to society as "votaries," that is, as people of action.

The Soka Gakkai's first and second presidents, Tsunesaburo Makiguchi and Josei Toda, struggled against the country's militarist regime and propagated the Law for the people's happiness without begrudging their lives. Accordingly, they certainly have a place in this lineage of votaries of the Lotus Sutra.

Nichijun, the sixty-fifth chief priest of Taiseki-ji, lauded President Makiguchi as "an emissary of the Buddha from birth," and he praised President Toda as "the forerunner of the Bodhisattvas of the Earth."

President Toda initiated the great struggle to spread the Lotus Sutra of the Latter Day for the sake of those laboring under the dire conditions after World War II. "I want to banish the word 'misery' from this world and rid the world of poverty and sickness." This passionate cry of my mentor, who stood up alone after the war, still resounds in my ears. This cry of the spirit is none other than the heart of the Lotus Sutra.

Buddhism always means action and practice. Enabling people to overcome their difficulties and establish lives of supreme happiness requires dialogue, thoroughgoing dialogue. In such action and practice beats the heart of the Lotus Sutra.

The Buddhism Hidden in the Depths of the Sutra Is Open to All

In his lectures, President Toda often spoke as follows:

> Nichiren Daishonin read the Lotus Sutra from the standpoint of its most profound depths. The Great Teacher T'ien-t'ai read the surface or literal meaning of the Lotus Sutra and interpreted its passages and phrases skillfully. . . .
>
> When I say Nichiren Daishonin read the Lotus Sutra, bear in mind that he was not reading the Lotus Sutra Shakyamuni expounded just as it was. He was reading it in terms of the meaning contained in its depths, from his state of life as the Buddha of the Latter Day. This is what he indicates when he refers to the theoretical teaching as he read it and the "Life Span" chapter from the perspective of his enlightenment.

President Toda explained the correct way to read the sutra today, strictly distinguishing between the literal, surface meaning—Shakyamuni's and T'ien-t'ai's standpoint—and the implicit meaning, or Nichiren's standpoint.

Just what does it mean to read the sutra in terms of its implicit meaning? In a nutshell, it is to read it from the standpoint of Nichiren's vast life state, which desires to help all people attain true happiness.

Nichiren "read the Lotus Sutra with his life" as he practiced with the spirit to not begrudge his life. The essence he propagated at the risk of his life was Nam-myoho-renge-kyo—the Lotus Sutra of the Latter Day, or the essential teaching hidden in its depths.

Considered from this standpoint, the twenty-eight-chapter Lotus Sutra becomes in its entirety an explanation of Nam-myoho-renge-kyo. Reading the Lotus Sutra from the standpoint of Nam-myoho-renge-kyo, hence, is to read it from the standpoint of its implicit meaning.

When we recite the "Expedient Means" and "Life Span" chapters in the morning and evening, we do so not from the standpoint of the Lotus Sutra of the Former or Middle Day of the Law but from that of Nichiren Daishonin's teaching of Nam-myoho-renge-kyo.

A Living Interpretation Is Rooted in Daily Life

Nichiren Daishonin lectured on the twenty-eight-chapter Lotus Sutra from the standpoint of the teaching hidden in its depths, and Nikko Shonin recorded Nichiren's lectures in the form of *The Record of the Orally Transmitted Teachings*. To revive the heart of the Lotus Sutra and enable all people of the Latter Day to attain Buddhahood, Nichiren, out of his immense compassion, explains exactly how the sutra passages should be read.

Reading the Lotus Sutra in terms of its implicit meaning might be described as interpreting it from the standpoint of the Daishonin's enlightenment. It is not simply a theoretical explanation. This interpretation articulates the spirit of the sutra passages from the single perspective of enabling all people, who live amid the realities of daily life, to become happy.

In other words, it is a living interpretation—an interpretation for putting the sutra into practice in our lives, an interpretation from the viewpoint of the human being, an interpretation for ordinary people, an interpretation that focuses on people's daily lives. It is not an interpretation merely for the sake of intellectual knowledge. Rather, it's one based on great wisdom so as to ensure that the sutra's teaching may be developed correctly and boldly as the times and society require.

"Hidden in the depths" may imply a mystery closed off to most people, but that is certainly not the case. On the contrary, the true value of Buddhism hidden in the depths lies in its being widely accessible to all people, a living, pulsing force that invigorates the age and society.

Unfortunately, the priests of Nichiren Shoshu have subverted the intent of this concept. They have misused the idea of the Buddhist teaching hidden in the depths of the Lotus Sutra, mystifying it to bolster their own air of authority. In so doing, they have ascribed to priests and temples a special level of privilege and endeavored to use the Gohonzon—the object of devotion in Nichiren Buddhism—as a tool for controlling people. While failing to engage themselves earnestly in Buddhist practice, they have instead tended toward the pursuit of pleasure and personal gratification, allowing their humanity to erode at its root. This is a truly fearsome development. They have, in effect, killed the spirit of Nichiren Daishonin within their own order.[2]

With *The Record of the Orally Transmitted Teachings* and my mentor's lectures as my foundation, I hope to address these principles in a way relevant to modern times and society.

The Benefit of Reciting the Sutra

Chanting Nam-myoho-renge-kyo, the title of the Lotus Sutra, is termed the "primary practice," and reciting the "Expedient Means" and "Life Span" chapters, or gongyo, is called the "supplementary practice" or "supporting practice."

Nichikan, the twenty-sixth chief priest of Taiseki-ji, explains the relationship between the primary and supplementary practices by comparing them to food and seasoning, respectively. In other words, when eating rice or noodles, the "primary" source of nourishment, one uses salt or vinegar as seasoning to help bring out, or "supplement," the flavor.

The benefit from carrying out the primary practice is immense. When one recites the "Expedient Means" and "Life Span" chapters, it increases and accelerates the primary practice's beneficial power. Our format for morning and evening gongyo is chanting Nam-myoho-renge-kyo as the primary component and reciting the "Expedient Means" and "Life Span" chapters as the supplementary one.

The benefit of chanting Nam-myoho-renge-kyo is immeasurable. Indeed, there is infinite power in chanting Nam-myoho-renge-kyo just one time. Nichiren writes, "If you recite these words of the daimoku once, then the Buddha nature of all living beings will be summoned and gather around you" (WND-I, 131). Also, he teaches that the benefit of chanting Nam-myoho-renge-kyo even once is equal to that of reading the entire Lotus Sutra, that of chanting Nam-myoho-renge-kyo ten times is equal to reading the sutra ten times, that of chanting Nam-myoho-renge-kyo one hundred times is equal to reading the sutra a hundred times, and that of chanting Nam-myoho-renge-kyo one thousand times is equal to reading the sutra a thousand times.

Accordingly, we do not necessarily have to recite the sutra as normal if, for example, we are sick. If we should push ourselves excessively and our condition worsens, then rather than increasing our benefit, it may in fact have the opposite effect: It may destroy our joy in faith and thus generate negative value.

Buddhism is reason. The important thing, therefore, is for each person to make wise judgments and practice filled with joy at all times.

The Lotus Sutra as Read From Nichiren's Standpoint

The primary practice of Nichiren Buddhism is to chant Nam-myoho-renge-kyo, the ultimate truth of the highest Buddhist teaching. Since we are carrying out the supreme primary practice, anything less than the highest supplementary practice would be of no help at all.

The supplementary practice Nichiren chose is to recite portions of the "Expedient Means" and "Life Span" chapters. Of the sutra's twenty-eight chapters, these two represent the essence of the theoretical teaching and the essence of the essential teaching, respectively.

During Nichiren's time, as well, his followers recited portions from these two chapters. In one instance, he writes:

> Among the entire twenty-eight chapters, the "Expedient Means" chapter and the "Life Span" chapter are particularly outstanding. The remaining chapters are all in a sense the branches and leaves of these two chapters. Therefore, for your regular recitation, I recommend that you practice reading the prose sections of the "Expedient Means" and "Life Span" chapters. (WND-1, 71)[3]

Reciting the sutra and chanting Nam-myoho-renge-kyo are the roots that, as it were, enable each practitioner to grow into a great tree. The tree of one's life strengthens and grows as a cumulative result of continuing this daily practice. While it may not be possible to see changes from one day to the next, because of the daily nourishment a consistent practice affords, one's life will become towering and vast like a great tree. As we carry out a steady practice, we will develop a state of absolutely indestructible happiness.

As I mentioned earlier, however, the "Expedient Means" and "Life Span" chapters we recite are those of the Lotus Sutra as seen from the Daishonin's standpoint of the teaching hidden in the depths.

Nichikan explains that we read the "Expedient Means" chapter to "refute" its surface meaning and "borrow" its phrases; we read the "Life Span" chapter, he says, to "refute" its surface meaning and "use" the profound meaning implicit in the chapter. Reading these chapters from the standpoint of Nichiren Buddhism, we refute their surface meaning; it is as though we are saying, "The Lotus Sutra of Shakyamuni has no beneficial power in the Latter Day."

At the same time, from Nichiren's standpoint, we also recite the

Lotus Sutra because it praises the greatness of the Gohonzon. This way of reading it corresponds to "borrowing" and "using" its words.

While there are meticulous arguments to substantiate this explanation, for the time being I will simply confirm the point that in reading the "Expedient Means" and "Life Span" chapters, we do so from the standpoint of Nichiren Buddhism.

Your Chanting Voices Reach the Buddhas and Bodhisattvas

I imagine some may wonder how reading sutra passages you cannot understand could bring about any benefit. Let me reassure you that there is definitely benefit from carrying out this practice.

The Daishonin writes:

> A baby does not know the difference between water and fire, and cannot distinguish medicine from poison. But when the baby sucks milk, its life is nourished and sustained. Although one may not be versed [in various sutras] . . . if one listens to even one character or one phrase of the Lotus Sutra, one cannot fail to attain Buddhahood. (WND-1, 513)

Just as a baby will grow naturally of its own accord by drinking milk, if you earnestly chant Nam-myoho-renge-kyo with faith in the Gohonzon, your life will definitely come to shine with immeasurable good fortune and benefit.

To cite another example: Dogs have a language in the world of dogs, and birds have a language in the world of birds. While people cannot understand these languages, dogs and birds can certainly communicate within their own species. Also, though some people do not understand scientific jargon or a particular language, others can communicate very well in these languages.

Similarly, it might be said that when we are reciting the sutra or chanting Nam-myoho-renge-kyo, we are speaking in the language of Buddhas and bodhisattvas. Even though you may not understand what you are saying, your voice definitely reaches the Gohonzon, all Buddhist deities, and all Buddhas and bodhisattvas over the three existences and in the ten directions. In response, the entire universe bathes you in the light of good fortune.

At the same time, of course, if you study the sutra with this practice as your basis and with a seeking spirit, you can as a matter of course deepen your confidence and strengthen your faith.

Our Practice Revitalizes Us

When we do gongyo and chant Nam-myoho-renge-kyo, we conduct a ceremony in which we praise the Gohonzon and the great pure Law of Nam-myoho-renge-kyo. On one level, it could be said that our daily chanting is like a paean for the Buddha and for Nam-myoho-renge-kyo, the fundamental Law of the universe. At the same time, we are also praising the eternal life of the universe and the world of Buddhahood in our own lives.

When we chant to the Gohonzon, right then and there the doors of the microcosm within us open completely to the macrocosm, and we can experience a great and serene sense of happiness, as though gazing out over the entire universe. We savor tremendous fulfillment and joy and gain access to a great and all-embracing wisdom. The microcosm that is encompassed by the universe in turn encompasses the entire universe.

Our morning and evening practice is an invigorating ceremony of beginningless time that revitalizes us from the very depths of our being. Therefore, the important thing is to chant each day filled with a sense of rhythm and cadence—like a horse galloping through the heavens. I hope you will chant in a way that leaves you refreshed and revitalized in both body and mind.

The King of Sutras Makes People Strong and Wise

The Lotus Sutra is the king of sutras, the scripture that calls out to all people. It is a living teaching that embodies the Buddha's compassion and egalitarian outlook. It is a scripture of renaissance overflowing with the spirit of revitalization that makes human beings strong and wise. And the "Expedient Means" and "Life Span" chapters are the heart of the sutra.

No practice is as universally accessible to all people as the practice of reciting the sutra and chanting Nam-myoho-renge-kyo set forth by Nichiren Daishonin. This is the Buddhist practice that is most open and accessible to all people.

During Nichiren's lifetime, both priests and lay people assiduously recited the sutra and chanted Nam-myoho-renge-kyo. For most people in Japan today, sutras have become something distant and remote, their only exposure to them being when they hear priests intoning them at funerals.

This tendency to depend on priests—which has come to be regarded as so natural that no one questions it—has produced a spiritual foundation of blind obedience to religious authority. It is the fundamental evil that allowed the clergy to grow arrogant and decadent.

Today, however, thanks to the Soka Gakkai's development, people not only in Japan but throughout the world joyously chant the Mystic Law and recite the "Expedient Means" and "Life Span" chapters. This is a grand undertaking wholly without precedent in the history of Buddhism. It constitutes the great religious revolution of our time.

Nichiren Buddhism, the Buddhism of the people, is generating a great light of peace and happiness throughout the world. Millions are experiencing the beneficial power of the Mystic Law and acting out the wonderful drama of their human revolution. More than anything else, this fact attests most eloquently to the correctness of the SGI, which carries on the spirit of the Lotus Sutra in the present age.

As I work on these lectures, I have images of these many friends in mind. I will proceed as though carrying on a discussion with each of you while gazing up into a clear blue sky or strolling along a path through a field filled with fragrant blooming flowers.

THE "EXPEDIENT MEANS" CHAPTER

On the "Expedient Means" Chapter

PRACTICING THE LOTUS SUTRA causes the sun to rise in our hearts. No matter how stormy our situation, when the sun blazes in the depths of our lives, a clear, bright sky—like the blue sky of May—opens in our hearts. And when we possess in our hearts the four virtues of eternity, happiness, true self and purity, then the land, the place where we are, shines as the Land of Eternally Tranquil Light.

While everyone has a sun in his or her heart, all too few are aware it exists. The Lotus Sutra is the scripture that reveals the brilliant sun of Buddhahood inherent in our lives.

"You, yourself, are a Buddha. Revere the sun of Buddhahood in your own life." This is the essential teaching of the Lotus Sutra, the message of the "Expedient Means" chapter.

Shakyamuni perceived that everyone possesses Buddhahood just as he did. He made it possible for everyone to advance along the path of which he had become enlightened. Based on the irrefutable proposition that all human beings are respectable and that no human being is better than anyone else, Shakyamuni went out among the people and expounded the Law continuously.

Buddhism Is the Path of Limitless Self-Improvement

In the latter half of "Expedient Means," Shakyamuni explains that Buddhas appear in the world to "open the door of," "show," "cause living beings to awaken to" and "induce living beings to enter the path of" (LSOC, 64) the Buddha wisdom that inherently exists in human life. He further states that all people can equally develop the Buddha's state of life and that he has fulfilled a vow he made long ago by expounding the Lotus Sutra, which enables them to do so.

I think the spirit of "Expedient Means," as these passages express, is a profound form of humanistic education. Buddhism starts from the recognition of each person's infinite potential. And it teaches the means whereby people can awaken to and draw forth the supreme treasure of Buddhahood.

When people become aware of this treasure in their lives, they also come to recognize it in others and so will treat their fellow human beings with heartfelt respect. At the same time, they naturally take action to spark the same awareness in others.

When we make such efforts, the treasure in our own lives is polished, and this in turn enables us to develop still more confidence in our innate potential and dignity. Buddhist practice is thus the path of limitless self-improvement.

After hearing the Buddha expound "Expedient Means," Shariputra and the other voice-hearers attain enlightenment. Vowing to take action among the people, they become voice-hearers who devote themselves to the people; they emerge as true disciples of the Buddha.

Shariputra and the others no doubt were moved by the profound compassion of their mentor, Shakyamuni. The great light of the Buddha wisdom suddenly illuminated the darkness of their formerly self-centered and tightly closed hearts. Their hearts opened and expanded widely.

They understood it had been the Buddha's intention all along to guide them to Buddhahood, the vast and boundless state of life. They realized that attaining the two vehicles (the worlds of voice-hearers and cause-awakened ones) or the three vehicles (the worlds of voice-hearers, cause-awakened ones and bodhisattvas) was not the true aim of the Buddha's teaching.

This teaching that guides people to aspire to the Buddha's state of life—the one vehicle—rather than the three vehicles is called the "replacement of the three vehicles with the one vehicle." This is the central teaching of the first half, or theoretical teaching, of the Lotus Sutra. And of the fourteen chapters that make up the theoretical teaching, "Expedient Means" is the central pillar.

In Buddhism, the term "expedient means" refers to the skillful means or methods Buddhas employ to guide people to enlightenment. The "Expedient Means" chapter extols the wisdom of the Buddhas to thus instruct the people. Later, I will elaborate further on the profound meaning of "expedient means."

The Essence of the Entire "Expedient Means" Chapter

Every day we recite the opening portion of "Expedient Means"—the most important part of the entire chapter.

Briefly, the contents of this part of the chapter are as follows: First, Shakyamuni clarifies that the wisdom to which all Buddhas are enlightened is "infinitely profound and immeasurable" (LSOC, 56) and that it is well beyond the capacity of Shariputra and the other voice-hearers to comprehend. Shakyamuni then says he has employed similes and various other means to skillfully expound the Buddha wisdom to the people. Finally, he reveals that the wisdom of all Buddhas is none other than the comprehension of the "true aspect of all phenomena." This concludes the portion of "Expedient Means" we recite each day.

In a nutshell, the "true aspect of all phenomena" represents the principle that all people have the potential to be Buddhas. In other words, this passage reveals in theoretical terms the path whereby all people can attain Buddhahood. The portion we recite during gongyo is thus the very essence of the entire "Expedient Means" chapter.

Let us now proceed to the contents of "Expedient Means."

✹ Excerpts From the "Expedient Means" Chapter

The following are the passages from the "Expedient Means" chapter that SGI members recite during gongyo. The numbers next to each passage correspond to the numbered lectures that follow; page numbers where the lecture for each passage can be found also appear here. The appendix on p. 387 contains the full English translation.

(1) Niji seson. Ju sanmai. Anjo ni ki. Go shari-hotsu. Sho-but chi-e. Jinjin muryo. Go chi-e mon. Nange nannyu. Issai shomon. Hyaku-shi-butsu. Sho fu no chi. (p. 23)

(2) Sho-i sha ga. Butsu zo shingon. Hyaku sen man noku. Mushu sho butsu. Jin gyo sho-butsu. Muryo doho. Yumyo shojin. Myosho fu mon. Joju jinjin. Mi-zo-u ho. Zui gi sho setsu. Ishu nange. (p. 37)

(3) Shari-hotsu. Go ju jo-butsu irai. Shuju innen. Shuju hiyu. Ko en gonkyo. Mu shu hoben. Indo shujo. Ryo ri sho jaku. (p. 57)

(4) Sho-i sha ga. Nyorai hoben. Chi-ken hara-mitsu. Kai i gu-soku. (p. 71)

(5) Shari-hotsu. Nyorai chi-ken. Kodai jinnon. Muryo muge. Riki. Mu-sho-i. Zenjo. Gedas. Sanmai. Jin nyu musai. Joju issai. Mi-zo-u ho. (p. 79)

(6) Shari-hotsu. Nyorai no. Shuju fun-betsu. Gyo ses sho ho. Gon-ji nyunan. Ekka shushin. Shari-hotsu. Shu yo gon shi. Muryo muhen. Mi-zo-u ho. Bus shitsu joju. (p. 89)

(7) Shi shari-hotsu. Fu shu bu setsu. Sho-i sha ga. Bus sho joju. Dai ichi ke-u. Nange shi ho. (p. 99)

(8) Yui butsu yo butsu. Nai no kujin. Shoho jisso. Sho-i shoho. Nyo ze so. Nyo ze sho. Nyo ze tai. Nyo ze riki. Nyo ze sa. Nyo ze in. Nyo ze en. Nyo ze ka. Nyo ze ho. Nyo ze honmak kukyo to. (p. 103)

◼ 1 ◼

Niji seson. Ju sanmai. Anjo ni ki. Go shari-hotsu. Sho-buťchi-e. Jinjin muryo. Go chi-e mon. Nange nannyu. Issai shomon. Hyaku-shi-butsu. Sho fu no chi.

At that time the World-Honored One calmly arose from his samadhi and addressed Shariputra, saying: "The wisdom of the Buddhas is infinitely profound and immeasurable. The door to this wisdom is difficult to understand and difficult to enter. Not one of the voice-hearers or pratyekabuddhas is able to comprehend it." (LSOC, 56)

AT THE BEGINNING of "Expedient Means," Shakyamuni arises from *samadhi*, or deep meditation, on the truth that immeasurable meanings come from the one Law. Immediately, he tells Shariputra: "The wisdom of the Buddhas is infinitely profound and immeasurable. . . . [None of you] is able to comprehend it." The teaching thus opens with a scene of considerable tension.

Let us first consider just what kind of time is being indicated in the phrase "At that time." President Toda explained:

"At that time" refers to the concept of time as employed in Buddhism. This is different from time in the sense that we ordinarily use it to indicate some particular time such as two o'clock or three o'clock or in the sense of springtime.

Neither is "at that time" comparable to the typical nursery tale opening "Once upon a time." Time, in the sense signified here, refers to the time when a Buddha, perceiving the people's longing for the Buddha, appears and expounds the teaching.

Four conditions must be met for a Buddha to expound the Law—time, response, capacity and teaching. Time, in Buddhism, indicates when the Buddha appears and expounds the teaching in response to the capacity of people who seek it. In other words, time refers to when a Buddha and human beings encounter one another.

While Shakyamuni is engaged in his deep meditation, his disciples' seeking spirit no doubt reaches a climax. They probably thought to themselves: "I wonder what kind of teaching the World-Honored One will expound? I don't want to miss a single word. I will engrave the Buddha's teaching in my heart." Containing their blazing enthusiasm, they all listened intently, focusing their full attention and fixing their gaze on their mentor.

And so the time became ripe. Shakyamuni finally broke his long silence and began to expound the Lotus Sutra—the ultimate teaching that enables all living beings to attain Buddhahood. This is the meaning of "At that time," which begins the "Expedient Means" chapter.

In other words, it indicates the time when a Buddha stands up to guide people to enlightenment and the time when the disciples have established a single-minded seeking spirit for the Buddha's teaching. It signifies a profound concordance of the disciples' hearts with the mentor's heart. This scene opens the grand drama of mentor and disciple, who dedicate themselves to the happiness of humankind.

The Buddha is the one who most keenly comprehends the time. The Buddha awaits the proper time, discerns the nature of the time, creates the time and expounds the Law that accords with the time. Such is the Buddha's wisdom and compassion.

"Why do the people suffer?" "For what do the people yearn?" "What teaching enables the people to become happy, and when should it be taught?" The Buddha ponders these matters constantly and expounds the Law freely in accordance with the time.

In this sense, to know the time is also to understand people's hearts. The Buddha is a leader who has mastered understanding others' hearts. The Buddha is an instructor of the spirit and an expert on human nature.

From the Buddha's standpoint, "that time" is the time when the Buddha initiates the struggle to enable all people to attain enlightenment. For the disciples, it is the time when they grasp and become powerfully aware of the Buddha's spirit.

Regarding the importance of the time, Nichiren Daishonin writes, "When it comes to studying the teachings of Buddhism, one must first learn to understand the time" (WND-1, 538). Thus he indicates that Buddhism is expounded based on the time; the teaching that should be propagated is the one that accords with the time.

Proclaiming this period of the Latter Day of the Law to be the time when the great pure Law of Nam-myoho-renge-kyo should be spread, Nichiren launched the struggle to propagate the Mystic Law and enable all people of the Latter Day to attain enlightenment.

One's Inner Determination Opens the Way Forward

In other words, from the standpoint of the Buddhism hidden in the depths, we can interpret "that time" as indicating the time when Nichiren Daishonin commenced his great struggle to save all humankind. And it can also be said that "that time" indicates the time when Nichiren's disciples stand up in concert with the mentor to realize kosen-rufu.

In terms of our practice, therefore, I would like to stress that "that time" exists only when we pray to the Gohonzon and manifest determination and awareness of our mission for kosen-rufu. We have to make a determination, pray and take action. Unless we do so, our environment will not change in the least; though five or ten years may pass, "that time" will never arrive.

Our single-minded determination for kosen-rufu, and that alone, creates the "time." "That time" is when we set our lives in motion, when we stand up of our own volition and by our own will and strength. "That time" is when we summon forth strong faith and take our place on the grand stage of kosen-rufu.

Goethe writes, "The moment alone is decisive; Fixes the life of man, and his future destiny settles."[4] "That time" is the moment you resolve from the depths of your heart, "Now I will stand up and fight!" From that instant, your destiny changes. Your life develops. History begins.

This is the spirit of the mystic principle of the true cause. This is the principle of three thousand realms in a single moment of life. The moment you autonomously determine to accomplish something— not when you do it because you are told to—is "that time," the time of mission.

Immeasurable Meanings Derive From the One Law

At the outset of "Expedient Means," Shakyamuni arises serenely from samadhi and begins expounding the Lotus Sutra. Samadhi, or meditative concentration, means to focus one's mind on one point so that it becomes perfectly tranquil and still like a clear mirror and thereby enter a state of inner serenity. Shakyamuni enters samadhi early in "Introduction," the first chapter of the Lotus Sutra, and continues meditating throughout it.

Even though the sutra speaks of Shakyamuni entering samadhi, this does not mean that in the Latter Day people should seclude themselves in mountains and forests and practice sitting meditation.

Nichiren Daishonin, who struggled in the very midst of society to enable all people to attain enlightenment, rejects such practices as unsuited to the time.

In the present age, samadhi means doing gongyo and chanting Nam-myoho-renge-kyo. We do not carry out this practice secluded in mountains and forests. Rather, on the foundation of our daily practice, we polish our lives, draw forth infinite wisdom and courage, and go out into society. This is the discipline we carry out.

Contemplation or meditation for its own sake is to have one's priorities reversed, to confuse a means for the end. In the Vimalakirti Sutra, Shakyamuni clearly explains that true meditation is not solitary contemplation beneath a tree but playing an active role in society while embracing the truth.

When someone urged that he pursue a life of meditation, Mahatma Gandhi is said to have replied that he felt no need to withdraw to a cave for that purpose. He carried the cave with him, he said, wherever he went. This episode is characteristic of Gandhi, who devoted his life to moving and taking action among the people.

Buddhism does not close its eyes to people's suffering; it is a teaching that opens people's eyes. Therefore, Buddhism is the path that enables people to become happy. To turn away our eyes from the contradictions of society and rid ourselves of all worldly thoughts is not the way of Buddhist practice.

The true spirit of meditation lies in manifesting our innate wisdom in society, resolutely struggling for the happiness of ourselves and others, and building a better society.

Nichiren Daishonin Stood Up for All Humankind

The specific samadhi Shakyamuni entered is termed "samadhi of the place of immeasurable meanings." The Immeasurable Meanings Sutra reads, "Immeasurable meanings are born from a single Law"

(LSOC, 13). This Law from which immeasurable meanings derive is the foundation of all teachings. Shakyamuni expounded the Lotus Sutra from the standpoint of this great truth to which he had become enlightened.

Nichiren Daishonin clarified that this "single Law" is Nam-myoho-renge-kyo. He revealed this fundamental Law of the universe for all people and expressed it so that anyone can practice it. He stood up and expounded it for the happiness of the entire world and for all humanity. This is what the phrase "calmly arose from his samadhi" signifies in terms of its implicit meaning.

For us, "Immeasurable meanings are born from a single Law" means that by believing in and embracing the Mystic Law, we can acquire the Buddha's infinite wisdom. By doing gongyo and chanting Nam-myoho-renge-kyo daily, we cause our lives to shine with supreme wisdom and advance along the path of genuine victory in life. Each day, starting from this foundation, we can revitalize ourselves.

Therefore, please be confident that SGI members who pray with the determination "I will fight again today; I will do my best tomorrow too" and who stand up for kosen-rufu in society are themselves practicing "calmly arising from samadhi" each morning and evening.

The Unsolicited and Spontaneous Teaching

Shakyamuni, having arisen from samadhi, spontaneously begins to expound the Lotus Sutra without anyone first requesting that he do so. This manner of preaching, where the Buddha expounds the Law on his own initiative without any question having been put to him, is called "taking it upon himself to preach without being asked" (see OTT, 18–19).

The doctrine Shakyamuni spontaneously and serenely begins to expound is so profound that his disciples could not have imagined it, let alone have asked him to teach it. In this, we see the outpouring of wisdom and compassion that impelled Shakyamuni to expound the Lotus Sutra.

It is of profound significance that Shakyamuni takes it upon himself to preach without being asked. All sutras other than the Lotus Sutra are described as "preaching in accordance with the minds of others," that is, according to his listeners' capacities. As such, they do not represent the Buddha's true intention. By contrast, the Lotus Sutra is described as "preaching in accordance with one's own mind," because in this sutra Shakyamuni reveals the truth directly, in accordance with his own enlightenment.

Nichiren's declaration of the Buddhism of the Latter Day of the Law is another instance of taking it upon himself to preach without being asked. With regard to establishing his teaching, the Daishonin says, "If I speak out, I am fully aware that I will have to contend with the three obstacles and four devils" (WND-1, 239). He knew that if he spread the Mystic Law, he was certain to encounter persecution.

Nonetheless, without being asked by anyone, he began to expound the teaching of Nam-myoho-renge-kyo. In his lifetime struggles, the Daishonin preached in accordance with his own mind.

In our own practice, preaching in accordance with one's own mind indicates the spontaneous spirit to praise the Mystic Law out of profound recognition of its greatness, no matter what anyone might say. Such admiration for the Mystic Law is the essential reason we recite the sutra during morning and evening gongyo.

"Preaching in accordance with one's own mind" also indicates the attitude of propagating the Law to the full extent of one's ability, the irrepressible desire to teach and explain to others even a single word or phrase. By contrast, if you talk about the Mystic Law because you have been told to do so, or in the belief that it will make others think highly of you, then you are preaching in accordance with the minds of others.

Broadly speaking, "taking it upon himself to preach without being asked" and "preaching according to one's own mind" indicate autonomous and self-motivated action. It does not matter if your words are plain or if you are not a talented speaker. What is important is to pray earnestly with the determination for others to become happy and to tell others candidly about the greatness of Buddhism—with conviction and in your own words. This is the spirit of the Lotus Sutra and the spirit of the Soka Gakkai.

The Buddha Seeks to Enable All People to Attain the Same Enlightened State of Life

Shakyamuni starts out by telling Shariputra: "The wisdom of the Buddhas is infinitely profound and immeasurable. The door to this wisdom is difficult to understand and difficult to enter. Not one of the voice-hearers or cause-awakened ones is able to comprehend it." This statement extols the great wisdom of the Buddha.

The "wisdom of the Buddhas" is the wisdom that shines like a sun within the Buddha. Shakyamuni praises this wisdom as "infinitely profound and immeasurable." It is "infinitely profound" because it penetrates down to the truth that is the very foundation of life. It is "immeasurable" because its light broadly illuminates all things.

Because the wisdom of the Buddhas reveals life in its entirety, the Buddha's state of life is said to be expansive and profound. Likening the Buddha's state of life to a great tree or a mighty river, Nichiren says: "The deeper the roots, the more prolific the branches. The farther the source, the longer the stream" (WND-1, 736).

Shakyamuni doesn't praise the wisdom of the Buddhas to say that the Buddha alone is great. In fact, it is just the opposite; his purpose is to encourage others. In effect, he is saying: "Therefore, all of you, too, should make this same great wisdom of the Buddhas shine in your own lives and become happy."

Wisdom is the path to happiness. Money, status, skill at getting by in the world—none of these can enable us to overcome the fundamental sufferings of birth, old age, sickness and death. The only way is to cultivate the wisdom with which our lives are inherently endowed.

The Lotus Sutra's purpose is to enable all people to cultivate supreme wisdom in their hearts and advance along the great path of indestructible happiness. Nichiren writes, "The treasures of the heart are the most valuable of all" (WND-1, 851). That is why Shakyamuni began by extolling the wisdom of the Buddhas, the supreme wisdom.

The next part of the passage reads, "The door to this wisdom is difficult to understand and difficult to enter." Here Shakyamuni again praises the Buddha wisdom but from a slightly different perspective.

The "door to this wisdom" is the door to the realm of Buddha wisdom. Shakyamuni expounded various teachings as means to enable people to enter this realm. As we've discussed, prior to the Lotus Sutra, he taught in accordance with his listeners' diverse capacities. For example, at different times, he taught that life is suffering, that nothing is constant, that happiness lies in extinguishing all desires and that people should seek to awaken to the principle of dependent origination. In this way, Shakyamuni expounded teachings that the people could best understand.

These specific teachings, however, did not represent the Buddha's true purpose. The true purpose lay in enabling all people to enter the path of wisdom, the path for becoming a Buddha. This purpose, however, cannot be understood with the wisdom of voice-hearers or cause-awakened ones. Such people may understand the contents of a particular teaching, but they cannot fathom the Buddha's reason for expounding it.

Their very satisfaction with specific teachings—ones that explain life's impermanence or the need to eradicate desires, for instance—prevented them from entering the realm of the wisdom of the Buddha who had expounded these doctrines. They reached the gate, as it were, and then stopped. Therefore, Shakyamuni says this wisdom is "difficult to understand and difficult to enter."

Regard Suffering and Joy as Facts of Life

I have discussed until now the literal or surface meaning of this passage. President Toda explained this passage from the standpoint of its implicit meaning as follows:

> The line "The wisdom of the Buddhas is infinitely profound and immeasurable" means that the wisdom of Nam-myoho-renge-kyo is infinitely profound and immeasurable. The passage "The door to this wisdom is difficult to understand and difficult to enter" refers to the "door of faith" in the Gohonzon. By substituting faith for wisdom, we can enter the "door to this wisdom." This door is "difficult to understand and difficult to enter."

As the Daishonin says, "'wisdom' means the Wonderful Law" (OTT, 29). Nam-myoho-renge-kyo, the "Wonderful Law," contains the infinitely profound and immeasurable wisdom of the Buddhas in its entirety. And the door to enter the wisdom of Nam-myoho-renge-kyo is the door of faith. Thus the Daishonin says, "The door is the mind of faith" (OTT, 26).

If we believe in the Gohonzon and exert ourselves in practice and study as the Daishonin teaches, then, in accordance with the principle of substituting faith for wisdom, we can develop a state of supreme happiness. This is what it means to enter through the door of faith, to advance along the path of attaining Buddhahood in this lifetime.

Carrying through with faith becomes difficult, however, when we encounter waves of adversity. At such times, people may forget that faith is the door to wisdom. Instead, filled with complaint, they may be tossed about helplessly on the rough seas of their problems. Or they may fear suffering and give themselves over to lives of pleasure and ease. In this sense, the door of faith is "difficult to understand and difficult to enter."

For precisely this reason, Nichiren says, "Regard both suffering and joy as facts of life, and continue chanting Nam-myoho-renge-kyo" (WND-1, 681).

Nam-myoho-renge-kyo is the wellspring of the wisdom of all Buddhas. And our daily gongyo is a ceremony of beginningless time in which we return to the very foundation of our lives and draw wisdom from the great ocean of the world of Buddhahood.

The Transformation of the Voice-Hearers

In the final sentence of this passage, Shakyamuni announces to Shariputra that the vast wisdom of the Buddhas cannot be fathomed by the shallow wisdom of voice-hearers and cause-awakened ones—the people of the two vehicles.

Shariputra, a voice-hearer, is known as the foremost in wisdom among Shakyamuni's disciples. He is a brilliant intellectual, second to none. Still, Shakyamuni declares that not even Shariputra, with all his wisdom, can comprehend the wisdom of the Buddhas. As Shakyamuni continues his preaching in this and subsequent chapters, however, not only Shariputra but all the voice-hearers undergo a complete transformation. They begin to comprehend the wisdom of the Buddhas, and Shakyamuni acknowledges they can attain Buddhahood without fail. This is known as the "attainment of Buddhahood by persons of the two vehicles."

What brought about this change for the voice-hearers? What

happened to them as a result of hearing Shakyamuni expound the Lotus Sutra? This is clarified in "Simile and Parable," the third chapter, where Shakyamuni explains that even Shariputra has been "able to gain entrance through faith alone" (LSOC, 110). In other words, the voice-hearers can enter the supreme wisdom of the Buddhas not through their own shallow wisdom but through faith.

In Buddhism, faith means a pure heart, a flexible spirit and an open mind. Faith is the function of human life to dispel the dark clouds of doubt, anxiety and regret and sincerely open and direct one's heart toward something great.

Faith might also be characterized as the power that enables the microcosm of the self to sense the universal macrocosm. Through this power, the power of faith, the voice-hearers can enter the vast realm of Buddha wisdom. According to Nagarjuna and T'ien-t'ai, Buddhism is a vast ocean, and only those with faith can enter.

It would seem that Shakyamuni's preaching of the first half—or theoretical teaching—of the Lotus Sutra, which was specifically addressed to the voice-hearers, aroused in them a power of faith markedly more profound than they had previously manifested. In "Expedient Means," Shakyamuni vigorously exhorts Shariputra to further develop his faith. He is saying, in effect, "This is the time when you should summon up great power of faith."

Voice-hearers Who Hear the Teaching Become Voice-hearers Who Relate It to Others

What becomes of the voice-hearers who enter the realm of the wisdom of the Buddhas through faith? The voice-hearers themselves clarify this point when they say, "Now we have become voice-hearers in truth, for we will take the voice of the Buddha way and cause it to be heard by all" (LSOC, 132). In other words, they change from voice-hearers who hear the teaching to voice-hearers who cause others to hear the teaching. They become voice-hearers who talk about Buddhism among the people.

In one sense, "voice-hearer" indicates those who look to their teacher, the Buddha, for personal salvation and gain. From this standpoint, the statement suggests that they have changed from disciples who are saved to disciples who save others and join the mentor's struggle.

In the pre-Lotus Sutra teachings, "people of the two vehicles" means those who become attached only to partial enlightenment and lose their aspiration for the Buddha way. In the Lotus Sutra, they are revived. They are no longer people of the two vehicles who close themselves off in a shallow level of awakening. Rather, they become people of the two vehicles who seek the supreme enlightenment of the Buddha.

In essence, the voice-hearers gain a revitalized trust in human beings, respect for the people and hope for the future. In other words, they discover the Buddha nature shining within all people. Such is the power and benefit of the vast Buddha wisdom they attain through faith.

A Person of Wisdom Is a Person With an Excellent Heart

Wisdom, in the Lotus Sutra, does not simply mean being smart; it is far more profound. Essentially, it is to have an excellent heart. Wisdom signifies humanity and force of character born of strength, breadth and depth of spirit.

The Daishonin says, "The wise may be called human" (WND-I, 852). He also explains that one who perseveres in following a correct way of life based on the Mystic Law, unswayed by praise and censure, is truly wise (see WND-I, 794).

Shariputra enters the realm of the wisdom of the Buddhas through faith and becomes a disciple of action. From the standpoint of

Nichiren Buddhism, he represents Nichiren's followers, who believe in and embrace Nam-myoho-renge-kyo, the entity of the wisdom of the Buddhas, and who strive to realize kosen-rufu.

Thus the Daishonin says, "Now Nichiren and his followers, who chant Nam-myoho-renge-kyo, are all Shariputra" (OTT, 46). All who conduct Buddhist dialogue with friends and who earnestly chant the Mystic Law and tax their wisdom to help others become happy are Shariputras of the present age.

▪2▪

Sho-i sha ga. Butsu zo shingon. Hyaku sen man noku. Mushu sho butsu.
Jin gyo sho-butsu. Muryo doho. Yumyo shojin. Myosho fu mon.
Joju jinjin. Mi-zo-u ho. Zui gi sho setsu. Ishu nange.

"What is the reason for this? The Buddhas have personally attended
a hundred, a thousand, ten thousand, a million, a countless number of
Buddhas and have fully carried out an immeasurable number of Buddhas'
ways and doctrines. They have exerted themselves bravely and vigorously,
and their names are universally known. They have realized the Law that
is profound and never known before, and preach it in accordance with
what is appropriate, yet their intentions are difficult to understand."
(LSOC, 56)

I N THIS PASSAGE, Shakyamuni explains why the wisdom of the
Buddhas is infinitely profound and immeasurable and why it is difficult to understand by indicating the practices he and other Buddhas
have carried out in previous lifetimes.

To convey a sense of just how difficult is the path to attaining Buddhahood, Shakyamuni explains that Buddhas have served countless
other Buddhas in previous lifetimes, have bravely and vigorously carried out incalculable practices, and as a result have become enlightened to a law of unparalleled greatness.

The practice of Shariputra and the other people of the two vehicles is quite shallow in comparison. Accordingly, they cannot comprehend the true purpose of the teaching Shakyamuni is expounding.

Comprehension, Courage and Action Are Born of Heartfelt Agreement

It is interesting how Shakyamuni mentions his practices in previous lifetimes to indicate that the wisdom of the Buddhas is infinitely profound and immeasurable. Since the wisdom he attained cannot itself be easily articulated, he explains it by describing the practices that became the cause for his enlightenment.

This method of reasoning may seem obscure to us today. But the people of India commonly understood the idea that one repeatedly undergoes the cycle of birth and death. Therefore, by explaining that he had served countless Buddhas in the past, Shakyamuni could readily win the people's understanding and agreement.

Heartfelt agreement is important. When people are satisfied with an explanation, their comprehension deepens and their state of life expands. Heartfelt agreement produces courage and hope and is sure to give rise to action.

For this reason, dialogue is very important. The power to impart profound understanding and earn others' heartfelt agreement is the power of words and the power of the voice. As a result of Shakyamuni's power of speech, even Shariputra developed a seeking spirit to attain the vast wisdom of the Buddhas.

As we've seen, Shakyamuni clarifies that through having carried out an immeasurable number of practices under a countless number of Buddhas, he has attained the wisdom and enlightened state of life of the Buddha.

A Buddha is one who has experienced and carried out all manner of practices in previous lifetimes. In this sense, Buddha means an expert at Buddhist practice. Shakyamuni had the experience and benefit of all the practices he carried out in the past. That's why he could expound teachings that perfectly matched the time and people's capacity. A Buddha is one whose richness of experience in the past produces a spiritual abundance in the present.

True leaders are those who can offer appropriate advice based on their own rich experience, not people who just give orders and are all words and no substance. Leaders are first people of action who lead by personal example. They are not people who merely occupy some status or position. Leaders are people of hard work, not people of tactics and maneuvering. Above all, they are not authoritarians.

In any event, the Buddha's life is profound and wondrous. The Buddha's one life contains the benefit of immeasurable practices; all is contained in the one. Such is the mystery of life. Nichiren Daishonin expressed the mystic nature of life as Nam-myoho-renge-kyo. Thus, he writes:

> The five characters of Myoho-renge-kyo, the heart of the essential teaching of the Lotus Sutra, contain the benefit amassed through the countless practices and meritorious deeds of all Buddhas throughout the three existences. (WND-1, 481)

Viewed from the perspective of Nichiren Buddhism, therefore, the passage "The Buddhas have personally attended a hundred, a thousand, ten thousand, a million, a countless number of Buddhas and have fully carried out an immeasurable number of Buddhas' ways and doctrines" praises the benefit of Nam-myoho-renge-kyo.

Earnest Faith Is the Path to Attaining Buddhahood

In describing the immeasurable practices he has carried out, Shakyamuni's purpose is not to indicate that others should do the same.

Rather, he is saying in effect, "Based on your trust in this Buddha, you should put your faith in the teaching that I, Shakyamuni, am about to expound."

Shakyamuni is a Buddha who in the past carried out immeasurable practices. Such tales as the boy Snow Mountains and King Shibi describe these brave and vigorous practices.

In the Latter Day of the Law, there is no need to carry out "an immeasurable number of Buddhas' ways and doctrines" as Shakyamuni did. Embracing and upholding the Law of Nam-myoho-renge-kyo for oneself and for others provides the benefit of carrying out "an immeasurable number of Buddhas' ways and doctrines."

This is not to say, however, that Shakyamuni's practices are irrelevant to us. Throughout Nichiren's writings, he stresses the spirit of Shakyamuni's practice. For example, commenting on the meaning of the boy Snow Mountains' practice, he writes:

> As for the matter of becoming a Buddha, ordinary people keep in mind the words "earnest resolve" and thereby become Buddhas. When we carefully consider what exactly earnest resolve refers to, it is the doctrine of observing the mind. (WND-I, 1125)

In the Latter Day of the Law, earnest resolve—the will to understand and live up to the Law—is the cause for attaining Buddhahood.

Nichiren praises most highly those courageous individuals who maintain earnest resolve. For example, to Shijo Kingo, who made the long and difficult journey over mountains and across rivers and the treacherous sea to visit Nichiren in exile on Sado Island, he writes, "How could your resolve be inferior to . . . the boy who threw away his body on the Snow Mountains?" (WND-I, 1069). And to the lay nun Myoichi, he writes of her deceased husband, who had dedicated his life to the Mystic Law, "He must certainly have received blessings as great as theirs [those of the boy Snow Mountains and Bodhisattva Medicine King]" (WND-1, 536).

In light of the above, we can say that the earnest resolve of each person who lives based on the Mystic Law and struggles for kosen-rufu contains the benefit of all Buddhist practices and all meritorious deeds.

According to this passage, a Buddha has served and practiced under an incalculable number of Buddhas for an unimaginably long time. This practice, continued over many lifetimes, becomes the cause for enlightenment; as a result, the practitioner attains the supreme state of Buddhahood. This is termed "countless kalpas of practice."

We should bear in mind, however, that this is only a literal interpretation of the Buddha's causes (practices) and effects (virtues) as described in the Lotus Sutra's theoretical teaching.

Reading this passage from the standpoint of Nichiren Buddhism, President Toda explained that it is unnecessary for us to engage in such practices for countless kalpas to attain enlightenment. He said as follows:

> From the standpoint of the Daishonin's teaching, the Buddha [the Gohonzon] of Nam-myoho-renge-kyo is the fundamental Law that gives birth to a hundred, a thousand, ten thousand or a million Buddhas. Therefore, without undertaking any difficult or painful practices, by simply chanting Nam-myoho-renge-kyo, we gain more benefit than we could by personally attending that many Buddhas. The benefit of this single practice is equal to that of the immeasurable number of austerities carried out by all Buddhas.

Nam-myoho-renge-kyo is the fundamental Law that gives rise to all Buddhas. To put it another way, the fundamental cause that enables all Buddhas to attain enlightenment is not that they have carried out various austerities over countless kalpas. Rather, it's because they have awakened to the fundamental Law of Nam-myoho-renge-kyo. The Buddhist practice of the Latter Day of the Law is to embrace and uphold the Law of Nam-myoho-renge-kyo directly. In Nichiren Buddhism, therefore, it is not necessary to engage in austerities for countless kalpas to attain Buddhahood.

Nichiren Daishonin states in "The Object of Devotion for Observing the Mind": "Shakyamuni's practices and the virtues he consequently attained are all contained within the five characters of Myoho-renge-kyo. If we believe in these five characters, we will naturally be granted the same benefits as he was" (WND-1, 365). The practices to attain Buddhahood carried out by Shakyamuni and all Buddhas throughout time and space, and the virtues they acquired as a result, are all contained in Nam-myoho-renge-kyo. This is the principle that embracing the Gohonzon is in itself observing one's own mind (i.e. attaining enlightenment). It is also termed "attaining Buddhahood in one's present form" and the "immediate attainment of enlightenment."

Nichiren Daishonin says that, for a person who embraces the Mystic Law, "Becoming a Buddha is nothing extraordinary" (WND-1, 1030). Nichiren's teaching establishes a path leading to Buddhahood for all. Attaining Buddhahood is not something that happens in the distant future or somewhere far away. Nichiren Buddhism makes it possible for all people to attain Buddhahood in this lifetime.

The teaching of "embracing the Gohonzon is in itself observing one's own mind" represents a revolutionary view of what it means to attain Buddhahood. President Toda said, "In contrast to the Buddhas of the 'Expedient Means' chapter who have practiced for tens of millions of years, we can complete our practice for attaining Buddhahood by simply believing in the Gohonzon and chanting the single phrase Nam-myoho-renge-kyo."

There is immeasurable benefit in chanting Nam-myoho-renge-kyo even just once. Instantaneously, we gain all the benefit the Buddhas acquired over many lifetimes of practice. That's how great the Mystic Law is.

According to the conventional Buddhist view, the process of attaining enlightenment is like climbing a steep mountain path toward the peak of Buddhahood far in the distance. By contrast, Nichiren Buddhism enables all people to reach the summit of enlightenment instantaneously. From the state of Buddhahood, we can gaze down on the surrounding mountains far below and survey the spectacular panorama of nature stretching out in all directions.

We can attain this vast state of Buddhahood directly—right now, right where we are. Then we go out into society and tell others of this exhilarating state of life we experience. This practice represents the quintessence of Nichiren Buddhism.

Buddhist Practice Means Challenging Ourselves Daily

"They have exerted themselves bravely and vigorously, and their names are universally known" refers to the practices of the Buddhas of the pre-Lotus Sutra teachings and the Lotus Sutra's theoretical teaching. At the same time, it provides an important guideline in faith.

First, "bravely and vigorously" means "with faith." *The Six-Volume Writings* by Nichikan cites the interpretation that "'bravely' means to act with courage and 'vigorously' means to use every ounce of one's wisdom." Nichikan explains that "bravely and vigorously" means to courageously exercise one's powers of faith to the fullest.

Buddhist practice has to be carried out with determination and courage. When we challenge ourselves bravely with the spirit to accomplish more today than yesterday and more tomorrow than today, we are truly practicing. Without such a brave and vigorous spirit, we cannot break the iron shackles of destiny, nor can we defeat obstacles and devils. Our daily prayers are dramas of challenging and creating something new in our lives. When we bravely stand up with faith, the darkness of despair and anxiety vanishes from our hearts and in pours the light of hope and growth. This spirit to stand up courageously is the spirit of faith.

The Buddha Nature Manifests When We Practice With Sincerity and Consistency

From the standpoint of Nichiren Buddhism, "exert" means to chant Nam-myoho-renge-kyo diligently for the happiness of oneself and others. We can exert ourselves in this fashion only if we possess a brave and vigorous spirit.

Nichikan, citing Miao-lo's interpretation of the term "exert" as meaning "pure" and "continuous," teaches the proper attitude to have in chanting Nam-myoho-renge-kyo. He explains that "pure" means unalloyed and that "continuous" means to practice continuously and unceasingly. In other words, the important thing is that we chant Nam-myoho-renge-kyo each day with sincerity and consistency. Only then does it become the practice for polishing our lives and attaining Buddhahood in this lifetime.

The Daishonin says: "If in a single moment of life we exhaust the pains and trials of millions of kalpas, then instant after instant there will arise in us the three Buddha bodies with which we are eternally endowed. Nam-myoho-renge-kyo is just such a 'diligent' practice" (OTT, 214).

In chanting Nam-myoho-renge-kyo, we are carrying out "diligent" practice; that is, we are exerting ourselves as the sutra describes. Therefore, the three Buddha bodies, the immeasurable wisdom and compassion of the Buddha, manifest in our lives at each moment when we are earnestly concerned for the Law and bravely and tenaciously struggle for its sake. When we have a brave and vigorous spirit of faith, we instantaneously manifest the life state of the Buddha. This is what "embracing the Gohonzon is in itself observing one's own mind" means.

Put another way, Nichiren says that those who bravely and vigorously exert themselves in faith are all Buddhas.

A Life of Continuous Self-Improvement

Let us remember that the SGI has greatly developed precisely because we have bravely and vigorously exerted ourselves in faith—that is, with true earnestness.

Once when asked by a foreign journalist to explain the reason for our great development, I said, "It's because of our wholehearted dedication." The present tremendous progress of kosen-rufu has come about because we have earnestly and wholeheartedly taken action for the sake of friends, society and peace.

A youth once asked Mr. Makiguchi how one could develop the ability to judge good and evil. He replied, "If you have the tenacity and courage to practice the world's foremost religion, you will come to understand." He also once said: "You must bravely and vigorously exert yourself. You must take action. Even though I am now an old man, I, too, am practicing in this manner."

Exerting oneself bravely and vigorously truly is the wellspring of the Soka Gakkai spirit. When we bravely challenge ourselves through faith, our lives stir, wisdom is born, our beings overflow with joy and hope.

A person of bravery and vigor who continually, moment by moment, makes causes for self-improvement is an eternal victor. Those who struggle with earnestness and broad-mindedness, with the spirit of a lion king, are certainly exerting brave and vigorous effort.

Shine as a Celebrity of the Mystic Law

The next line, "their names are universally known," means that the names of those who bravely and vigorously exert themselves in their practice will be known far and wide. Because of their brave and vigorous efforts, they win renown. Because of their splendid Buddhist practice, they move the hearts of all Buddhas.

Nichiren writes to a follower whose husband was seriously ill:

> No matter what may happen on the road between this life and the next, he should declare himself to be a disciple of Nichiren. . . . My name resounds throughout the pure lands of the ten directions, and heaven and earth no doubt know it. If your husband declares that he is Nichiren's disciple, I do not think that evil demons of any kind can claim ignorance of my name. (WND-1, 938)

President Toda often told us that when we go to Eagle Peak, we should proudly declare ourselves "disciples of Josei Toda, the leader of kosen-rufu." The names of those who bravely and vigorously dedicate themselves to kosen-rufu are known to all Buddhas and bodhisattvas in the ten directions, and to Brahma and Shakra and all the heavenly gods and benevolent deities. Their reputation extends throughout the universe.

The reason for this, the sutra explains, is that spreading the correct Buddhist teaching in the Latter Day of the Law is the most difficult undertaking. Accordingly, the great achievement of those who actually spread the Lotus Sutra cannot fail to be known to the beings in the worlds of the ten directions, the entire universe. Therefore, all Buddhas, bodhisattvas and heavenly gods and benevolent deities throughout the three existences and the ten directions—throughout time and space—are sure to protect the courageous men and women who propagate the Mystic Law.

In "The Emergence of the Treasure Tower," the eleventh chapter, Shakyamuni says: "This sutra is hard to uphold; if one can uphold it even for a short while [after I have entered extinction] I will surely rejoice and so will the other Buddhas. A person who can do this wins the admiration of the Buddhas" (LSOC, 220).

And Nichiren Daishonin writes: "Now, no matter what, strive in faith and be known as a votary of the Lotus Sutra, and remain my disciple for the rest of your life" (WND-1, 385) and "Bring forth the great power of faith, and be spoken of by all the people of Kamakura, both high and low, or by all the people of Japan, as 'Shijo Kingo, Shijo Kingo of the Lotus school!'" (WND-1, 319).

Nichiren's intent is for each person to shine as a celebrity of the Mystic Law in their community and in society at large. By making dedicated efforts in faith, we are certain to develop such a reputation.

To win a name for oneself through dedication to the Lotus Sutra is the highest honor. The lives of those who struggle for kosen-rufu alongside the original Buddha, Nichiren Daishonin, bloom eternally with a beautiful fragrance of Buddhahood. They are definitely known to all Buddhas in the ten directions.

The SGI's movement and ideals have now spread throughout the world, and as a result, voices far and wide are extolling Buddhism's value. This certainly corroborates the words "their names are universally known."

This propagation, which has brought the Mystic Law to some 115 countries and territories,[5] is unprecedented in the history of Buddhism. You, the millions of friends who have emerged from the earth, have accomplished this sacred undertaking. No other individuals or groups have dedicated themselves to spreading Buddhism and elevating the Law with such earnestness.

Your names and the SGI's name will definitely shine with a golden light in history and resound throughout the universe, reaching the ears of all Buddhas in the ten directions. This is clear in light of the words "their names are universally known."

According to the passage "They have realized the Law that is profound and never known before," the Mystic Law in which we believe is a teaching "never known before." When I read these words, I feel as though the dawn were breaking before my eyes.

In the past, Shakyamuni served countless Buddhas and carried out an immeasurable number of religious practices. This passage says that as a result of his arduous practice for enlightenment over a period of countless kalpas, he "realized the Law that is profound and never known before."

T'ien-t'ai explains that "profound" means "reaching the very foundation of enlightenment." And "never known before" indicates that, until then, no one knew of this Law and that Shakyamuni himself didn't know of it until he attained enlightenment.

It was therefore certainly beyond the people of the nine worlds, including the people of the two vehicles and the bodhisattvas. That's why a little later in "Expedient Means" Shakyamuni says, "The true aspect of all phenomena can only be understood and shared between Buddhas" (LSOC, 57).

The Lotus Sutra Reveals the Secret Teaching for Attaining Buddhahood

The Lotus Sutra is the teaching that reveals this "Law . . . never known before," this Law that "can only be understood and shared between Buddhas."

The pre-Lotus Sutra teachings were all "preached in accordance with the minds of others"—that is, according to the capacities of the people of the nine worlds. For people of the nine worlds, therefore, the Lotus Sutra is a teaching they have never heard before; and in this sense, too, it is a Law "never known before."

The Lotus Sutra reveals to all people the "secret" teaching "understood and shared [only] between Buddhas" that has never been known before. But a genuine secret teaching is not something kept to oneself, hidden from others and used to create an aura of mystery or to appropriate authority. When the proper time arrives, a genuine secret teaching should be expounded passionately and spread to cure all humankind's ills, its brilliant force thus proven. That is the purpose of this secret teaching, of this "Law that is profound and never known before."

In many of his writings, Nichiren Daishonin refers to the Gohonzon of the Three Great Secret Laws as a "great mandala never before known" (WND-1, 832). He writes: "Even in the Lotus Sutra he [Shakyamuni] did not allude to it in the earlier chapters of the theoretical teaching. He began things in the 'Treasure Tower' chapter, he revealed it in the 'Life Span' chapter, and he brought things to a close in the 'Supernatural Powers' and 'Entrustment' chapters" (WND-1, 467).

In another place, he states:

> Now, during the three periods following the Buddha's passing, in the two thousand years of the Former and Middle Days of the Law, not even the term "object of devotion of the essential teaching" yet existed. How then could the object of devotion have been revealed? . . . T'ien-t'ai, Miao-lo, and Dengyo . . . never put it into words . . . I was the first to reveal . . . this great mandala. (WND-1, 831)

Nichiren Daishonin bestowed the great secret teaching known only to Buddhas upon all people of the Latter Day in the form of the object of devotion that has never before been known. Toward that end, he underwent great persecutions.

It is important to always remember the immense compassion the Daishonin revealed in spreading this teaching. For the same reason, it is important to practice faith based on a profound sense of gratitude and joy.

The "Law that is profound and never known before" manifests in our lives when we have ardent faith in the "great mandala never before known."

Advance With the Pride of the Bodhisattvas of the Earth

President Toda explained the passage "They have realized the Law that is profound and never known before" as follows: "This refers to the establishment of the Gohonzon of the Buddhism of sowing in Nichiren Daishonin's own life."

The Law that is profound and never known before does not exist somewhere else. It manifests in the living bodies, the actual lives of us who embrace the Gohonzon. In "On the Treasure Tower," Nichiren writes, "Whether eminent or humble, high or low, those who chant Nam-myoho-renge-kyo are themselves the treasure tower, and, likewise, are themselves the Thus Come One Many Treasures" (WND-1, 299).

In other words, we should erect the treasure tower of Nam-myoho-renge-kyo within our lives. This is the spirit that imbues the passage "They have realized the Law that is profound and never known before."

Not only Shakyamuni but all people can awaken to the Law that is profound and never known before. All people can establish the treasure tower in their lives and shine brilliantly as entities of the treasure tower. In time, the earth will teem with countless shining treasure towers of life. From the standpoint of Nichiren Buddhism, this will constitute the actual proof of the passage "They have realized the Law that is profound and never known before." We are opening a never before known dawn in human history by means of the great, never before known Mystic Law.

Because it is such a teaching, votaries and courageous Bodhisattvas of the Earth never known before must appear in order to spread it. President Toda said, "We are members of the Soka Gakkai family, Bodhisattvas of the Earth, who have emerged from the earth to accomplish the unprecedented widespread propagation of the Law." We have inherited President Toda's spirit and are striving to carry out this practice never known before.

Please be confident that in advancing this "unprecedented widespread propagation of the Law," we will receive immeasurable and boundless good fortune and blessings, the likes of which have never been known before.

The SGI Puts Nichiren's Intention Into Practice

In the passage "And [they] preach it [the Law] in accordance with what is appropriate, yet their intentions are difficult to understand," Shakyamuni explains why the door to the wisdom of the Buddhas is difficult to understand and difficult to enter.

Shakyamuni indicates that the pre-Lotus Sutra teachings were expounded according to the capacities of the people of the nine worlds. He also indicates that he has not yet explained his intention in expounding his teaching and that no one has yet comprehended it.

It is no simple matter to directly expound the Law that is profound and never known before, which the Buddha has attained as the result of bold practice. That's because the levels of understanding differ so greatly between the Buddha and other beings.

Even were the Buddha to expound the true teaching, should the people not fully understand, there would be the danger they would develop doubt, destroy the Law and fall into the three evil paths of existence.

Shakyamuni, after attaining enlightenment beneath the bodhi tree, at first hesitated to expound the Law. He realized, however, that unless he expounded his teaching right then and there, people would be forever locked in the darkness of delusion. Herein lay the inner conflict of Shakyamuni, who pioneered the way for the enlightenment of all human beings. Overcoming his dilemma, he began to teach the Law.

Shakyamuni wanted people to gain a correct and unerring understanding of the Law. He therefore exercised every ounce of his wisdom, continuously pondering how to convey his enlightenment to as many people as possible. He taxed his ingenuity. Such was Shakyamuni's compassion. Wisdom is born of compassion.

He set forth teachings for people of the three vehicles according to their various capacities. He expounded the way of the voice-hearers, the way of the cause-awakened ones and the way of the bodhisattvas, tailoring each teaching to each group's understanding. He thereby enabled them to arrive at the "door to this wisdom" of the Buddhas. This was the expedient purpose of the provisional teachings that preceded the Lotus Sutra.

In this passage, Shakyamuni says that Buddhas preach the sutra "in accordance with what is appropriate." That is, they expound the Law in accordance with what is appropriate to the capacities of the people.

The Buddha's true intention is always to expound the supreme vehicle of Buddhahood, the path for all people to become Buddhas. The voice-hearers and the cause-awakened ones do not understand this, however. Having grown attached to provisional teachings, they fail to understand that the Buddha's true intention is to enable all people without exception to become Buddhas. They do not comprehend the true teaching that makes all people Buddhas. This is the meaning of "their intentions are difficult to understand."

Needless to say, the Buddha did not try to make his teaching difficult to understand. Rather, the intention is difficult to understand because his listeners harbor attachments and do not believe.

When people's hearts are closed, they cannot readily accept even sound reasoning. This shows just how fearful is attachment to mistaken ideas. Such attachment can destroy a person's life.

In fact, the three powerful enemies persecute the Lotus Sutra's votaries precisely because these enemies remain attached to provisional teachings, failing to understand the heart of the Lotus Sutra. The sutra says, "The evil monks of that muddied age, failing to understand the Buddha's expedient means, how he preaches the Law in accordance with what is appropriate, will confront us with foul language" (LSOC, 234).

Those who fail to understand and who distort the Buddha's true intention will persecute those who practice exactly as the Buddha taught. And in any age, the former will be numerous and the latter few.

Speak Out for the True Teaching

In a polluted and evil society, those who persecute the votaries of the Lotus Sutra will spread malicious rumors, try to turn public opinion against the votaries and seek to drive off people of justice.

Since this is a muddied world of such inverted proprieties, we need to raise the cry of truth and justice persistently. We must win and show proof of the correct teaching.

After Nichiren died, his correct teaching was protected because Nikko Shonin stood up alone. Had Nikko Shonin remained silent, then no doubt history would have labeled the five senior priests as correct. Instead, Nikko Shonin strictly refuted their erroneous teachings.

The five senior priests did not understand Nichiren's intention, the true intention of the original Buddha. The Daishonin's sole intention was to accomplish the widespread propagation of the object of devotion and enable all people of the Latter Day to become happy.

The five senior priests lost sight of Nichiren's spirit. Nikko Shonin alone followed and served the Daishonin continually, endured persecutions together with him and boldly propagated his teaching in strict accordance with the mentor's instructions. Because he struggled one in spirit with the mentor, he understood Nichiren's intention.

You can tell whether the mentor's spirit has been understood correctly by looking at the disciple's conduct. No matter how people may claim to uphold Nichiren Buddhism, if they don't take action for kosen-rufu for the happiness of all people, then we must conclude that they have lost sight of the Daishonin's intention.

Seven hundred years after Nichiren's struggle to spread the Law amid persecution, when his spirit was almost extinguished, the Soka Gakkai appeared. The Soka Gakkai has directly inherited his true teaching and advances in accord with his will and decree.

The Soka Gakkai is directly connected to Nichiren and bases itself on the Gohonzon and Nichiren's writings, and it is the only body of harmoniously united believers that correctly passes on what he intended.

As glorious verifiers of the correct teaching, let us speak out for kosen-rufu with lofty pride and dignity and with golden eloquence, not begrudging our voices.

"If We Do Not Harbor Doubts in Our Hearts," We Can Attain the Summit of Happiness

President Toda explained the meaning of the line "their intentions are difficult to understand" as it applies to our practice:

> Whereas the Buddha sees what is to come, for us the future
> is totally dark, and we can see only what has already passed.
> For this reason, it is difficult for us to awaken to the heart of

the Gohonzon. It is enough that we believe wholeheartedly
in the Gohonzon, no matter what. If we do so, then we will
definitely receive benefit. It is no good if we start doubting
along the way.

He is discussing the ultimate meaning of faith. Firm faith in the
Gohonzon leads to the highest wisdom. This is the principle of substituting faith for wisdom.

Nichiren's intent is to enable all people to become Buddhas. Therefore, it is impossible that those who embrace his Buddhism throughout their lives could fail to realize true happiness.

In the course of our practice, however, various things arise on
account of the negative causes and tendencies in our own lives. There
may be times when we think, "What did I do to deserve this?" But
we should not be swayed every time such phenomena arise, for it
is already certain that we will become happy in the end. We should
regard everything that happens to us in our practice as our training.
If we do so, then later we will see the profound meaning and intention
underlying each of these phenomena.

As Nichiren writes, "If we do not harbor doubts in our hearts, we
will as a matter of course attain Buddhahood" (WND-1, 283). Those
who avoid succumbing to doubts no matter what happens are win-
ners in faith. They are people who truly understand the Daishonin's
intention.

3

Shari-hotsu. Go ju jo-butsu irai. Shuju innen. Shuju hiyu. Ko en gonkyo. Mu shu hoben. Indo shujo. Ryo ri sho jaku.

"Shariputra, ever since I attained Buddhahood I have through various causes and various similes widely expounded my teachings and have used countless expedient means to guide living beings and cause them to renounce their attachments." (LSOC, 56)

HERE, SHAKYAMUNI elaborates on the passage immediately preceding this one, in which he discussed the "wisdom of the Buddhas." In this passage, by contrast, he reveals this wisdom in his own life.

"Ever since I attained Buddhahood" refers to the period after Shakyamuni attained enlightenment and before he taught the Lotus Sutra. During this time, he expounded various provisional sutras, and here he clarifies the distinctive character of those teachings.

An expedient means is a device that the Buddha employs to help people attain enlightenment. From the outset, Shakyamuni's ultimate purpose lay in enabling all people to attain Buddhahood. But he does not reveal this in the provisional sutras; he reveals it for the first time in the Lotus Sutra.

The purpose of the provisional sutras is to enable people to part with various attachments. People differ in terms of the types of attachments they have, so Shakyamuni employed various explanations of causes and similes that specific people could best understand.

These teachings were all no more than means for drawing people toward the goal of attaining Buddhahood. In this sense, the pre-Lotus Sutra teachings are regarded as expedient means.

Still, the expedient teachings expounded before the Lotus Sutra arose from the Buddha's compassion. Shakyamuni strove to respond to the different capacities of people, to select teachings that precisely matched their needs and to satisfy everyone. He was waging a struggle of compassion and wisdom.

"What is this person seeking? How should I instruct this person to ensure that he will not deviate from the correct path?" He deeply considered each person's circumstance and gave instruction with an earnest must-win spirit.

Though we may speak of "the people" in the aggregate, they are not an abstract, homogeneous multitude; they are not a colorless mass. "How can the heart of this person before me be opened? How can I reinvigorate this specific individual?" This is the spirit of Buddhism. When speaking to a large number of people, only if we have the attitude that we are addressing each individual can we offer living words that reverberate in their hearts.

Since attaining enlightenment, Shakyamuni devoted himself to teaching the Law for individuals. Because his words and phrases were uttered for individuals, with their happiness in mind, the Law inspired one person after another. Because he waged such a struggle, he sent people's hearts a fresh breeze, dispelling the dark clouds of doubt and anxiety and causing the sun of hope and happiness to emerge. Because he regarded the individual with such warmth, people from all walks of life—young and old, men and women—gathered with joy and enthusiasm to hear Shakyamuni speak.

Shakyamuni preached the expedient teachings because he

sympathized with the people, whose lives were steeped in illusion and suffering. He was impelled by the desire to somehow help them. This led him to consider, "By what means can I save them from suffering? How might I liberate them from illusions?" In other words, expedients arose from his desire to help people; his compassion gave birth to wisdom.

Shakyamuni aroused a great mercy and resolved to save all people from suffering. At that time, the Buddhas of the ten directions appeared and urged Shakyamuni on, saying: "But following the example of all other Buddhas, you will employ the power of expedient means. We too . . . make distinctions and preach the three vehicles" (LSOC, 77–78). Thereupon Shakyamuni, preparatory to expounding the Law "never known before," began to expound the pre-Lotus Sutra teachings via expedient means.

Expedient means are expressions of wisdom serving to raise people up. Shakyamuni, armed with words of compassion and wisdom, thus resolutely took the first step on the difficult journey to expound the Law for the salvation of all people. And so he raised the curtain on Buddhism, which sends out a message of happiness to all humankind.

The Secret and Wonderful Expedient Means of the Lotus Sutra

As I have already mentioned, the expedient means to which this passage refers are the expedient means of the pre-Lotus Sutra teachings. These are not to be confused with the expedient means indicated by the title of the second chapter of the Lotus Sutra. Profound significance is attached to the expedient means of the Lotus Sutra.

T'ien-t'ai identifies three types of expedient means: "adaptations of the Law expedient means," "expedient means that can lead one in" and the "secret and wonderful expedient means." The first two correspond to the pre-Lotus Sutra teachings and constitute provisional teachings. The "secret and wonderful expedient means" is the teaching that contains the truth.

"Adaptations of the Law expedient means" are the various teachings expounded according to the differing capacities of the people. Through these teachings, Shakyamuni brought benefit to people of various capacities.

"Expedient means that can lead one in" indicate the teachings the Buddha preached as a gateway to the true teaching.

These expedients of the pre-Lotus Sutra teachings serve to guide people to the wisdom of the Buddha; they are the means for directing people until they have reached the Lotus Sutra. And, as Shakyamuni indicates when he says, "Honestly discarding expedient means" (LSOC, 79), the expedients of the pre-Lotus Sutra teachings should be discarded once the Lotus Sutra has been expounded.

Shakyamuni Dared to Express the Truth in Words

By contrast, the expedient of the Lotus Sutra is not an expedient that ought to be discarded; it is the teaching of the truth. At the same time, however, it is still always just an expedient. Although the second chapter explains the truth, it is titled not "Truth" but "Expedient Means." Herein lies the profound significance of the secret and wonderful expedient means.

In the opening of "Expedient Means," we are told that the wisdom of the Buddhas is infinitely profound and immeasurable and difficult for all voice-hearers and cause-awakened ones to comprehend. It is the ultimate teaching that defies expression through words and so cannot be explained. But unless the wisdom of all Buddhas is expressed, all people will forever remain shut away in darkness. For this reason, the Buddha ventures to put it into words.

Compared with the inexpressible truth, the words the Buddha uses to expound it are expedients. At the same time, it is through these words that people can be saved. The words of the Lotus Sutra that the Buddha expounded "in accordance with one's own mind" constitute the secret and wonderful expedient. More than simply a means, these words are an expedient at one with the Buddha's wisdom.

Regarding the words of the Lotus Sutra, Nichiren Daishonin says things like: "Its words are the ultimate reality" (WND-1, 3); all "69,384 characters of the sutra, each of which is a Buddha" (WND-2, 602); and "When you cast your eyes upon the words of the Lotus Sutra, you should consider that you are beholding the living body of the Thus Come One Shakyamuni" (WND-1, 333). Nichiren thus repeatedly emphasized the oneness of the Buddha's wisdom and the words whereby it is expressed.

In a sense, it could be said that the expedients of the pre-Lotus Sutra teachings and the expedient of the Lotus Sutra are entirely opposite in their directionality. The Japanese term for "expedient means," *hoben*, derives from the Sanskrit *upaya*, meaning, "approach." The pre-Lotus Sutra teachings enable people to move away from illusion and approach enlightenment. The direction, in other words, is toward the wisdom of the Buddhas. This is the direction of the adaptations of the Law expedient means and the expedient means that can lead one in. These expedients are no longer of any use once we arrive at the teaching of the Lotus Sutra.

In the Lotus Sutra, by contrast, Shakyamuni articulates the wisdom of the Buddhas according with his own mind. The directionality of this expedient is thus that of the Buddha approaching the world of human beings. This is the secret and wonderful expedient.

Through the power of the Lotus Sutra, pre-Lotus Sutra teachings take on importance as partial expressions of the truth. They are said to be revealed and unified in the teaching of the Lotus Sutra.

Revealing the Power of the Mystic Law Through Our Struggles

The wisdom of the Buddhas revealed in the "Expedient Means" chapter is the "true aspect of all phenomena." Put another way, it is the truth that all living beings are Buddhas.

The "secret" of the secret wonderful expedient means indicates that the Buddha concealed, or kept secret, the truth for the first forty-two years of his preaching life, expounding it only in the Lotus Sutra. When viewed from the standpoint of the Lotus Sutra, however, all the provisional teachings are included in the sutra as partial explanations of the truth. This inclusion is termed "wonderful."

This is exemplified in the parable of the Jewel in the Robe related in "Prophecy of Enlightenment for Five Hundred Disciples," the eighth chapter of the Lotus Sutra. A man is given a priceless jewel by a close friend, who sews it into the lining of the man's robe while the man drowses in a drunken stupor. Not realizing he possesses the jewel, the man suffers hardships and is always in want. Much later, he meets the friend again, and only then does he discover that all along he has had the jewel of great value.

The man's friend (the Buddha) knew that the man (representing the beings of the nine worlds) possessed the jewel (the world of Buddhahood) in his robe, even though the man failed to realize it.

An ordinary human being is a Buddha. This is difficult and wonderful to understand. Unless we believe we possess the Buddha nature, it will remain forever secret. However, once we recognize it, it is no longer secret, and our wonderful powers appear.

President Toda said: "That we are merely ordinary, unenlightened beings is the secret and wonderful expedient. The truth is that we are Buddhas." To realize this truth is to understand the secret and wonderful expedient.

Although we are Buddhas, we are born as common mortals. This is so that, through doing our human revolution and showing proof of the Mystic Law, we can accomplish kosen-rufu. If we had everything from the outset, including good health and riches, then other people could not understand the power of the Mystic Law. Therefore, we reveal it to them through our struggles as common mortals. This is the secret and wonderful expedient.

Victory in Life Through Victory in Faith

In other words, all of us who believe in the Gohonzon—the Lotus Sutra of the Latter Day—and who are struggling amid the reality of the nine worlds exemplify the secret and wonderful expedient.

As long as we live based on the Gohonzon, then any and all sufferings become expedient means for us to strengthen and deepen the world of Buddhahood in our lives. Sufferings and joys and everything that happens to us become expedient means for us to reveal the power of the Mystic Law.

It is said that life is like a drama. Whether in the world of business, education or the home, each person plays a role in a drama. Though the role is itself an expedient means, should the "actor" abandon it, he or she will be at a loss for a mission. When acting out our respective roles, we manifest our own inner truth most fully.

Daily life equals faith. And the world of Buddhahood appears nowhere except on the stage of the reality of the nine worlds. We enact the drama of human revolution on the stage of our lives.

From misery to happiness, from disappointment to hope, from fate to mission, from suffering to eternal joy—the driving force that makes these dynamic transformations possible is faith in the Mystic Law.

Dialogue is the lifeline of Buddhism. The Buddha's fundamental objective is to develop in the lives of all people a wisdom equal to his own.

As this implies, we tell others about Buddhism because, fundamentally, we venerate their lives. If, on the other hand, we had the attitude "Even if I tell this person about Buddhism, it couldn't possibly do any good," then we simply would not bother talking to them.

We tell people about Buddhism because we respect them as human beings. Because we trust the person, we can conduct tenacious dialogue.

Saying, "I have . . . widely expounded my teachings and have used countless expedient means to guide living beings," Shakyamuni indicates that he has guided people through free and boundless dialogue. Shakyamuni and Nichiren Daishonin both spread the Law through talking and speaking out in the very midst of the people.

Tsunesaburo Makiguchi and Josei Toda were also experts at dialogue. Regardless of the social standing of the person they were addressing, they always spoke with dignity and conviction. They created a history of such conversation.

The power of dialogue changes people's hearts. Sincere dialogue is the sunlight that can soften and melt hearts that are thoroughly frozen over. Clear, confident words are the fresh breeze that dispels clouds of illusion. Buddhist dialogue is the foundation for bringing change to people's lives.

Shakyamuni says here that he has conducted compassionate dialogue and spoken earnestly with a must-win spirit in order to help others; he has exercised every ounce of wisdom and ingenuity to ensure that his words might reach people's hearts. This is the significance of the "various causes and various similes" to which he refers. In other words, he continually spoke out and conducted dialogue, explaining the reason behind the unfolding of actions and events and employing examples to make his teaching easy to understand.

The Cause to Dedicate One's Life to Kosen-rufu

"Various causes" refers to causes and their effects, to the origin of things and to the relations or connections that exist between self and other, or between all things.

One Buddhist scripture, for example, explains the causes and relations associated with King Ashoka through the story of two young boys, Virtue Victorious and Invincible, who made offerings to Shakyamuni. Virtue Victorious offered the Buddha a mud pie, while Invincible pressed his palms together in reverence. Shakyamuni then explains to his disciple Ananda that Virtue Victorious is sure to be reborn as a king named Ashoka. Later, according to traditional accounts, Virtue Victorious, due to the causes he formed in making an offering to the Buddha, was born as Ashoka, the son of King Bindusara.

In the pre-Lotus Sutra teachings, through examples such as these, Shakyamuni strove to help people awaken to the strict law of cause and effect operating in their lives.

Still greater significance attaches to the causes expounded in the Lotus Sutra. These concern what might be referred to as the life-to-life bond between the Buddha and the people—the relationship that has existed between the Buddha and living beings since the remote past.

In this connection with this, President Toda said:

> Regarding the meaning of "various causes": In the remote past of beginningless time we were followers of the original Buddha, Nichiren Daishonin. Because of this cause, now in the Latter Day of the Law, more than six hundred years after Nichiren's passing, here in Japan, a country steeped in misery, we as his disciples have appeared as poor people. We demonstrate that by believing in this Gohonzon we can become wealthy. When we recall the cause we made in having promised to accomplish kosen-rufu, our poverty and other sufferings will vanish in an instant.

To prove the power of the Mystic Law, we need to experience various worries and struggles in our present existence. Having promised in the primal moment of the infinite past to accomplish the widespread propagation of the Mystic Law, we have now been born to carry out this mission.

It is impossible that a Bodhisattva of the Earth could remain submerged in suffering or be defeated by hardships. Once we realize the cause—namely, that we freely chose our circumstances so we could prove the validity of Buddhism—we can definitely win.

One Person's Victory Provides an Illustration for All

Next, "various similes" refers to the allegories and parables Shakyamuni expounded in the pre-Lotus Sutra teachings. Using natural reason and examples from immediate life experience to explain difficult Buddhist principles makes them easy to understand. This is Shakyamuni's purpose in employing similes.

The use of similes, therefore, arises from compassion for others. Precisely because the Buddha's compassion is so strong, he expounds skillful similes in hopes of making his teachings as easy as possible to understand.

The Buddha, adapting his preaching to the people's capacity, draws comparisons with a wide variety of natural phenomena and common observations. For example, in the pre-Lotus Sutra teachings, he variously compares earthly desires to a fierce current that sweeps people along, to a shade that conceals the light of the Buddha nature, to flames that consume one's body and mind, to poison that harms one greatly and to a dense forest where those who become lost can never find their way out. In this way, he taught people the fearfulness of, and tried to cause them to renounce, earthly desires.

Simply renouncing earthly desires, however, does not amount to attaining enlightenment. The similes of the pre-Lotus Sutra teachings explain the Buddha wisdom from one angle only. In fact, there is the danger that if we become preoccupied with these similes, it will actually make it harder to attain Buddhahood.

By contrast, the similes of the Lotus Sutra are at one with the Buddha wisdom. That's because they reveal and express the Buddha's enlightenment and wisdom just as they are.

Our Experiences Are Like the Parables Explaining the Power of Faith

Moreover, viewed from the standpoint of the Law of Nam-myoho-renge-kyo, it might be said that all sutras, including the Lotus Sutra, are grand similes to help people understand the Gohonzon of Nam-myoho-renge-kyo.

In Nichiren Buddhism, instances of actual proof of faith manifesting in our daily lives are also similes and parables explaining the Gohonzon's power. These illustrations of actual proof eloquently testify to the truth of the Gohonzon.

Regarding "various similes," President Toda explained that the life-or-death struggles of Nichiren's contemporaries and the benefit they received serve as similes and parables for us in modern times.

There is Shijo Kingo, who overcame hardships in his place of work; the Ikegami brothers, who brought their father, who had opposed their faith, to convert to the Daishonin's teaching; Nanjo Tokimitsu, who defeated the devil of illness and dedicated his life to the mission of a successor; the lay nun Myoichi, who struggled in the cause of faith for herself and on behalf of her deceased husband; and the list goes on. The actual proof shown by each follower who overcame difficult circumstances is a source of great encouragement for us as we face similar problems.

This same principle applies to our sharing our own experiences. One person's victorious experience can provide courage, hope and heartfelt understanding to many others.

Our victories become splendid illustrations of how many others can win. Our triumphs over hardships provide many others with confidence: "If that's the case, then I can win, too. If that person can win, everyone can be victorious."

When talking about the power of the Mystic Law, people may discuss your victory as a parable, saying, "Just look at him, for example," or "Look at the human revolution she is carrying out."

In this sense, let us compose many dramas of human revolution for the sake of others. Let us adorn our lives with many "various causes" and "various similes." And let us decorate our communities like flower gardens filled with many and varied dramas of human revolution, with one person after another realizing victory and becoming happy.

The Wisdom to Discern the True Nature of Attachments

Shakyamuni says that he tried to free people from desires and illusions by employing causes and similes.

The fundamental cause of people's unhappiness lies in their tendency to develop attachments of various kinds. An attachment, just as it sounds, is a fetter on one's heart; it indicates earthly desires, cravings and the like. In the pre-Lotus Sutra teachings, Shakyamuni taught the people of the nine worlds, whose lives were steeped in misery, the path for freeing themselves from such attachments. That is, he caused them "to renounce their attachments."

The spirit of the Lotus Sutra, however, is not to eradicate earthly desires. When we base ourselves on the Mystic Law, we can transform desires—just as they are—into enlightenment. This is the principle that earthly desires are enlightenment.

The "Former Affairs of the Bodhisattva Medicine King" chapter of the Lotus Sutra says, "It [the Lotus Sutra] can cause living beings to cast off all . . . pain" (LSOC, 328). Regarding this, Nichiren says that "cast off" should be interpreted as "becoming enlightened concerning" (OTT, 174).

In Nichiren Buddhism, therefore, "cause them to renounce their attachments" should be interpreted as "cause them to become enlightened concerning their attachments." It's not a matter of eradicating attachments but of seeing them clearly. In other words, rather than cause us to abandon our earthly desires and attachments, our Buddhist practice enables us to discern their true nature and use them as the driving force to become happy.

The truth is that we could not in fact eradicate our attachments even if we so wished. For the sake of argument, even if it were feasible, doing so would make it impossible to live in the real world.

What is important is that we make full use of our attachments rather than allow them to control us. In order to do that, it is necessary that we clearly recognize them for what they are.

Make Full Use of Your Attachments

President Toda said:

> The Gohonzon enables us to perceive our attachments just as they are. I believe that each of you has attachments. I, too, have attachments. Because we have attachments, we can lead interesting and significant lives. For example, to succeed in business or to introduce Buddhism to many others, we must have attachment to such activities. Our faith enables us to maintain these attachments in such a way that they do not cause us suffering. Rather than being controlled by our attachments, we need to fully use our attachments to become happy.

The essence of Mahayana Buddhism lies in developing the state of life to clearly discern and thoroughly use our attachments, thus leading lives made interesting and significant by cultivating strong attachments.

In short, we should cause the firewood of earthly desires to burn high and, to that same extent, chant Nam-myoho-renge-kyo sincerely and take action. In so doing, our earthly desires become a springboard to propel us toward our attainment of Buddhahood.

Faith means creating a mountain for ourselves, climbing it and then starting out again. In this process, we develop from a state of life in which we are caught up with our own small worries to one in which we can challenge progressively greater worries—for the sake of a friend, for many others, for all humankind.

Toward that end, it is important that we always consider the purpose of our actions. When we clearly establish our fundamental objective in life, we can use our attachments most fully and profitably. We can turn them into tailwinds to propel us toward happiness.

This principle offers an extremely valuable guide for living in modern society, where people are constantly swept along by various wants and cravings.

▪4▪

Sho-i sha ga. Nyorai hoben. Chi-ken hara-mitsu. Kai i gu-soku.

"Why is this? Because the Thus Come Ones are fully possessed of both expedient means and the paramita of wisdom." (LSOC, 56)

IN THIS SECTION, Shakyamuni continues to praise the immense wisdom of the Buddhas, or Thus Come Ones. Until this point, he has praised their wisdom from the standpoint of the immeasurable practices that they've carried out. Here he discusses the power of their wisdom to guide people and the state of life they've attained as a result.

Knowledge and Wisdom Are Not the Same

Continuing from the preceding passage, Shakyamuni now clarifies why the Buddha could use various causes and similes to guide people and have them renounce attachments.

In "expedient means and the paramita of wisdom," "paramita of wisdom" means the perfection of wisdom. The Sanskrit word "paramita" means to attain or to perfect. Also, "fully possessed" in the above passage means endowed with. The Buddha, having perfected various practices and attained an extremely profound state of enlightenment, possesses skillful means and perfect wisdom for guiding people in a way that exactly matches their capacity.

In the section that follows, Shakyamuni explains specifically what he means by wisdom. There he says that the Buddha possesses "immeasurable [compassion], unlimited [eloquence], power, fearlessness . . ." (LSOC, 56). I will discuss the contents of this passage in detail later. For the time being, let it suffice that these powers are functions of the wisdom the Buddha uses to guide people to happiness.

Buddhism is a religion of wisdom. President Toda would often make the following point: "One cause of people's misfortune today is that they confuse knowledge and wisdom. . . . Knowledge is not wisdom. Knowledge may serve as a door that opens the way to wisdom, but knowledge itself is definitely not wisdom."

For example, taking business classes in college doesn't guarantee you will prosper in the business world. In fact, many realize commercial success without ever having gone to business school.

Reading many books on child rearing doesn't guarantee that someone can parent well. The truth is that innumerable factors contribute to children's growth. There are even accounts of mothers who experience acute depression or anxiety because, in raising children, they encounter situations that completely contradict what they have read in books.

Knowledge is of course necessary. To *know* something is a great strength. In modern society, in particular, it might be said that knowledge has increasingly come to be used as a weapon. At the same time, merely having knowledge does not produce value. Happiness cannot be created by knowledge alone. An increase in knowledge definitely does not equate to an increase in happiness. The important thing is for people to possess the wisdom to use their knowledge most effectively.

To take one example, theories on childhood education often stress the importance of talking to children at their eye-level. Someone with experience in this area comments as follows:

What should you do when a child starts pleading with you to buy him or her something at a store or somewhere and then sits down on the floor and cries, refusing to budge until you give in? Under such circumstances, no amount of standing above the child and scolding will do any good. The best approach is to sit down right there together with the child. When you do so, the child, in amazement, will stop crying. And if you then quietly admonish the child, you will find that he or she is surprisingly ready to do as you say.

This method, of course, will not necessarily work every time. Still, it doubtless represents individual wisdom arising from the parent's desire to connect on a heart-to-heart level with the child. Knowledge of the importance of talking at the child's eye-level produced this kernel of practical wisdom.

Always Ask, "What Purpose Does This Knowledge Serve?"

Unless we continually ask ourselves, "What purpose does this knowledge serve?" we are liable to fall into the trap of pursuing knowledge for its own sake.

To illustrate, a teacher's mission is to provide instruction. The teacher's purpose is to cultivate the pupils' character and wisdom and help them acquire skills they will need to lead happy lives.

This is the purpose of the teacher's knowledge. But unless the teacher also possesses the wisdom necessary to attain this objective, he or she is not a true educator.

Politicians, as public servants, have the duty to devote themselves selflessly to the people's happiness and prosperity. Toward that end, they must seek the counsel of many others and work to implement their ideas. If politicians lack the wisdom to take such actions, then they are not true politicians.

The purpose of scholars, likewise, is to contribute to humanity through their academic endeavors.

We need to constantly ask ourselves whether we have realized our fundamental mission, our purpose. If we should forget this and instead gloat over how much we know, over our standing or access to information, then our basic spirit will become distorted.

By rights, education, science, politics, economics and all fields of human endeavor exist to serve the happiness of all humanity.

For what purpose, then, did the Buddha appear in the world? His objective, too, was to enable people to become happy and, specifically, to enable all people to realize a state of eternal happiness. Thus there is no contradiction between Buddhism and other areas of human endeavor. Knowledge in all areas yields the greatest value when based on the wisdom of Buddhism.

In the "Expedient Means" chapter, Shakyamuni explains that the Buddha's purpose in appearing in this world is "to open the door of Buddha wisdom to all living beings" . . . "to show the Buddha wisdom to living beings" . . . "to cause living beings to awaken to the Buddha wisdom" and . . . "to induce living beings to enter the path of Buddha wisdom" (LSOC, 64). These four aspects of opening, showing, causing to awaken to and inducing to enter together are referred to as the "one great reason" for the Buddha's appearance in the world.

In short, Shakyamuni taught that the path to happiness lies in each person developing his or her own wisdom. The Buddha himself could develop his wisdom because of his strong sense of purpose and awareness of his mission.

Tend the Ills of Humankind With the Medicine of the Law

Buddhism teaches the supreme way to live.

The question-and-answer sessions President Toda held were truly forums of wisdom to lead people to happiness. With great confidence, he candidly gave guidance regarding people's various worries and sufferings in life—from sickness and loss of work to debt and marital problems—hitting the nail on the head every time. Through his encouragement, participants immediately recovered their spirits and gained renewed courage and hope.

He would remark: "You know people from how they walk, from how they perk up their shoulders, from their voices. Similarly, from the slightest gesture, from how they open a door, you can tell what their worries are."

A true leader of Buddhism can discern with such depth and deft the state of people's lives and can explain the Law to them in a way tailored to their situation.

It is difficult to explain Buddhism correctly, that is, in a manner that accords with the time and people's capacity. There is an account of how even Shariputra blundered in expounding the Law.

Shariputra was once explaining Buddhism to a blacksmith and a laundryman. Neither could grasp the teaching, however, and they both developed doubts.

Shariputra ought to have taught the blacksmith the practice of breath-counting meditation and the laundryman the practice of meditating on the vileness of the body. The reason is that a blacksmith's job entails continually striking hot iron with a hammer while fanning the fire with a bellows. A blacksmith, therefore, constantly works to control the movement of air. Had Shariputra explained the breath-counting meditation to the blacksmith, he could have understood it immediately and advanced in his Buddhist practice. Likewise, since the work of a laundryman involves cleaning dirty clothes, had Shariputra taught him the meditation on the vileness of the body, he without doubt could have grasped it.

But Shariputra taught each the teaching appropriate to the other. As a result, they failed to gain any result from their practice. For all his efforts, Shariputra succeeded only in causing them suffering.

To expound a teaching appropriate to each person is extremely difficult. Nichiren Daishonin, however, established a method of practice accessible to all people regardless of their capacity. Thus, he said, "Nam-myoho-renge-kyo is recommended for people of all capacities" (GZ, 875). And for precisely this reason, the benefit of telling others about the Mystic Law is immense.

An experienced doctor can diagnose a patient's malady accurately and prescribe a treatment that matches the person's constitution. Such a doctor possesses not only medical knowledge but also the wisdom to use that knowledge effectively. True knowledge is at one with wisdom.

There probably are no physicians who would simply tell a patient, "You have appendicitis," without doing anything about it. It might be said that true medical knowledge, or wisdom, lies in curing people of their conditions and returning them to a state of health.

The Buddha is a great physician of life who guides all to happiness. The Buddha clearly discerns the fundamental cause of people's suffering and teaches them the path to eternal happiness, how to live a boundlessly fresh and exhilarating life. This is the wisdom of the Buddha.

In this age, when it has become natural for people to lack compassion, no one can match SGI members in bringing a fresh, revitalizing breeze to many others. There is no other popular organization in the world whose members are so sincere or who pray and take action as we do for others. There are many eminent people and intellectuals in the world, but I believe that SGI members are even more respectable. You are "doctors" and "nurses" of wisdom worthy of the greatest admiration.

Faith Contains the Paramita of Wisdom

How do Shariputra and the others gathered at the assembly react when hearing Shakyamuni expound the "Expedient Means" chapter? Do they think, "I couldn't possibly have even an iota of the perfect wisdom of the Buddha in me"?

No. In fact, they say to themselves: "If this teaching represents the wonderful Buddha wisdom that can save people, then I want to learn it, too. I want to make it my own."

In "Expedient Means," Shariputra and the others "wish to hear the teaching of perfect endowment" (LSOC, 61). In other words, they arouse a seeking mind for the path leading to the Buddha's state of life, which is "fully possessed of both expedient means and the paramita of wisdom."

Rather than think, "I've heard all I need to hear," they become even more spirited and encouraged.

In "The Opening of the Eyes," Nichiren Daishonin says that this "teaching of perfect endowment" is Nam-myoho-renge-kyo (WND-1, 250).

In the pre-Lotus Sutra teachings, Shakyamuni expounded the six paramitas as practices for bodhisattvas to attain the state of life of the Buddha. The idea was that through carrying out the six practices of almsgiving, keeping the precepts, forbearance, assiduousness, meditation and obtaining wisdom they could approach the state of life of the Buddha. Such a practice, carried out in lifetime after lifetime over a vast period of time, is called "countless kalpas of practice."

However, the Immeasurable Meanings Sutra, which serves as an introduction to the Lotus Sutra, states, "Although they have not yet been able to practice the six paramitas, the six paramitas will of themselves appear before them" (LSOC, 26). In other words, even though we do not practice the six paramitas, by embracing the Lotus Sutra, we are naturally endowed with their benefit.

Believe in the Gohonzon and Advance With the SGI

"Distinctions in Benefits," the seventeenth chapter of the Lotus Sutra, explains that the benefit of those who understand and believe in the Lotus Sutra when they hear it expounded is great beyond measure. It says that their benefit will be a hundred, a thousand, ten thousand, a million times greater than the benefit of practicing the five paramitas (i.e., excluding the paramita of obtaining wisdom) for a period of "eight hundred thousand million nayutas of kalpas" (LSOC, 278).

The paramita of obtaining wisdom is excluded because this is the fundamental paramita; it is in a class by itself relative to the other five paramitas. It might also be said that the five paramitas are practiced to attain the paramita of wisdom. Buddhism always places great importance on wisdom.

Therefore, Nichiren Daishonin says that practitioners in the Latter Day of the Law "who have just aroused the aspiration for enlightenment" need not practice the five paramitas (see WND-1, 786). This view of Buddhist practice—expressed at a time when making offerings to priests, upholding the precepts and the other paramitas were being promoted in earnest—represents a great religious revolution.

Moreover, Nichiren Buddhism teaches the principle of substituting faith for wisdom. Correct faith itself becomes wisdom. Through believing in the Gohonzon, we in the Latter Day of the Law can gain the same benefit as we would by carrying out all of the six paramitas, including the paramita of obtaining wisdom.

In conclusion, those who now believe in the Gohonzon and advance toward kosen-rufu together with the SGI can gain the benefit of the six paramitas. Those who persevere in carrying out activities for kosen-rufu with others lead lives of the highest wisdom. The examples of your many seniors in faith attest to this. When we look back on our lives later on, we can see this clearly.

Because we practice faith, let us strive to live most wisely each day based on the principles of faith finds expression in daily life and action for kosen-rufu brings about good health.

▪5▪

Shari-hotsu. Nyorai chi-ken. Kodai jinnon. Muryo muge. Riki. Mu-sho-i. Zenjo. Gedas. Sanmai. Jin nyu musai. Joju issai. Mi-zo-u ho.

"Shariputra, the wisdom of the Thus Come Ones is expansive and profound. They have immeasurable [compassion], unlimited [eloquence], power, fearlessness, concentration, emancipation, and samadhis, and have deeply entered the boundless and awakened to the Law never before attained." (LSOC, 56–57)

THIS PASSAGE explains the expansive powers of the Buddha. That is, it describes the wonderful state of life that those who embrace the Gohonzon can develop.

Interpreting this passage from the standpoint of Nichiren Buddhism, Mr. Toda taught that it explains the state of life embodied in the Gohonzon:

> The difference between the state of life of [the Buddha of] Nam-myoho-renge-kyo and that of the Buddha of the Lotus Sutra's theoretical teaching is as vast as that between heaven and earth. [Just as the sutra says] without our having made the slightest effort, "This cluster of unsurpassed jewels has come to us unsought" (LSOC, 124). We are given in its entirety the benefit of all Buddhas throughout the existences of past, present and future.

Even though we have not carried out any practices in the past, by believing in the Gohonzon, our lives become endowed with many, varied powers. And, through the principle of the simultaneity of cause and effect, we enter the world of Buddhahood just as we are—as ordinary people.

From the standpoint of Nichiren Buddhism, these powers are embodied in the Gohonzon. These powers well forth in our lives as we maintain our faith. What a wonderful teaching this is.

The Functions of Buddhahood in Our Lives

Here, Shakyamuni identifies "immeasurable [compassion]," "unlimited [eloquence]," "power," "fearlessness" and so on, as attributes of the Buddha's state of life. To put it simply, the Buddha has infinite concern for the people (immeasurable [compassion]), can freely expound the teaching through words (unlimited [eloquence]), has penetrating insight into life and the power to discern the causes of people's unhappiness (power) and has the courage to fully articulate the truth (fearlessness).

Armed with these powers of wisdom, the Buddha dives into the great ocean of the people and, while facing persecution, leads them to enlightenment through wholehearted efforts.

The Buddha's immeasurable compassion includes the four infinite virtues of giving living beings delight, removing their suffering, rejoicing at seeing beings become free from suffering and gain happiness, and abandoning attachments to love and hatred and being impartial to everyone. The Buddha's consideration toward the people is expansive and infinite; it knows no bounds.

In concrete terms, what does "immeasurable" mean for us as ordinary people? It means not to give up halfway. In spreading the teaching or giving individual guidance—in all aspects of the struggle for kosen-rufu—the important thing is that we follow through. Whenever we become deadlocked, we can tap inner strength through our practice to the Gohonzon and then challenge ourselves to see how many walls we can break through. Such faith to advance limitlessly may be characterized as "immeasurable."

Also, it may be hard to get a practical sense of the meaning of the spirit of compassion. President Toda used to say that "courage substitutes for compassion." Our courageous actions as emissaries of the Buddha are comparable to the Buddha's compassionate practices.

In society today, if anything, people tend to try to avoid developing relations with others. Ours might be also characterized as a society of envy where people view the happiness of others with jealousy.

In such an environment, SGI members actively seek to develop relations with others out of the desire to help them become happy. Yet in such a society, these compassionate actions are liable to be misunderstood and, indeed, may meet with great resistance.

Nevertheless, each day we pray and take action for others: giving people delight, removing their sufferings, rejoicing at their happiness as if it were our own and dedicating ourselves to their well-being without discrimination. An immeasurable spirit of removing suffering and imparting joy pulses in the SGI. In this regard, we definitely stand alone.

Wherever people, instead of feeling jealous, rejoice at seeing others gain happiness, wherever people can encourage one another—that is a realm pervaded with happiness. By contrast, those who go through life constantly comparing themselves to others, consequently seesawing between joy and sorrow, find themselves utterly deadlocked in the end.

As President Toda taught, we need to live our own lives.

Just as cherry, plum, peach and damson blossoms all possess their own unique qualities, each person is unique. We cannot become someone else. The important thing is that we live true to ourselves and cause the great flower of our lives to blossom. If we fail to do so, then what is the purpose of our lives? What is the purpose of our existence?

There is no need whatsoever to compare ourselves to others. Rather, we should consider whether we have grown by comparing how we are now to how we were in the past. The Buddhist way of life is to grow each day, accomplishing more today than yesterday and more tomorrow than today.

Earnest Faith Is the Key to a Life of Freedom

Next, "unlimited [eloquence]" indicates the power to freely understand and freely express oneself without hindrance. Unlimited eloquence comprises four unlimited kinds of knowledge: (1) complete understanding of the teachings, (2) complete mastery of the meanings deriving from the teachings, (3) complete freedom in expressing the teachings in various languages and dialects and (4) the ability to preach to all people at will by employing the other first three powers.

The Buddha has the wisdom to freely understand the teachings and freely expound them. We should note that while the Buddha appears to do so with composure, this is not something that happens automatically. President Toda said that even lectures on Nichiren's writings could be classified as unskilled, skillful or artistic, pointing out that one does not all of a sudden arrive at the level of artistic. Reaching that stage requires earnest practice and training.

Buddhas are earnest. Precisely because they are earnest, wisdom wells forth in their lives. "How can I send out a message that will touch a chord in each person's life?" they continually ask. The Buddhas earnestly weave a tapestry of words. They rack their minds and exercise ingenuity. They bring to bear the power of expedient means. Such efforts find expression in unhindered preaching of the Law.

Throughout his life, Nichiren Daishonin continued to send highly detailed encouragement to his followers. Sometimes he would join them in their sadness, other times he would admonish them, show them tolerance or encourage them—all the while sending them words of revitalization. He had a thorough knowledge of the daily life, family makeup, worries and personality of each follower.

To the lay nun Sennichi, for example, after her husband, Abutsu-bo, had died, Nichiren declared that Abutsu-bo had definitely attained Buddhahood. He also pointed out that her son, Tokuro Moritsuna, had himself become a votary of the Lotus Sutra, saying, "There is no treasure greater than a child, no treasure greater than a child!" (WND-I, 1045). He thus expresses delight at the growth of a capable successor.

Another follower, the lay nun Konichi, was worried about her deceased son's future existence because, as a soldier, he had taken the lives of others. To this mother, the Daishonin explains the teaching that "even a small error will destine one to the evil paths if one does not repent of it. Yet even a grave offense can be eradicated if one repents of it sincerely" (WND-I, 662–63). He explains to her that the child can definitely be saved from falling into the evil paths of existence through the parent's strong faith.

Children bring their parents joy, and they also cause them worry. But Nichiren Buddhism teaches that, so long as they have faith, parent and child can definitely both become happy.

The Buddha's preaching is free and unrestricted. It certainly is not rigid or narrow. The Buddha knows how to explain the Law in concrete terms and based on firm principles so as to help individuals revive their spirits and create value in their situations. For this reason, the Buddha puts people's hearts at ease.

Nichiren's words encourage and invigorate people. One can imagine his followers' joy upon receiving a letter from him—right down to the look of determination that must have appeared on their faces.

Nichiren's writings, transcending their time and place of origin, are a message of happiness for all humanity. They are a living textbook of humanism. They are the supreme inheritance of humankind.

Open a Path Among the People

Next, "power" refers to the so-called ten powers a Buddha possesses. For example, the Buddha has the power to judge people's understanding of the teaching, to understand their various hopes and to know the states of life of all people.

The ten powers all revolve around the ability to understand people's minds and hearts. This ability, again, represents the crystallization of the Buddha's tenacious efforts in that regard.

The important thing is that Shakyamuni used his powers of wisdom to pioneer a path of great happiness among the people. He went out himself among the people to single-handedly spread the teaching, and he called upon his disciples to do the same. Nichiren, too, continually expounded the Law to the people.

Unless you go out among the people, you cannot understand their hearts. For example, because Nikko Shonin spared no effort in visiting Atsuhara, the lay followers there could carry through with their faith without succumbing to the great persecution that befell them. Through Nikko's example, these followers, all of them farmers, came to understand the wondrousness of Buddhism and the Daishonin's greatness soon after they converted. And Nikko stood in the lead among them even at the height of the persecution.

Detailed reports went out from Nikko to Nichiren, who was at Mount Minobu. Because Nikko was present on the scene, the Daishonin could gain accurate information and then take appropriate measures. It thus became possible for him to send continuous encouragement to, and open the hearts of, his followers who were in the eye of the persecution.

Because Nichiren and Nikko deeply understood the people's hearts, they could provide the greatest encouragement, and the followers of Atsuhara could overcome the persecution.

In any age, understanding the hearts of the people is the basis for victory. A genuine leader, a true leader of Buddhism, makes the greatest efforts to understand people's hearts, to understand their thoughts and to understand their struggles.

Next, "fearlessness" means to expound the Law bravely and without fear. It indicates the Buddha's unshakable self-confidence in expounding the Law.

The Buddha is fearless in his preaching in four ways. The first is in declaring he is enlightened to the truth of all phenomena; that is, he has great confidence in the Mystic Law. The second is in proclaiming he has extinguished all desires and illusions; that is, he definitely will not be defeated by worries or sufferings. The third is in proclaiming that he has elucidated the obstacles to Buddhist practice and enlightenment; in other words, he encourages others to defeat the three obstacles and four devils. The fourth is in declaring that he has clarified the way of liberation from the world of suffering, and thus the way of attaining emancipation.

Fearlessness means that when talking about these things, he has no fear. In short, fearlessness means courage arising from great confidence.

If you propagate Buddhism, you are certain to meet with difficulties. Shakyamuni and Nichiren Daishonin, while fully aware of this, launched a campaign of words—their voices like the dignified roar of a lion—against the religious authorities and the political rulers of their times. This is the epitome of fearlessness.

Nichiren also urged his disciples to have no fear. He says, "If Nichiren's disciples are cowardly, their prayers cannot be answered" (GZ, 840). He teaches that, while vigorously chanting Nam-myoho-renge-kyo, we should speak out for justice.

He indicates that such actions exemplify the spirit of this passage from "Emerging from the Earth," the fifteenth chapter: "'They [the Bodhisattvas of the Earth] are clever at difficult questions and answers, their minds know no fear'" (LSOC, 263).

This passage explains that the Bodhisattvas of the Earth are skilled at discussing difficult doctrine and that they have not the slightest fear of their opponents in debate. They are clever at questions and answers, and they bravely stand up to even the most powerful of enemies.

If you are fearful, you cannot say anything that will strike a chord in another person's heart. Nor will any wisdom well forth in your life.

Nikko Shonin says, "You should treasure those practitioners who are skilled in difficult debate, just as the late master [Nichiren Daishonin] did" (GZ, 1619).

We should treasure boundlessly those who spread the teaching. This is Nichiren Daishonin's spirit and Nikko Shonin's decree. The SGI is a gathering without peer or precedent of people who spread the teaching.

Highly articulate and eloquent people are treasures of kosen-rufu. Eloquence does not mean verbosity; it is the power to win others' wholehearted understanding. Sometimes even a single word from a person of strong faith is enough to win the full understanding of someone whom not even a great scholar could reach. This is the power of wisdom, the power of character, the power of faith.

Amid a storm of calumny, all of you have persistently carried out dialogues of justice, unafraid of the winds of arrogant criticism. Without doubt you qualify as people of fearlessness, as people who "are clever in difficult questions and answers."

The Buddha Freely Spreads the Law Among the People

This passage further explains that the Buddha possesses "concentration," "emancipation" and "samadhis," and that he has entered a boundless state of life and become enlightened to a great Law never before attained. Because he possessed such a firm and unshakable state of life, Shakyamuni could continuously expound the Law among the people with boundless freedom.

There simply are no Buddhas who spend all their time sitting in meditation. Buddhas are Buddhas precisely because they continually ponder and take action to help others resolve their worries.

In that sense, all of you who concern yourselves over and pray to resolve the various problems encountered in the course of advancing kosen-rufu are most laudable. Each day, you grapple earnestly with issues relating to the happiness of friends, the advancement of kosen-rufu and the raising of capable people. Having these concerns makes you bodhisattvas. For the same reason, you can develop the Buddha's state of life.

Your actions to challenge the great undertaking of kosen-rufu are comparable to those of the Buddha.

As I said previously, the wisdom and powers of the Buddha indicated by this passage are attributes of the state of life embodied in the Gohonzon; and we who embrace the Gohonzon can develop this same state of life. Also, as I have already noted, concentration, emancipation and samadhis are included in our daily practice of gongyo and chanting Nam-myoho-renge-kyo.

In other words, to the extent that we earnestly rack our brains for kosen-rufu, to the extent that we take our problems to the Gohonzon, these attributes of the wisdom and power of the Buddha well forth in the depths of our being. This is what it means to read this passage with one's life.

In concrete terms, the Buddha's enlightened state of life and wisdom "never before attained" indicate nothing other than great confidence in the Gohonzon.

▪6▪

Shari-hotsu. Nyorai no. Shuju fun-betsu. Gyo ses͡sho ho. Gon-ji
nyunan. Ekka shushin. Shari-hotsu. Shu yo gon shi. Muryo muhen.
Mi-zo-u ho. Bus͡shitsu joju.

"Shariputra, the Thus Come Ones know how to make various distinctions
and to expound the teachings skillfully. Their words are soft and gentle
and can delight the hearts of the assembly.

"Shariputra, to sum it up: the Buddhas have fully realized the Law
that is limitless, boundless, never attained before." (LSOC, 57)

IN THIS PASSAGE, Shakyamuni continues to praise the vast Buddha
wisdom. It is because he, the Thus Come One, possesses "the Law
that is limitless, boundless, never attained before" that he could skillfully expound his teachings according to the people's understanding
and circumstances and delight them with "soft and gentle" words.

He can do this also because the wisdom of the Buddhas infuses his
life. In this way, he indicates the vastness of the unparalleled Law he
has attained.

This is the third time in "Expedient Means" that Shakyamuni has
referred to a Law never attained before. Why has he said essentially
the same thing to Shariputra three times since the start of the chapter?

For the voice-hearers and cause-awakened ones the wisdom of
the Buddhas is an "infinitely profound and immeasurable" teaching that they cannot comprehend. Shakyamuni desperately wants to

communicate to Shariputra and the others that there exists a realm of wisdom so vast as to be beyond even their imagination.

That is why he repeatedly alludes to the existence of a great Law never before known or attained. Shariputra and the others cannot comprehend the vast wisdom of the Buddha as long as they remain satisfied with their own shallow wisdom. For that reason, Shakyamuni courteously and repeatedly explains just how wondrous is the wisdom of the Buddhas.

Saying "Since I explained it once, that's sufficient" lacks compassion. We should continue to conduct dialogue until the other person's life changes. Attaining the objective is what counts; to speak solely for purposes of self-satisfaction is pointless.

As he spoke each word, Shakyamuni must have been observing the changes in Shariputra's expression. While repeatedly praising the wisdom of the Buddhas, he was doubtless waiting for a great seeking spirit to arise in Shariputra's heart.

Shariputra certainly knew of Shakyamuni's greatness before this juncture. Still, both his respect for the grand scale of the Buddha's wisdom and his seeking spirit must have grown as he listened. "I wish I could hear this 'Law never before attained,'" Shariputra probably thought as he aroused in himself a seeking mind he had never before attained.

Praying Consistently for the Happiness of Others

"Their words are soft and gentle" means that, to his listeners, the Buddha's words are soft and gentle. These are words that, while tender, reverberate with piercing conviction.

With such words, the Buddha caused people to feel joy and so had led them to this point. Even though he is saying this with regard to the pre-Lotus Sutra teachings he expounded "in accordance with the minds of others," it offers us an important guideline.

Here, "soft and gentle" does not simply mean nice and easygoing.

Soft and gentle words are completely different from compliant words intended merely to be agreeable. They are words that touch a chord in others' lives, words that move people. That is, they express an understanding of others' feelings.

Moreover, since deep down everyone desires true happiness, words uttered with ardent prayer for someone's happiness, even if they are strong, are soft and gentle.

Nichiren writes:

> Even though one may resort to harsh words, if such words help the person to whom they are addressed, then they are worthy to be regarded as truthful words and gentle words. Similarly, though one may use gentle words, if they harm the person to whom they are addressed, they are in fact deceptive words, harsh words.
>
> The Buddhist doctrines preached by scholars these days are regarded by most people as gentle words, truthful words, but in fact they are all harsh words and deceptive words. I say this because they are at variance with the Lotus Sutra, which embodies the Buddha's true intention. (WND-1, 178)

Even words that on the surface seem polite may be vicious and destroy a person's heart. By contrast, strongly spoken words can warm the heart.

There is a saying: Good advice grates on the ear, good medicine tastes bitter. Sugarcoated words are dangerous.

Conduct Hope-Filled Dialogue in a Society Lacking Truthful Words

Soft and gentle words are not determined by how harsh or kind the words sound. Rather, it depends on whether they are laden with value and whether there is compassion in the heart of their speaker.

In society today, truthful words are few. Words of self-interest and calculation deluge us, as do frivolous words and words intended to cause injury. These days, we simply don't hear words of truth that issue from the depths of one person's heart and penetrate the heart of another.

Truthful words coincide perfectly with the actions of the speaker. Words spoken out of personal conviction, words upon which we have lived our lives are certainly truthful words. Truthful words are living words that issue from a lively and exuberant heart.

Nikko Shonin admonished against indulging in "idleness and chatter" (GZ, 1617; see WND-1, 760). Similarly, President Toda compared words not based on faith to smoke.

In conclusion, "truthful words and gentle words" means words spoken in good faith. Such words are sincere, they are earnest, and they are suitable. Moreover, words that clearly convey what you want to say are truthful and gentle words.

With abundant self-confidence, let us conduct dignified dialogue, never losing our inner latitude, poise and humor. Such dialogue is the true "weapon" of a Buddhist.

Confusion of language portends confusion in society. In an age lacking truthful words, our movement, which is based on dialogue, is becoming a great light of hope for the world.

A leader is one who causes people to feel joy. The mission of a leader is to encourage people and elevate their spirits. A leader absolutely must not scold others. Nothing qualifies a leader to castigate a friend.

"Delight the hearts of the assembly" indicates that Shakyamuni delights people and wins their heartfelt understanding by means of soft and gentle words.

Based on firm conviction and with true soft and gentle words, a leader shows appreciation to everyone for their efforts, makes them feel refreshed, puts their hearts at ease, dispels their doubts and arouses their hopes and aspirations. This is a leader's struggle. Those who pressure others or drive them into a corner are disqualified as leaders and are turning their backs on this passage.

In terms of its literal meaning, this passage describes Shakyamuni's preaching of the pre-Lotus Sutra teachings. In other words, it refers to how Shakyamuni expounded various teachings for people of different capacities and with different worries and sufferings in order to cause them to feel delight and guide them to happiness.

For example, in the pre-Lotus Sutra teachings, he taught those who were preoccupied with what others thought of them—those who had lost sight of themselves—to "wander alone," or be self-reliant. To those caught up in their own narrow way of thinking, he taught that even fools will become wise if they associate with and become close to good friends.

Additionally, Shakyamuni encouraged those suffering on account of desire and greed to extinguish desires, and he directed those leading hedonistic existences toward ascetic practices. And, he admonished those carrying out extended fasting or other extreme austerities to cease such painful practices and instead pursue the Middle Way.

On the surface, these different teachings might seem contradictory. But in every case, he taught people in accordance with their situations how they could improve their lives. While "delight[ing] the hearts of the assembly," he helped them advance. Shakyamuni's spirit in every instance was the same. The pre-Lotus Sutra teachings consist of the many teachings he expounded in this manner.

On the foundation of these earlier teachings, he expounds the Mystic Law in the Lotus Sutra. The Mystic Law is the teaching that enables people fundamentally to become happy, irrespective of whether his listeners can readily understand.

Because the Buddha taught the Lotus Sutra "in accordance with [the Buddha's] own mind," those hearing it could not readily comprehend it. In fact, Shariputra was incredulous when he first heard the "Expedient Means" teaching that all people can become Buddhas. He thought, "Is this not a devil pretending to be the Buddha, trying to vex and confuse my mind?" (LSOC, 85).

We cannot laugh at Shariputra. Hardly anyone upon first hearing of Nam-myoho-renge-kyo understands the greatness of this Buddhism or feels genuine delight. In time, however, all people can gain unsurpassed joy through this teaching. They can attain the greatest of all joys. In that sense, the Mystic Law is the teaching that can truly "delight the hearts of the assembly." From the standpoint of Nichiren Buddhism, this passage means that through the benefit of the Gohonzon, our lives become filled with joy.

Even though we have faith, we cannot avoid painful, sad or unpleasant things in the course of life. Yet through the principle that earthly desires are enlightenment, we can definitely manifest a state of delight in our lives. This is the greatness of Nichiren Buddhism. By advancing based on faith, we can definitely change a life of suffering into a life of great joy.

Regarding "delight the hearts of the assembly," Mr. Toda said:

> When we practice faith in earnest for ten years, our lives become truly pure. Our skin, the look of our eyes, our actions all become soft and pure and yet come to possess a certain dignity. This is the benefit of the Gohonzon. When this happens, we feel delight in our hearts; this is the meaning of "delight the hearts of the assembly."
>
> Since those who attain this state of life are always bright, they cannot help feeling joy. Such people are happy and therefore always smiling and cheerful; if they should go into business, they are sure to prosper. That's because others think, "If I'm going to buy the same item anyway, then I might as well go and buy it from that person." This is what "delight the hearts of the assembly" means.

Pure joy wells forth abundantly from lives polished by chanting Nam-myoho-renge-kyo. People like those Mr. Toda described are experts at life who make friends even in the midst of suffering. While skillfully dealing with life's hardships, they can find cause for delight in any situation whatsoever. They enjoy a truly elevated state of life.

Nichiren Daishonin says, "Regard both suffering and joy as facts of life, and continue chanting Nam-myoho-renge-kyo" (WND-1, 681). The central meaning is that we should regard suffering and joy as inescapable facts of our existence.

Without hardships, life would be bland and colorless. People learn from hard work; hard work provides nutrients needed to cause the flower of joy to blossom. Suffering and joy are like two sides of a coin. When we recognize this truth, we manifest the true strength of the human being and the true profundity of life.

The great Russian author Leo Tolstoy continually fought against suffering. Even when excommunicated by ecclesiastical authorities, he contemplated events with composure and poise. He retained his blazing single-minded spirit of struggle. He concluded that he would "rejoice" no matter what; this was his creed.

> Rejoice! Rejoice! One's life's work, one's mission is a joy. Toward the sky, toward the sun, toward the stars, toward the grasses, toward the trees, toward animals, toward human beings—you may as well rejoice.[6]

We train ourselves through faith to develop the state of life in which we can change everything into joy.

The Strong Create Value Even From Obstacles

Nichiren writes: "The greater the hardships befalling him [the votary of the Lotus Sutra], the greater the delight he feels, because of his strong faith" (WND-1, 33); and "The three obstacles and four devils will invariably appear, and the wise will rejoice while the foolish will retreat" (WND-1, 637).

Making up our minds that the greater our worries, the greater our opportunities to develop our state of life, we should advance with increasing joy and high spirits. While giving friends peace of mind, let us endure all with bright smiles and persistent effort. This is the conduct of Buddhists. Such people lead lives that "delight the hearts of the assembly." Let us live robustly.

There is a saying that "the block of granite which was an obstacle in the pathway of the weak becomes a steppingstone in the pathway of the strong."[7] Strong people make the most of obstacles. The stronger we are, the more joyful our lives. It all comes down to life force, spiritual energy. And these fundamentally derive from the powers of faith and practice.

Commenting on the parable of the Jewel in the Robe from the standpoint of his teachings, Nichiren explains that the joy of the poor man upon discovering that he possesses the priceless jewel is "the great joy that one experiences when one understands for the first time that one's mind from the very beginning has been a Buddha. Nam-myoho-renge-kyo is the greatest of all joys" (OTT, 211–12).

True happiness is inner happiness. We need to establish an inner state of life that is not swayed by external conditions.

People these days tend to pursue momentary pleasures and to regard outward displays of wealth as equivalent to happiness. There-fore, it is all the more important that we teach others the wonder of life's inner happiness by manifesting in our lives "the greatest of all joys."

Joy is contagious. Those who "delight the hearts of the assembly" can transform those around them into people who also delight the hearts of the assembly. And those who make efforts to delight the hearts of the assembly experience delight in their own hearts.

The SGI has the true capacity to delight the hearts of the assembly. It has the joy of life and the joy of action; and because its activities are fundamentally joyful, people gather. That the SGI is joyful is great proof that Buddhism pulses vigorously within it.

▪7▪

Shi shari-hotsu. Fu shu bu setsu. Sho-i sha ga. Busˆsho joju.
Dai ichi ke-u. Nange shi ho.

"But stop, Shariputra, I will say no more. Why? Because what the
Buddhas have achieved is the rarest and most difficult-to-understand
Law." (LSOC, 57)

As we've already seen, the "Expedient Means" chapter is an
unsolicited and spontaneous teaching, because the Buddha
begins expounding it on his own initiative without being asked, saying, "The wisdom of the Buddhas is infinitely profound and immeasurable" (LSOC, 56).

Up to this point, he has emphasized that the Buddha's wisdom
is beyond the ability of Shariputra and others of the two vehicles to
comprehend. Here, however, in order to arouse in Shariputra a still
stronger seeking mind, Shakyamuni tells him, "I will say no more."

Live True to Yourself

Shakyamuni explains that he will preach no more "because what the
Buddhas have achieved is the rarest and most difficult-to-understand
Law."

President Toda, smiling, commented on this passage as follows:

The Buddha began preaching the "Expedient Means" chapter without any question having first been put to him. Until this point, he has praised the Buddha's state of life up and down, but now he says, "I'm not going to let you hear any more." His listeners were no doubt taken aback.

Wanting to enable his beloved disciples to attain the supreme state of life, Shakyamuni utters the words of strict compassion, "But stop, Shariputra."

As I have noted already, the mentor's wish is to enable the disciples to attain the same state of life as the mentor. That is the true way of the mentor. A true mentor does not do anything to trouble or obstruct the growth of disciples.

Shariputra, regarded as the foremost in wisdom among Shakyamuni's disciples, listens to the preaching that follows and comes to realize that the sole purpose of Buddhist practice is to open up the world of Buddhahood in one's own life. Because he accepted the strictness of the mentor, Shakyamuni, with his whole being, the disciple, Shariputra, could develop his state of life.

Further, from Shakyamuni's standpoint, it was because he trusted Shariputra and his other disciples that he ventured to begin preaching the true Law, the teaching that is difficult to comprehend. If the mentor believed his disciples could not grasp his true intention, he would not have begun expounding it. With such feeble disciples, he could not even have taken them to task for their immature state of life. Under those circumstances, he would have no choice but to expound teachings "in accordance with the minds of others," that is, teachings that matched his disciples' state of life.

On one level, the Lotus Sutra, and this scene in particular, might be thought of as a spiritual drama unfolding between the mentor who begins to expound the truth and the disciples who receive his teaching with their entire beings.

From the standpoint of its deepest meaning, this passage indicates that the great Law of Nam-myoho-renge-kyo that Nichiren upholds is the "rarest" teaching, beyond people's ability to comprehend with their ordinary state of life.

The vast and boundless power of the Gohonzon cannot be fathomed with a shallow state of life. It is foolish to try to estimate or determine the power of the Gohonzon with our minds. Such thinking betrays conceit. When we practice, summoning forth the great power of faith, we can definitely produce results in the form of inconspicuous and conspicuous benefit. To the extent we are convinced of this, we can expand our inner state of life.

The Mystic Law is the "rarest and most difficult-to-understand Law." Nichiren writes, "If the Law that one embraces is supreme, then the person who embraces it must accordingly be foremost among all others" (WND-1, 61). The lives of those who embrace the supreme Law are supremely happy.

I want all of you to shine as the foremost people on your respective stages of activity. Please lead lives of brilliant proof of the supreme Law. This is what it means to practice the "rarest and most difficult-to-understand Law."

The SGI is a gathering of such foremost people. We should not demean ourselves. Never say such things as, "My capability is so limited." Everyone has a mission that only he or she can fulfill.

President Toda said: "I want even those who seem the least remarkable among Soka Gakkai members to do things beyond the ability of members of other groups. I would like to develop an organization such that even the weakest person in it is stronger than anyone outside it."

Determined to shine as foremost people in our respective fields and to live in a manner true to ourselves, let us fulfill our missions with dignity.

∎8∎

Yui butsu yo butsu. Nai no kujin. Shoho jisso. Sho-i shoho. Nyo ze so.
Nyo ze sho. Nyo ze tai. Nyo ze riki. Nyo ze sa. Nyo ze in. Nyo ze en.
Nyo ze ka. Nyo ze ho. Nyo ze honmak kukyo to.

"The true aspect of all phenomena can only be understood and shared
between Buddhas. This reality consists of the appearance, nature, entity,
power, influence, internal cause, relation, latent effect, manifest effect,
and their consistency from beginning to end." (LSOC, 57)

WE NOW COME to the most important passage of the "Expedient Means" chapter, the section dealing with "the true aspect of all phenomena" and "the ten factors of life."

Just what exactly is the wisdom of the Buddha that Shakyamuni has been praising from the start of the chapter as "infinitely profound" and "difficult to understand"? Here he tries to explain.

The true aspect of all phenomena is the wisdom of the Buddhas that can only be understood and shared between Buddhas. Shakyamuni clarifies that the true aspect specifically consists of the ten factors of life—appearance, nature, entity, power, influence, internal cause, relation, latent effect, manifest effect and their consistency from beginning to end.

"All phenomena" indicates life in the Ten Worlds and its environment, or all living beings and the realms in which they dwell. In other words, it refers to all nature, to all things and phenomena.

Also, "true aspect," just as it sounds, means the true reality just as it is. The true aspect of all phenomena might be thought of as the undisguised truth of all things.

The ten factors of life that follow indicate the contents of the true aspect. For this reason, this passage is termed the "true aspect of the ten factors."

What Are the Ten Factors of Life?

The meaning of the ten factors might be summarized as follows:
(1) Appearance: attributes of things discernible from the outside, such as color, form, shape and behavior. (2) Nature: the inherent disposition or quality of a thing or being that cannot be discerned from the outside. (3) Entity: the essence of life that permeates and integrates appearance and nature. These first three factors describe the reality of life itself.

The next six factors, from the fourth, power, through the ninth, manifest effect, explain the functions and workings of life. (4) Power: life's potential energy. (5) Influence: the action or movement produced when life's inherent power is activated. (6) Internal cause: the cause latent in life that produces an effect of the same quality as itself, i.e., good, evil or neutral. (7) Relation: the relationship of indirect causes to the internal cause. Indirect causes are various conditions, both internal and external, that help the internal cause produce an effect. (8) Latent effect: the effect produced in life when an internal cause is activated through its relationship with various conditions. (9) Manifest effect: the tangible, perceivable result that emerges in time as an expression of a latent effect and therefore of an internal cause, again through its relationship with various conditions. (10) Consistency from beginning to end: the unifying factor among the ten factors. It indicates that all the other nine factors from the beginning (appearance) to the end (manifest effect) are consistently and harmoniously interrelated. All nine factors thus consistently and harmoniously express the same condition of existence at any given moment.

In the passage, each factor is prefixed by the term *nyo ze*, meaning, "it is like." Shakyamuni is saying in effect: although the Buddha wisdom cannot be articulated in words, if one were to venture to describe it, this is how it might be expressed.

Let me try to explain the ten factors of life through an example. Your own existence is a phenomenon. Your features, posture and so on compose the "appearance" of the phenomenon of your life.

Invisible to the eye, such traits as shortness of temper, magnanimity, kindness or reticence or the various aspects of your personality or temperament make up your "nature." Your physical and spiritual totality—that is, your "appearance" and "nature" together—make up your "entity," the person you are.

Also, your life has various energies (power), and these produce various external functions (influence). Your life thus becomes a cause (internal cause) and, activated by conditions internal and external (relation), changes arise in your life (latent effect), and these eventually appear externally (manifest effect).

Moreover, these nine factors interweave your life and your environment without any inconsistency or omission (consistency from beginning to end). This is the true aspect of the ten factors of your life.

Each of us lives within the framework of the ten factors. No one could say that he or she has no appearance. Such a person would be invisible. Similarly, no one could truly claim not to have a personality, not to have any energy or not to carry out any activity. Nor could there be a situation where the appearance was one person, the nature someone else and the entity another person still. There is consistency among all factors, and together they make up the irreplaceable totality of your being.

People in each of the Ten Worlds are endowed with the ten factors according to their state of life. For example, people in the world of hell have the dark and depressed appearance of those overwhelmed by suffering. Since their nature is filled with suffering and anger, their power and influence tend to mire those around them in darkness too.

Those in the world of heaven are typically bright and smiling in their appearance. In their nature, since they feel uplifted—as though ascending into the sky, as it were—anything they see makes them happy. Their power and influence tend to make those around them feel buoyant and cheerful too.

Similarly, each of the Ten Worlds has its own factors of appearance, nature, entity, power, influence, internal cause, relation, latent effect and manifest effect, and there is consistency from beginning to end. This is the true nature of all phenomena.

President Toda explained this as follows: "Suppose there is a thief in front of us. He is a thief from appearance to manifest effect. That's consistency from beginning to end in a thief's life. There is no discontinuity."

Rather than simply looking at surface appearances, understanding the true aspect of all phenomena means to grasp the vastness and profundity of life in its entirety.

The ten factors of life are not limited only to human beings. Flowers blooming on the roadside, for example, have the appearance, nature and entity of beauty. They also possess power, influence, internal cause, relation, latent effect and manifest effect, without any omission. And in their totality, all of these factors are coherently integrated with the life of the flower.

The same is also true of inorganic things. A pebble, the sky, the moon, the stars, the sun, the sea with its salty scent, rugged mountains, skyscrapers overlooking noisy streets, houses and cars and every utensil and piece of furniture—the ten factors of life describe the existence of all things.

This is the wisdom of the true aspect of all phenomena that the Buddha has attained. In other words, when observing any phenomenon, the Buddha understands its true aspect. When looking at people, the Buddha understands their state of life and sees their Buddha nature within. When looking at something in nature, the Buddha can sense its noble brilliance. And, when considering social phenomena, the Buddha can deftly discern their underlying significance.

It might be said that the wisdom of the true aspect of all phenomena is the ability to discern the true nature of all things.

The Importance of Seeing the Truth

Buddhism explains that there are five types of vision, or perceptive faculty, that people may possess depending on their state of life: (1) the eye of ordinary people, which distinguishes color and form; (2) the heavenly eye, which perceives things in the darkness, at a distance or beyond obstructions; (3) the wisdom eye, with which people of the two vehicles can perceive that nothing has independent existence and all phenomena are non-substantial; (4) the Dharma eye, with which bodhisattvas perceive the nature of all teachings in order to save the people; and (5) the Buddha eye, which perceives the true nature of life spanning past, present and future and includes the other four eyes. The wisdom of the true aspect of all phenomena is to view everything with the Dharma eye and the Buddha eye.

Seeing is one example, but there is also hearing, smelling, tasting, feeling and sensing. Through all our faculties, we should strive to perceive the true aspect of all phenomena.

The French poet Comte de Lautréamont wrote, "The phenomenon passes. I seek the laws."[8] What is important is the vision to profoundly and deftly perceive the true nature of shifting phenomena. The Buddha is one who has mastered this vision.

Often people experience failure or loss in even simple, everyday affairs due to misunderstandings or misperceptions, prejudice or speculation. It is all the more difficult to see the truth when it comes to fundamental problems of human life or society. When observing the same phenomena, the Buddha succeeds in seeing the true aspect while others fail.

To take one example, the scientist Isaac Newton is said to have formulated the law of universal gravitation after observing an apple fall from a tree. In the falling apple (the phenomenon), he discerned the truth (the true aspect) that the force of gravity acts consistently upon all objects. This could be thought of as a part of the wisdom of the true aspect of all phenomena.

No matter how many apples someone sees fall, if the person lacks insight, he or she will not be able to discern the true aspect. Newton's discovery resulted in the opening of a new world and has greatly benefited humankind.

Similarly, and on an even grander scale, the Buddha wisdom to discern the true aspect of all phenomena is inestimably important for people's happiness in life, for the advancement of humanity.

To speak of discovering the true aspect "behind" phenomena might give the impression that the Law exists somewhere apart from the phenomena. This is definitely not the case. Phenomena and their true aspect are always inseparable. The Buddha observes the true aspect as it manifests through phenomena and correctly perceives that the true aspect exists only as the phenomena. They do not exist separately.

To illustrate, if phenomena, which are constantly changing, are likened to waves, then the true aspect is comparable to the ocean. Waves are born of the ocean and consist of ocean water. Conversely, there are no oceans without waves. The two are one in essence.

Again, if the true aspect is likened to the surface of a mirror, then phenomena would be comparable to the images appearing therein. The mirror reflects all things; there is no mirror that does not reflect images as long as there is light. Conversely, there can be no reflected images without the mirror.

From the standpoint of life, "all phenomena" means individual lives, and "true aspect" refers to the truth of life that the Buddha perceives. This truth of life pervades the universe, and the Buddha perceives the universal life in even the smallest living manifestation.

To put it another way, all living beings are entities of the Mystic Law to which the Buddha is enlightened, and the Buddha perceives that they are inherently endowed with the Buddha nature. This is the wisdom of the true aspect of all phenomena.

The vision that enables the Buddha to perceive the true aspect that manifests in all phenomena is also the eye of compassion to save all people and enable them to become Buddhas.

The Daishonin says: "Life is the foremost of all treasures. It is expounded that even the treasures of the entire major world system cannot equal the value of one's body and life" (WND-1, 1125). The life of one person, he says, is more precious even than all the treasures of the universe. This is the wonderful Buddhist view of life, which is based on the perception of the true aspect of all phenomena.

Life is mysterious. It is the wisdom of the Buddha to perfectly and fully understand the truth of life. What a vast and infinitely profound wisdom this is!

As seen with the Buddha eye, this world, this universe, is shining with life, resounding with the chorus of all things. The Buddha perceives the irreplaceable uniqueness and value of all things in the world. The Buddha's wisdom is a state of life filled with boundless exhilaration and joy in living.

As I will discuss next, from the deepest standpoint, the true aspect of all phenomena means the Gohonzon. For us who embrace the Gohonzon, the wisdom of the true aspect of all phenomena means to view everything with the eye of Buddhism and the eye of faith.

The Gohonzon Is the True Aspect of All Phenomena

In the previous section, I discussed the true aspect existing in all things from the surface standpoint of the sutra passage that reveals the ten factors of life.

In his letter titled "The True Aspect of All Phenomena," Nichiren Daishonin clarifies the fundamental meaning of the true aspect of the ten factors of life. He wrote the letter in reply to a question from his disciple Sairen-bo regarding the above passage. Sairen-bo, thought to have been originally a scholar-priest of the Tendai school, was an avid student of Buddhism.

Nichiren plainly states at the outset of his letter that this passage "means that all beings and environments in the Ten Worlds, from hell, the lowest, to Buddhahood, the highest, are without exception manifestations of Myoho-renge-kyo" (WND-1, 383). In other words, all life (all phenomena), which undergoes constant and manifold changes, is the manifestation of Nam-myoho-renge-kyo (the true aspect).

The entire universe is itself the Mystic Law. All things in nature are the song, the dance, the drama, the poem, the sparkling, the birth and death, the suffering and joy, the constant vicissitudes, the advance and the supreme joy of the Mystic Law.

We practice faith to become genuinely aware of the true aspect of all phenomena and to manifest it actively in our own lives. Through faith, we can develop a great state of absolute freedom in our lives.

Of the ten factors of life, "consistency from beginning to end" does not mean simply that the nine factors from "appearance" to "manifest effect" are perfectly integrated in each of the Ten Worlds—so that if someone or something is in the world of hell, for instance, then all factors of that person or thing will be in the state of hell. Nichiren clarifies that it indicates consistency on a more fundamental level, that all nine factors in any of the Ten Worlds are manifestations of Myoho-renge-kyo.

To view all things as manifestations of Myoho-renge-kyo is to perceive the true aspect of all phenomena. This is the wisdom of the Buddha.

In another writing, Nichiren clearly says, "These ten factors represent Myoho-renge-kyo" (WND-2, 87). Nam-myoho-renge-kyo is the fundamental Law of the universe (the true aspect) that ceaselessly manifests as life in the Ten Worlds (all phenomena).

One who becomes enlightened to the Mystic Law as the fundamental truth of the universe is the Buddha. The Buddha's enlightened state of life is expressed as the Gohonzon. Therefore, the ten factors of life ultimately indicate the Gohonzon.

President Toda explained this, saying:

> The ten factors thus become an abbreviated explanation of the form of the Gohonzon. That's why the "Expedient Means" chapter is very important.
>
> On the surface, they are just the ten factors; this is on the level of doctrinal study of sutras. But from the standpoint of Nichiren's enlightenment, on the level of his perception of the truth in the depths of his being, they become a description of the Gohonzon.

From the deepest standpoint, the true aspect of all phenomena is none other than the Gohonzon.

In terms of the Gohonzon, "Nam-myoho-renge-kyo Nichiren" inscribed down the center of the Gohonzon corresponds to the true aspect, and the beings of the Ten Worlds appearing on either side represent all phenomena. In terms of the doctrine of three thousand realms in a single moment of life, "single moment of life" corresponds to the true aspect and "three thousand realms," to all phenomena.

When we pray to the Gohonzon as beings of the nine worlds, our daily activities, illuminated by Nam-myoho-renge-kyo, reveal the true aspect of all phenomena. Nichiren says, "The living beings of the Ten Worlds are all Buddhas of the true aspect of all phenomena" (GZ, 830). Our lives just as they are—whether in the world of hell or the world of humanity—can shine as the embodiment of the true aspect, that is, of Myoho-renge-kyo.

It is not necessary to go far away or to become someone special. Regardless of whether we experience suffering or joy, as long as we sincerely continue to pray to the Gohonzon and take action for kosen-rufu, then, just as we are, we will definitely become Buddhas of the true aspect of all phenomena, and we can fulfill our own unique mission.

In fact, through our practice of faith, we become able to express the unimpeded workings of three thousand realms in a single moment of life in our day-to-day existence and throughout our lives.

Nichikan says in his commentary on "The Object of Devotion for Observing the Mind": "When we single-mindedly chant Nam-myoho-renge-kyo, our lives in their entirety become the object of devotion." Through carrying out the practice of the Mystic Law for ourselves and others, our lives become the Gohonzon. We can in fact make our lives shine as entities of the Mystic Law.

President Toda said: "By embracing the Gohonzon and chanting Nam-myoho-renge-kyo, the Gohonzon permeates our lives. When we open our eyes and look at the universe, there we find the Gohonzon. And when we close our eyes and look deeply within, the Gohonzon appears there too. The Gohonzon in our hearts grows stronger and comes to shine still more brightly."

The entire universe is the true aspect of all phenomena and the Gohonzon. Our lives are also the true aspect of all phenomena and the Gohonzon. Therefore, when we embrace the Gohonzon, through the dynamic exchange between the universe and our lives, our true aspect—that is, our lives as entities of Nam-myoho-renge-kyo— comes to shine. The wisdom of the Buddha inherent in our lives wells forth. The courage to take compassionate action arises in our hearts, and we enter the golden path of happiness.

How great, indeed, is the Gohonzon! How wondrous is the wisdom of the Lotus Sutra! Let us deeply engrave in our hearts that the Gohonzon itself is the embodiment of inexhaustible happiness and wisdom, and it is the Lotus Sutra of the Latter Day of the Law.

The Mutual Possession of the Ten Worlds and the Three Thousand Realms In a Single Moment of Life

Through explaining the ten factors and the true aspect of all phenomena, Shakyamuni has more or less expressed the contents of the wisdom of the Buddha. Later in the "Expedient Means" chapter, he explains the Buddha's true teaching (the one Buddha vehicle) to "open the door of," "show," "cause living beings to awaken to" and "induce living beings to enter the path" of the Buddha wisdom (see LSOC, 64). And he clarifies that the three types of teachings (the three vehicles) expounded before the Lotus Sutra for the voice-hearers, cause-awakened ones and bodhisattvas are expedient means. This is called the "replacement of the three vehicles with the one vehicle."

Since the passage explaining the true aspect of the ten factors indicates the gist of the replacement, it is termed "the concise replacement of the three vehicles with the one vehicle." T'ien-t'ai established his doctrine of three thousand realms in a single moment of life on the basis of this passage and the concept of the mutual possession of the Ten Worlds.

The teaching that opens the Buddha wisdom to all people is the revelation that all beings of the nine worlds are endowed with the world of Buddhahood. Based on this mystic principle, T'ien-t'ai expressed the inscrutable true aspect through the concepts of the mutual possession of the Ten Worlds (that each of the Ten Worlds is endowed with all Ten

Worlds) and the hundred worlds and thousand factors (that each of the hundred worlds is endowed with the ten factors).

The realm of the environment is then clarified when we come to the "Life Span of the Thus Come One" chapter. Here it states that the saha world—this world, which is full of suffering—is the land where the Buddha dwells eternally. On this basis, T'ien-t'ai developed the doctrine of three thousand realms in a single moment of life, explaining that the thousand factors operate within the three realms.

Regarding this, Nichiren Daishonin writes, "These doctrines of three thousand realms in a single moment of life and threefold contemplation in a single mind are based on the ten factors, or ten thusnesses, enumerated in the first volume of the Lotus Sutra" (WND-2, 82).

And so we see that the passage explaining the true aspect of the ten factors is a crucial one indicating that the beings of the Ten Worlds can all become Buddhas.

To say that the beings of the Ten Worlds all possess the ten factors affirms that, as seen with the Buddha eye, there is no difference between the life of the Buddha and the lives of others. The enlightenment of all people, therefore, is a certainty.

The Daishonin emphasizes the importance of this passage, saying: "The Lotus Sutra represents the true reason why the Buddha made his appearance in the world. It embodies the basic teaching by which all living beings are able to attain the Buddha way. And that teaching is found nowhere but in these four characters that express the idea of the true aspect of all phenomena . . . this one phrase, a single phrase with ten thousand meanings" (WND-2, 591).

Refutation of the Tendai School for Its Lack of Practice

Truly epochal significance attaches to the fact that, from the deepest standpoint, the true aspect of all phenomena is the Gohonzon.

The purpose of T'ien-t'ai's Buddhism was to perceive the true aspect of all phenomena in one's own heart through the practice of observing one's mind and perceiving the Law therein. The ultimate target was to awaken to the true aspect that is one with all phenomena.

This spirit, however, was distorted by later scholars of the Tendai school, the Japanese counterpart to the Chinese T'ien-t'ai school. The Tendai school in Nichiren's day had declined to the point of repudiating the value of Buddhist practice. Their view, simply put, was that since the true aspect was at one with all phenomena, it was fine for things to be just as they were; one was a Buddha even if he or she carried out no practice. They had become completely degenerate and had killed the spirit of the founder, T'ien-t'ai.

Simply saying that reality, mired in pollution and suffering, is itself the true aspect and therefore need not change cannot possibly lead to improvement in people's lives or in society. To this day, the tendency to readily view present conditions with rose-colored glasses and neglect the action needed to bring about positive change remains deeply ingrained in Japanese people's outlook on religion and on life.

Nichiren Daishonin fought against this decadent Tendai school. It could even be said that priests of the Tendai school used the teaching of the true aspect of all phenomena to justify their own negligence. In this respect, they resemble the Nichiren Shoshu priesthood today.

Nichiren revived the idea that the Buddha wisdom—the true aspect of all phenomena—is the goal for people to strive toward in their Buddhist practice and to use to attain Buddhahood. That is, he inscribed the Gohonzon that embodies the enlightened life of the Thus Come One of Nam-myoho-renge-kyo (Nichiren) for all people throughout the world during the Latter Day of the Law.

Nichiren Buddhism teaches not that we should merely observe the true aspect of all phenomena within our lives. Rather, it teaches that we should strive to make the reality of our lives and our environment shine as the true aspect of all phenomena. It is a philosophy of change and improvement for causing all phenomena—our lives and society—to shine as entities of the Mystic Law.

With the light of the wisdom of the true aspect of all phenomena, we can dispel the darkness of illusion arising from ignorance of this wisdom. In that sense, our existence itself is a source of light. Ours is a struggle to brighten and illuminate the place we are now. When we shine, then, wherever we are, no darkness can exist.

Nichiren initiated a great struggle of religious reformation to counter the decadence and degeneration of the Buddhist world. And we, who have a direct connection in faith with the Daishonin, carry on this struggle.

The Nichiren Shoshu priesthood today, similar to the Tendai school in Nichiren's time but incomparably more reprehensible, has trampled upon the founder's spirit. Neglecting practice and whiling away their lives in dissipation, they have thoroughly defiled the spirit of Buddhism. Therefore, we have struggled dauntlessly against them. Fighting evil is proof of a true disciple of Nichiren Daishonin.

The Benefit of Reading the Passage Three Times

What significance attaches to our reading this passage explaining the true aspect of the ten factors three times when we do gongyo each morning and evening?

In "The Doctrine of Three Thousand Realms in a Single Moment of Life," Nichiren explains. He says that reading the ten factors three times signifies the manifestation of the three truths—non-substantiality, temporary existence and the Middle Way—in our lives. This means that our lives express the three bodies of a Buddha: the Dharma body, the reward body and the manifested body. It also means that our lives manifest the three virtues, or three attributes of a Buddha: the Dharma body, wisdom and emancipation.

Our lives shine as Buddhas embodying enlightenment (the Dharma body and the virtue of the Dharma body) endowed with wisdom (the reward body and the virtue of wisdom) and compassion (the manifest body and the virtue of emancipation). Nichiren taught, "Reading them three times will produce great benefit" (WND-2, 83). In short, we read this passage three times to proclaim that our lives are noble Buddhas and increase our benefit of faith.

In general, every time we do gongyo and chant Nam-myoho-renge-kyo, we praise the Buddha nature in our own lives. We also praise the Buddha nature in the lives of all others, and we commune with the Buddha nature of the universe. What a solemn ceremony this is! How fortunate we are to live according to the principle that faith expresses itself in daily life.

In Suffering or Joy, We Can Find Meaning

What does the wisdom of the true aspect of all phenomena add to our lives? It gives us the power to skillfully use everything that happens to create value.

Many things occur in the course of life. There are sufferings and joys, tailwinds and headwinds. All such phenomena provide opportunities for us to make the true aspect of the world of Buddhahood in our lives shine; we can use everything that happens to expand our happiness. This is what it means to lead a life illuminated by the wisdom of the true aspect of all phenomena.

Worth is not found in joy alone, nor is success the only valuable outcome. Suffering is the mother of realization; worries and failures, so long as we are not defeated by them, enable us to deepen our faith. Our sufferings become the raw material with which to build our happiness. This is the principle that earthly desires are enlightenment. Earthly desires, like other phenomena, are themselves the true aspect.

Fundamentally, for people with faith in the Gohonzon, everything that happens is a benefit. This is the difference between those who believe in the Mystic Law and those who do not.

As a young man, I once asked President Toda what makes a person great. Smiling brightly, he replied: "It's having confidence. In life and in everything, it's confidence that counts." There are many important things in life. Among all possible answers, Mr. Toda, without a moment's hesitation, cited confidence. By this, he meant of course great confidence in the Mystic Law.

"I will show victory in my life without fail." "I will help everyone definitely become happy." "I will cause my workplace and my community to develop greatly." "I will change the current of the times toward the emergence of a joyous society of humanism." Those who possess confidence and who take unwavering action based on such confidence are great.

Confidence is single-minded resolve. Confidence is courage. Confidence is hope. Confidence is inner latitude and mercy. As Nichikan indicated when he said "Buddhahood means a strong mind of faith in the Lotus Sutra," confidence is itself the world of Buddhahood.

Although confidence and the world of Buddhahood are invisible to the eye, they are certain to become manifest in concrete form. This accords with the principle of the true aspect manifesting in all phenomena. Buddhism is not empty idealism.

Faith Reveals Itself in Daily Life

Buddhism finds expression in society. It could be said that Buddhism is the "true aspect," and society (secular matters), "all phenomena." Similarly, faith is the "true aspect" and daily life, "all phenomena." The principle of faith manifesting itself in daily life is therefore another way of expressing the principle of the true aspect of all phenomena.

There can be no Buddhism divorced from the real world. Nichiren, citing T'ien-t'ai's words "No worldly affairs of life or work are ever contrary to the true reality," writes, "A person of wisdom is not one who practices Buddhism apart from worldly affairs but, rather, one who thoroughly understands the principles by which the world is governed" (WND-1, 1121). He also writes, "In the end secular matters are the entirety of Buddhism" (WND-1, 1126). "In the end" here indicates "just as they are." In other words, secular matters, just as they are, are Buddhism. Only in the real world can the validity of Buddhism be proven.

Nichiren teaches: "When the skies are clear, the ground is illuminated. Similarly, when one knows the Lotus Sutra, one understands the meaning of all worldly affairs" (WND-1, 376). President Toda commented on this passage of "The Object of Devotion for Observing the Mind" as follows: "Nichiren is saying that those who have embraced the Gohonzon ought to know, for example, how to improve their lives or how to develop their business."

The sun instantaneously illuminates the earth. Likewise, those who uphold the Mystic Law have to understand secular matters. Faith causes the sun of wisdom—which enables us to clearly see what we need to do in order to win—to rise in our hearts.

One of the Buddha's ten honorable titles is Understanding the World. The Buddha has a profound understanding of all secular affairs.

The Ten Factors Also Exist in the Land

Incidentally, the true aspect of the ten factors exists in the land and in society, just as it does in our lives. The land and society, for instance, have the factors of inherent cause and latent effect. They also have power. A land's or society's fortune and destiny are expressed in its factor of appearance. Nichiren Daishonin writes: "Buddhism is like the body, and society like the shadow. When the body bends, so does

the shadow" (WND-1, 1039). A body and its shadow are inseparable. If bends in the "body"—distortions of philosophy, thought and
religion—are not rectified, then all attempts to produce a straight
"shadow" are bound to fail.

Through our movement to conduct dialogue, we contribute to
society on a fundamental level by helping straighten out this "body."
We are creating the inherent cause for peace and prosperity.

No land is more wretched than one wracked by ceaseless hostili-
ties and bloodshed. War destroys everything. Nothing is crueler than
war. President Toda, thinking of the suffering of the North and South
Korean people during the Korean War, composed the following elegy:

> I grieve for the many people there must be who have lost
> their husbands or wives or who search in vain for their chil-
> dren or parents on account of this war.
>
> There must be those who, losing the wealth that they have
> accumulated, are reduced to beggary and suddenly die.
>
> There are doubtless young people who have died without
> knowing why and elderly women who have been killed while
> crying out, "I haven't done anything wrong!"
>
> There must be bands of children who cannot even imag-
> ine what it would be like to have parents and siblings. And
> there are doubtless not a few housewives who have come
> to regard it as normal to be living with just the clothes on
> their backs, and elderly people surprised to find themselves
> dreaming about the rice they once ate.
>
> Are there not some who show surprise when asked,
> "Whose side are you on?" and who reply without hesitation,
> "I am on the side of food and shelter."

These lines express the grief, sadness, anger and resentment of
people mercilessly trampled upon, divided and killed. President Toda

regarded the sufferings of the people of Asia as his own, and he was deeply pained by their plight. In his heart, he shed tears of sympathy. And to wipe away the tears of all people, he stood up alone to undertake the great struggle to widely propagate the Mystic Law.

Carrying on the spirit of our mentor, we help friends become happy through the Mystic Law and send brilliant waves of peace, culture and education around the globe.

Creating a True and Lasting Peace

The true aspect of all phenomena is the philosophical principle of the sanctity of life.

In the world today, ethnic conflicts and fear of terrorism are intensifying. The tragedy of people hating and killing their fellow human beings goes on with no sign of abating. In Japan, murders involving firearms are increasing, and there is a growing sense of anxiety about the emergence of a "handgun society."

In contrast, as seen with the eye of the Buddha who recognizes that each person is an entity of the Mystic Law, each person—irrespective of ethnicity, social standing or birth—is truly invaluable and irreplaceable. There must be no discrimination. The killings in society are absolutely intolerable.

"May all people shine! May all life shine!" This cry of love for humanity is the cry of the Lotus Sutra. It is the cry of those who understand the true aspect of all phenomena. Buddhism exists to enable all people to share in the boundless joy of life.

Therefore, it is the duty of Buddhists to struggle dauntlessly against those who would rob life of its sanctity. In his famous "Declaration for the Abolition of Nuclear Weapons," President Toda proclaimed that he wanted "to rip out the claws that are hidden in the very depths" of nuclear weapons.

It was a challenge against the devilish nature inherent in life that would prompt people to employ nuclear weapons against one another, and a challenge against the power of devilish function called *mara*, the "robber of life," pervading the universe. It was a battle against the insidious nature of authority that readily uses people and sacrifices their lives in the interest of its own self-preservation.

The twenty-first century is upon us. Humankind must overcome on its own this devilish nature, this cancer of humanity, that festered and grew to sickening proportions during the twentieth century.

The Lotus Sutra's wisdom of the true aspect of all phenomena will undoubtedly become an important guideline for this new century—for realizing a century free of murder, a century in which people can peacefully coexist with one another and with nature. In that sense, all of you spreading the Mystic Law are pioneers. You will definitely win the applause of the new century.

From the standpoint of the true aspect of all phenomena, to harm someone is to harm the universe and to harm oneself. When such a sense of oneness with the universe is lost, people become isolated and alienated from one another like grains of sand, and violence erupts from the depths of their impoverished, empty hearts.

When people establish a sense of oneness with the infinite life that is the Mystic Law, it doubtlessly will feel as though humankind has been released from a prison.

Nichiren writes: "Ultimately, all phenomena are contained within one's life, down to the last particle of dust. The nine mountains and the eight seas are encompassed in one's body, and the sun, moon, and myriad stars are found in one's life" (WND-I, 629).

What a vast and grand state of life Nichiren described! The Gohonzon reveals the vast life of the original Buddha, who realizes the unity of the universe with the self, the self with the universe. Nichiren, out of his immense compassion, bestowed the Gohonzon on humankind so that we, too, might develop the same state of life.

We find similar insights outside the Buddhist tradition as well. For example, the English author D. H. Lawrence writes:

> I am part of the sun as my eye is part of me. That I am part of the earth my feet know perfectly, and my blood is part of the sea. My soul knows that I am part of the human race, my soul is an organic part of the great human soul, as my spirit is part of my nation.[9]

He is expressing a sense of the oneness of the individual life and the universe. This true aspect of human life has been pursued through various philosophies, religions and literatures of East and West since time immemorial. Nichiren Buddhism perfectly expresses the unity of life with the universe both theoretically and in practical terms. Nichiren Buddhism, therefore, might be characterized as the religion of universal humanism.

Lawrence, who looked forward to the arrival of a new age of humankind, concluded, "Start with the sun, and the rest will slowly, slowly happen."[10]

Buddhism comes down to state of life. "Start with the sun." While carrying out a dialogue with the heavens and with the gods of the sun and moon as our allies, we are developing a magnificent state of life. This is our Buddhist practice.

What is the purpose of life? It is to construct and solidify a state of absolute happiness, a condition in which to be alive is itself great joy.

Whatever happens, we experience joy. In the depths of our lives, we are always happy. And we have confidence in the future. Like the ocean that remains calm in its depths even when waves rage over its surface during storms, and like the sun that continues shining on high even during heavy rain when dark clouds fill the sky, at every turn we can create value and develop our state of life, enjoying our existence to the fullest in times of both suffering and joy. This is a life based on the true aspect of all phenomena.

How wonderful, indeed, are the lives that we who dedicate ourselves to Nichiren Daishonin's "Buddhism of the Sun" can lead! And what a brilliant dawn for human civilization this great Buddhism will bring on! As we forge on in the twenty-first century, we will see increasingly clear actual proof of this. Burning with this great confidence, let us advance toward our tomorrow.

THE "LIFE SPAN" CHAPTER
PROSE SECTION

On the "Life Span of the Thus Come One" Chapter

L IFE IS THE ultimate mystery. It is the greatest wonder, an unparalleled enigma, the supreme drama.

What do our lives mean? What is the essential nature of our existence? Where do we come from and where do we go? These are the most fundamental questions we face as human beings.

No matter what material abundance we might enjoy, no matter how happy and carefree an existence we might lead, if we divert our eyes from these questions, then genuine happiness and a true sense of fulfillment in life will forever elude us.

It is the sixteenth chapter of the Lotus Sutra, "The Life Span of the Thus Come One," that provides answers to these questions. Nichiren Daishonin says:

> Were it not for the presence of the "Life Span" chapter among all the teachings of Shakyamuni, they would be like the heavens without the sun and moon, a kingdom without a king, the mountains and seas without treasures, or a person without a soul. (WND-I, 183)

If we compare other scriptures to stars in the sky, then the "Life Span" chapter is like the sun and the moon, which shine most brightly in the heavens. It is king among all philosophies, the most precious jewel among all systems of thought and the soul of Buddhism.

Again, were it not for the "Life Span" chapter, then, as Nichiren says, all sutras would be like "grass without roots" or "a river without a source" (WND-1, 184).

The "Life Span" chapter perfectly elucidates the answers to the questions of life that lie at the very root of all sutras and, more broadly, all systems of thought, philosophy and religion.

Let us now commence our study of the "Life Span" chapter — of the great drama of life. My aim is to articulate as clearly as possible the essential meaning of the "Life Span" chapter, from which we recite every morning and evening.

The Status of the "Life Span" Chapter

To begin with, just what does the "Life Span" chapter teach? It explains the eternity of life. The chapter's Japanese title, *nyorai juryo*, means to fathom the span of life (*juryo*) of the Thus Come One, or the Buddha (*nyorai*). The "Life Span" chapter clarifies that the life span of the Buddha is immeasurable.

Shakyamuni explains the eternity of life in terms of his own existence. This is important. The eternity of life is not in any sense an abstract theory, nor is it fictitious or imaginary. The "Life Span" chapter is an account of Shakyamuni's own experience.

The gist of this account is as follows: Shakyamuni begins by noting that most people believe that he renounced the world at a young age and practiced and attained Buddhahood beneath the bodhi tree near the city of Gaya. But he refutes this view and clarifies that in fact he attained Buddhahood in the inconceivably remote past and that ever since then he has been instructing countless people in this saha world and in innumerable other lands. In this way, he indicates that his life span is immeasurable and that his life itself is eternal and nonperishing.

Now, some may wonder: "Although we say that Shakyamuni's life is eternal, didn't he in fact die? Doesn't this indicate that the Buddha's life span is finite?" This is a very natural question. We can find an answer in the "Life Span" chapter itself.

The chapter explains that the Shakyamuni who attained enlightenment for the first time in India is a provisional, or "expedient," Buddha, whereas the Shakyamuni who attained enlightenment in the remote past and whose life is eternal and nonperishing is a true Buddha.

An expedient, as we have already learned, is a means that the Buddha employs to guide people. While the life of the Buddha is in fact eternal, the Buddha appears in a transitory form and then "enters extinction" as a means to develop people's seeking spirit. This is the answer that the "Life Span" chapter provides.

While accepting the eternity of the Buddha's life, some may question if this revelation has any significance for the lives of us ordinary people. It has a very important bearing, for the Buddha who attained enlightenment in the remote past ultimately is none other than us, the ordinary people who embrace the Mystic Law.

Nichiren Daishonin says, "The term 'Thus Come One' refers to all living beings" (OTT, 124). Eternity is not an attribute exclusively of the Buddha's life; it is the true aspect of the lives of all living beings.

The Buddha Who Attained Enlightenment in the Remote Past Eternally Guides People to Happiness

To clarify the eternity of life to which he has become enlightened, Shakyamuni reveals his true identity as the Buddha who attained enlightenment in the remote past and who eternally continues to guide the people. This is the literal teaching of the sutra; it explains eternity as an attribute of the Buddha's life acquired as a result of his having attained Buddhahood.

Ultimately, however, this attribute is a function of the Mystic Law, the fundamental Law of the universe. The eternal Mystic Law, spanning the three existences—past, present and future—blossoms like a lotus flower in people's lives. The true aspect of the Buddha is found in the ability to lead a pure and noble existence, to emit the fragrance of compassion and to shine with wisdom, even amid painful circumstances. It is this function of the Mystic Law that is eternal.

In other words, Myoho-renge-kyo is itself the true aspect of the Buddha who attained enlightenment in the remote past. Shakyamuni and all Buddhas are functions of the Mystic Law. This is the teaching of the "Life Span" chapter from the deepest standpoint. Therefore, the Daishonin says, "It is Myoho-renge-kyo that is the true Buddha" (WND-I, 384). From this standpoint, he proclaimed that "Thus Come One" in the chapter's title means the "Nam-myoho-renge-kyo Thus Come One," or Nichiren Daishonin himself.

The Daishonin further says, "Now Nichiren and his followers, those who chant Nam-myoho-renge-kyo, are the original lords of teachings of the 'Life Span' chapter" (OTT, 126). The original Buddha thus plainly declares that we who accept and uphold Nam-myoho-renge-kyo are the subject of the "Life Span" chapter. Each of us is the protagonist of "Life Span," a grand epic of the eternity of life.

We who strive to actively manifest in our lives the eternal Mystic Law lead lives of eternal tranquillity, joy and contentment. As though traversing the infinite universe, we advance along the great path of happiness with a state of life of total freedom. "Life Span" expounds the secret teaching that enables us to experience supreme joy both in life and in death.

Who Will Spread This Teaching in the Latter Day of the Law?

The Lotus Sutra is the teaching that enables all people to become happy. Specifically, it is in the "Life Span" chapter that Shakyamuni reveals the great pure Law that can lead all people to happiness after his passing. This is the Law of Nam-myoho-renge-kyo implicit in the depths of the "Life Span" chapter.

Nichiren says: "But once the world entered the Latter Day of the Law, the doctrines of the sutras preached prior to the Lotus Sutra and those of the theoretical teaching of the Lotus Sutra no longer were capable of freeing one from the sufferings of birth and death. Only in the 'Life Span' chapter of the essential teaching is to be found the vital doctrine needed to free one from the sufferings of birth and death" (WND-2, 985).

Even within the Lotus Sutra, the teaching that can save the people of the Latter Day of the Law can be found only in the "Life Span" chapter. Overcoming the sufferings of birth and death means gaining liberation from the fundamental sufferings of existence. This is the teaching that enables people to develop a state of happiness arising from the very depths of their being. The "Life Span" chapter elucidates the eternal life from which all lives fundamentally spring.

What benefit may be gained from hearing the "Life Span" chapter expounded? In "Distinctions in Benefits," the seventeenth chapter, we find the passage, "Hearing that the Buddha's life is immeasurable, all beings are filled with joy" (LSOC, 278). In other words, understanding life's eternity fills people with joy from the depths of their being. This joy is the power of the Mystic Law to dispel any suffering, no matter how deep-seated.

Needless to say, this refers to the benefit of Nam-myoho-renge-kyo hidden in the chapter's depths; Nichiren Daishonin states, "Nam-myoho-renge-kyo is the greatest of all joys" (OTT, 212).

President Toda described the inner state of those who embrace the Gohonzon, saying, "From the depths of their lives, they feel total peace of mind, and to live is itself a joy."

Nam-myoho-renge-kyo is the great Law that illuminates the lives of all people. It is the great beneficial medicine that can fundamentally save all people of the Latter Day, who are steeped in the sufferings of birth and death.

The protagonists of the Lotus Sutra who will teach and spread the great beneficial medicine of Nam-myoho-renge-kyo among the people of the Latter Day are none other than the Bodhisattvas of the Earth.

The Bodhisattvas of the Earth are bodhisattvas who possess the eternal Mystic Law in their lives. Nichiren said that if they had not been entrusted with the supreme Law, they could not possibly appear and propagate it in the Latter Day (see WND-1, 372). The "supreme Law" means Nam-myoho-renge-kyo.

As I mentioned earlier, the Law of Nam-myoho-renge-kyo implicit in the "Life Span" chapter is the great beneficial medicine that can lead all people of the Latter Day to enlightenment. Nam-myoho-renge-kyo is the Law of life. Accordingly, one cannot save the people of the Latter Day unless he or she has been entrusted with this Law and can manifest it for the sake of the people of the Latter Day.

Nichiren Daishonin associated himself with Superior Practices, leader of the Bodhisattvas of the Earth. For the liberation of all people of the Latter Day, he perceived that his own life was Nam-myoho-renge-kyo of the "Life Span" chapter and embodied his life in the form of the Gohonzon.

Nichiren says: "The accepting and upholding of this original Law is expressed in the single word 'belief' or 'faith.' The single word 'belief' is the sharp sword with which one confronts and overcomes fundamental darkness or ignorance" (OTT, 119–20). And "If you are of the same mind as Nichiren, you must be a Bodhisattva of the Earth" (WND-1, 385).

Thus, we who practice faith in the Gohonzon and advance kosen-rufu with the same mind as Nichiren Daishonin are also Bodhisattvas of the Earth entrusted with the supreme Law.

The Practice of the Bodhisattvas of the Earth in the Modern Age

The Lotus Sutra's "Emerging from the Earth" chapter says of the Bodhisattvas of the Earth, in "this saha world they have been dwelling in the empty space in its lower part" (LSOC, 260). Regarding "lower part," or lower region, Nichiren says, "The lower region represents the principle of truth" (OTT, 119).

The Bodhisattvas of the Earth are bodhisattvas from the world of truth who have appeared in this saha world. That is, they are courageous people arising from the great Law of the universe, from Nam-myoho-renge-kyo, who have jubilantly appeared among the people.

Therefore, they are never deadlocked. They can limitlessly draw forth life force and wisdom from the world of the Mystic Law, and they can spread the Mystic Law and endure great persecution in the polluted world of the Latter Day.

All those who spread Buddhism in the defiled world of the Latter Day as Nichiren Daishonin taught are, without exception, Bodhisattvas of the Earth. In this day and age, SGI members match the sutra's description of the Bodhisattvas of the Earth perfectly.

The Bodhisattvas of the Earth are described as "firm in their intent and thought" (LSOC, 256). That is, they are people of firm determination who, once set on a course of action, follow through; they are people of persistence. They include the pioneers of our movement who, come what may, have persevered in faith since the early days. Though subject to slander and abuse, they have never turned their backs on their determination. Their lives shine, adorned with the medal of perseverance that adorns the Bodhisattvas of the Earth.

The sutra also describes the Bodhisattvas of the Earth as "skillfully learning the bodhisattva way, unsoiled by worldly things like the lotus flower in the water" (LSOC, 263).

In a society defiled by the five impurities, SGI members, untarnished, sincerely live out their lives in the realm of Buddhism. They help those suffering in the cloudy waters of society become happy.

Those who are loath to go out among the people and who instead abandon society and seclude themselves in the mountains cannot fulfill the mission of the Bodhisattvas of the Earth.

Moreover, the sutra says that the Bodhisattvas of the Earth "are clever at difficult questions and answers, their minds know no fear. They have firmly cultivated persevering minds, upright in dignity and virtue" (LSOC, 263).

"Clever at difficult questions and answers," simply put, means that they are experts at conducting dialogue. They have wisdom from having lived on the very forefront of society. They have the wisdom to turn back unjust abuse gracefully, offering instead, "Why don't we first discuss what it means to lead a happy life?" SGI members are all certainly people of wisdom who are skilled at difficult questions and answers.

"Their minds know no fear" describes you courageous men and women who, fearing no one, resolutely fight against those evil powers that seek to trample upon the people.

"They have firmly cultivated persevering minds." Such tenacity is your true forte. There may be those around you who always complain or who constantly think only of themselves. Yet you definitely would not abandon a friend. You are people of the foremost perseverance. And by persevering you have won over difficulties in your own lives too. You are truly champions of compassion and conviction.

"Upright in dignity and virtue" means that your hearts and your lives shine. Your lives overflow with a human magnetism that powerfully draws people to you. No one can fail to be convinced of the greatness of this Buddhism when they see such rich human virtue.

In this way, each of you has the power of the Bodhisattvas of the Earth. When you hear this description, doubtless many of you are reminded of a certain chapter leader, pioneer member or local women's leader.

Each of the Bodhisattvas of the Earth is "a treasure among persons" (LSOC, 262). They are treasures of the community, the nation and the world. This is just how precious and respectable they are.

Each of you has the spirit of a Bodhisattva of the Earth. You have the mettle to staunchly protect the Mystic Law and the bodhisattva spirit to encourage others and try to assuage the pain in their lives. You respect all people from the bottom of your heart. This is the spirit of the Lotus Sutra and the spirit of the Bodhisattvas of the Earth.

Again, each of you is carrying out the practice of the Bodhisattvas of the Earth, who appear when people are suffering most and where there is the greatest sadness.

The Great Task of Transmitting Hope to Humanity

Nichiren Daishonin describes conditions during the Latter Day of the Law, saying: "Those who espouse Hinayana reject Mahayana, and those who espouse provisional teachings attack the true teaching, until the country is overrun with slanderers of the Law" (WND-1, 400).

While Nichiren is referring specifically to confusion regarding the Hinayana and Mahayana teachings and the provisional and true teachings, his words perfectly describe the spiritual confusion of the present age. Being strongly attached to bankrupt systems of values, people prefer what is base and shrink from what is lofty. They are fond of the trivial and inauthentic and detest the genuine. The Latter Day of the Law is an age when people are receptive to shallow thought and shallow ways of living, and they disparage a way of life that is profound.

In a society with such topsy-turvy values, SGI members have persisted in their efforts to explain the correct way of life to those who have lost their sense of direction and gone adrift. Just as the sutra indicates where it says "Each one of these bodhisattvas was the leader of his own great assembly" (LSOC, 253), as leaders of the people you are shedding light on many others.

World War II ended in 1945, and that same year Josei Toda stood up alone amid the devastation of war and took the first step to reconstruct the Soka Gakkai. The history of members' spiritual struggle is engraved in countless places throughout the country.

In Okinawa, the only place in Japan where a land war was fought; in Hiroshima and Nagasaki, the first cities in the history of the world to experience the horrors of nuclear warfare; and in all parts of the country, the seeds of peace have been planted and great trees of happiness and prosperity have grown up.

In areas facing the greatest of challenges—rural villages that, amid rapid economic development, suffered from an exodus to urban areas; mountainous regions devastated by the closure of coal mines; remote islands and big cities where people's hearts have withered—you have followed Nichiren's encouragement to "grit your teeth and never slacken in your faith" (WND-1, 498). Because society's values are upside down, you have had to endure storms of untoward criticism and calumny.

And you have won!

Your cheerful, smiling faces have greatly changed Japan. And the same smiles are spreading to all parts of the world.

President Toda declared:

> I perceive that we have appeared in this world charged with the great responsibility to propagate the seven-character Lotus Sutra during the Latter Day of the Law. If our status is assessed in terms of this role, then we are certainly Bodhisattvas of the Earth.

All of you are proving in reality our mentor's declaration, which is like a lion's roar. How highly the original Buddha and all Buddhas must be praising and applauding the great achievements of the Bodhisattvas of the Earth of the present age!

Yet the world is still rife with tragedy and suffering. In Japan and elsewhere, the degree of turmoil is only intensifying. The long march of the Bodhisattvas of the Earth continues—for peace and for people's happiness.

Toward that end, I hope you will advance in even better health and even more cheerfully, and that you will lead long lives. The world and coming era eagerly await your smiling faces.

On the Title

What associations or meanings have the words *Myoho-renge-kyo nyorai juryo-hon* (The Lotus Sutra of the Wonderful Law, The Life Span of the Thus Come One Chapter) had for those who, since ancient times, read and recited the Lotus Sutra?

Without a doubt, many have read them casually, unaware of their significance. On the other hand, more than a few have passionately debated the meaning of this chapter title. Unique among them was T'ien-t'ai, who correctly grasped the meaning of the chapter's content and explained its title on that basis.

In all of history, however, no one has ever read the title of the "Life Span" chapter with the clarity of Nichiren. He says: "The title of this chapter deals with an important matter that concerns Nichiren himself. This is the transmission described in the 'Supernatural Powers' chapter" (OTT, 123). Only Nichiren could read the title of the "Life Span" chapter with the understanding that it constituted "an important matter" that applied directly to his own life. And this matter, he says, is closely related to the transmission described in "Supernatural Powers of the Thus Come One" chapter.

In the "Supernatural Powers" chapter, Shakyamuni entrusts Bodhisattva Superior Practices and the other Bodhisattvas of the Earth with the task of propagating the Lotus Sutra after his death.

The essence of the teaching entrusted to the Bodhisattvas of the Earth, which can lead all people in the Latter Day to enlightenment, is the Law of Nam-myoho-renge-kyo. This is the great Law of beginningless time implicit in the depths of the "Life Span" chapter.

Nichiren embodied Nam-myoho-renge-kyo in his own life. And, fulfilling the role of Bodhisattva Superior Practices, he took the first step to spread the Mystic Law for the people of the Latter Day. That's why the Daishonin says that the title of the "Life Span" chapter "deals with an important matter that concerns Nichiren himself."

The title of the "Life Span" chapter also indicates the benefit of Nam-myoho-renge-kyo. Regarding this, there are a few points I'd like to mention.

The words *nyorai juryo* in the chapter's Japanese title literally mean to fathom the Thus Come One's life span. To fathom the length of the Buddha's life span also means to fathom the vastness of the benefit the Buddha accumulated. That's because the longer the Buddha's life span, the more people he can lead to happiness and, hence, the greater his virtue and benefit.

Accordingly, T'ien-t'ai says that the term *juryo* (fathom the life span) means to reveal and fathom that benefit, to measure and clarify the benefits of various Thus Come Ones.

According to T'ien-t'ai, the benefit of the Buddha specifically consists of the Buddha's three bodies: the Dharma body, the truth to which a Buddha is enlightened; the reward body, the Buddha wisdom obtained as the reward of completing bodhisattva practices; and the manifested body, the physical forms and compassionate actions that a Buddha manifests in this world in order to save people. He clarifies that the Buddha—who dwells in this world eternally and possesses these three bodies—is Shakyamuni who attained enlightenment in the remote past.

By contrast, from the deepest standpoint, the source of this eternal Buddha's benefit is Nam-myoho-renge-kyo. That is, the benefit of the Buddha who attained enlightenment in the remote past derives from Nam-myoho-renge-kyo.

Therefore, the Daishonin indicates that the title of the "Life Span" chapter should read "The Life Span of the Thus Come One Nam-myoho-renge-kyo" (OTT, 123).

President Toda stressed: "The addition of the [Sanskrit] word *nam* completely changes the meaning of 'Thus Come One.'" When we read the title as *Nam-myoho-renge-kyo nyorai juryo*, it means to fathom the benefit of the "Nam-myoho-renge-kyo Thus Come One," that is, of the Buddha implicit in the depths of the chapter.

Because Nichiren himself is the Nam-myoho-renge-kyo Thus Come One, he says that the title "deals with an important matter that concerns Nichiren himself."

This Buddha implicit in the chapter is said to be eternally endowed with the three bodies. "Eternally endowed" means originally and naturally possessing. Nichiren says: "'Eternally endowed with the three bodies' refers to the votaries of the Lotus Sutra in the Latter Day of the Law. The title of honor for one who is eternally endowed with the three bodies is Nam-myoho-renge-kyo" (OTT, 124).

He also says: "'Thus Come One' refers to all living beings. More specifically, it refers to the disciples and lay supporters of Nichiren" (OTT, 124). If we earnestly chant Nam-myoho-renge-kyo, then, he says, "instant after instant there will arise in us the three Buddha bodies with which we are eternally endowed" (OTT, 214).

How wondrous! We can each manifest and fathom the benefit of the Law of Nam-myoho-renge-kyo implicit in the "Life Span" chapter. From the deepest standpoint, the "Life Span" chapter fathoms and praises the immeasurable benefit that we who base our lives on the Mystic Law possess. Accordingly, from this perspective, the chapter's title radiates the brilliant light of the Buddhism of the people.

EDITOR'S NOTE

The following is a brief overview of developments within the Lotus Sutra regarding the Bodhisattvas of the Earth: Beginning in "Expedient Means," Shakyamuni makes various predictions about how Shariputra and other disciples will in the future become Buddhas. In "The Teacher of the Law," the tenth chapter, however, the theme changes, and the question of who will propagate the Lotus Sutra after Shakyamuni's passing becomes the main focus.

In "The Emergence of the Treasure Tower," the eleventh chapter, a majestic treasure tower appears from out of the earth and the Ceremony in the Air gets under way. Then, in response to Shakyamuni's exhortations, the bodhisattvas of the theoretical teaching (Bodhisattvas who are followers of a provisional Buddha) and the voice-hearers pledge one after another to propagate the Lotus Sutra after the Buddha's passing. Bodhisattvas from other worlds (those instructed by Buddhas dwelling in worlds other than this saha world) then join the assembly and pledge to propagate the Lotus Sutra without begrudging their lives even if they should be attacked by the three powerful enemies.

Shakyamuni, however, refrains from entrusting these bodhisattvas with the sutra's propagation after his death. In "Emerging from the Earth," the fifteenth chapter, he says: "In this saha world of mine there are bodhisattvas mahasattva who are as numerous as the sands of sixty thousand Ganges Rivers . . . After I have entered extinction these people will be able to protect, embrace, read, recite, and widely preach this sutra" (LSOC, 252).

Suddenly, the earth splits open and a great multitude of bodhisattvas emerge from its depths. They are all leaders, each followed by a large retinue. The Bodhisattvas of the Earth are led by four bodhisattvas named Superior Practices, Boundless Practices, Pure Practices and Firmly Established Practices. They are endowed with splendid dignity and merit. The bodhisattvas of the original assembly are much taken aback. On behalf of the others, Bodhisattva Maitreya asks about the meaning of the appearance of the Bodhisattvas of the Earth.

Praising Maitreya, Shakyamuni says, "Excellent, excellent, . . . that you should question the Buddha about this great affair" (LSOC, 258), and then begins to explain who these bodhisattvas are. Shakyamuni indicates that he himself had converted and instructed these countless bodhisattvas since the time of his enlightenment in the remote past.

Filled with surprise and doubt, Maitreya then asks where and when Shakyamuni instructed them, beseeching him to answer clearly. In response, Shakyamuni begins to expound the "Life Span" chapter. Later, in "Supernatural Powers of the Thus Come One," the twenty-first chapter, Shakyamuni entrusts the Bodhisattvas of the Earth with propagating the Lotus Sutra after his death.

❧ The "Life Span" Chapter Prose Section

The following are the passages from the "Life Span" chapter prose section that SGI members used to recite during gongyo. (See the Editor's Note on p. ix for more information about why these passages are no longer recited during gongyo.) The numbers next to each passage correspond to the numbered lectures that follow; page numbers where the lecture for each passage can be found also appear here. The appendix on p. 387 contains the full English translation.

(**9**) Niji butsu go. Sho bo-satsu gyu. Issai daishu.
Sho zen-nanshi. Nyoto to shinge. Nyorai jotai shi go. Bu go daishu. Nyoto to shinge. Nyorai jotai shi go. U bu go. Sho daishu. Nyoto to shinge. Nyorai jotai shi go. Zeji bo-satsu daishu. Mi-roku i shu. Gassho byaku butsu gon. Seson. Yui gan seś shi. Gato to shinju butsu-go. Nyo ze san byaku i. Bu gon. Yui gan seś shi. Gato to shinju butsu-go. Niji seson. Chi sho bo-satsu. San sho fu shi. Ni go shi gon. Nyoto tai cho. Nyorai hi-mitsu. Jinzu shi riki. (**p. 147**)

(**10**) Issai seken. Tennin gyu. Ashu-ra. Kai i kon shaka-muni-butsu. Shuś shaku-shi gu. Ko gayajo fu on. Za o dojo. Toku a-noku-ta-ra san-myaku sanbodai. Nen zen-nanshi. Ga jitsu jo-butsu irai. Muryo muhen. Hyaku sen man noku. Nayuta ko. (**p. 159**)

(**11**) Hi nyo go hyaku sen man noku. Nayuta. Asogi. Sanzen dai sen sekai. Ke shi u nin. Matchi mijin. Ka o tobo. Go hyaku sen man noku. Nayuta. Asogi koku. Nai ge ichi-jin. Nyo ze to gyo. Jin ze mijin. Sho zen-nanshi. O i unga. Ze sho sekai. Ka toku shiyui. Kyokei chi go. Shu fu. Mi-roku bo-saŕ to. Ku byaku butsu gon. Seson. Ze sho sekai. Muryo muhen. Hi sanju sho chi. Yaku hi shin-riki sho gyu. Issai shomon. Hyaku-shi-butsu. I mu-rochi. Fu no shiyui. Chi go genshu. Gato ju. A-yui-ot-chi-ji. O ze ji chu. Yaku sho fu daś seson. Nyo ze sho sekai. Muryo muhen. (**p. 173**)

(12) Niji butsu go. Dai bosas̄ shu. Sho zen-nanshi. Konto funmyo. Sengo nyoto. Ze sho sekai. Nyaku jaku mijin. Gyu fu jaku sha. Jin ni i jin. Ichi-jin ikko. Ga jo-butsu irai. Bu ka o shi. Hyaku sen man noku. Nayuta. Asogi ko. (p. 177)

(13) Ji ju ze rai. Ga jo zai shi. Shaba sekai. Seppo kyoke. Yaku o yosho. Hyaku sen man noku. Nayuta. Asogi koku. Dori shujo. (p. 181)

(14) Sho zen-nanshi. O ze chugen. Ga setsu nen-to-butᴗto. U bu gon go. Nyu o nehan. Nyo ze kai i. Hoben fun-betsu. Sho zen-nanshi. Nyaku u shujo. Raishi ga sho. Ga i butsu-gen. Kan go shin to. Sho kon ridon. Zui sho o do. Shosho ji setsu. Myoji fudo. Nenki daisho. Yaku-bu gen gon. To nyu nehan. U i shuju hoben. Setsu mimyo ho. No ryo shujo. Hokᴗkangi shin. (p. 189)

(15) Sho zen-nanshi. Nyorai ken sho shujo. Gyo o shobo. Toku hakᴗku ju sha. I ze nin setsu. Ga sho shukke. Toku a-noku-ta-ra san myaku sanbodai. Nen ga jitsu jo-butsu irai. Ku-on nyaku shi. Tan ni hoben. Kyoke shujo. Ryo nyu butsu-do. Sa nyo ze setsu. (p. 197)

(16) Sho zen-nanshi. Nyorai sho en kyoden. Kai i dodas̄ shujo. Waku sekᴗkoshin. Waku setᴗtashin. Waku ji koshin. Waku ji tashin. Waku ji koji. Waku ji taji. Sho sho gon-setsu. Kai jitsu fu ko. (p. 203)

(17) Sho-i sha ga. Nyorai nyojitᴗchi-ken. Sangai shi so. Mu u shoji. Nyaku tai nyaku shutsu. Yaku mu zai-se. Gyu metsu-do sha. Hi jitsu hi ko. Hi nyo hi i. Fu nyo san-gai. Ken no sangai. Nyo shi shi ji. Nyorai myo ken. Mu u shaku-myo. (p. 207)

(18) I sho shujo. U shu-ju sho. Shuju yoku. Shuju gyo. Shuju oku-so. Fun-bekᴗko. Yoku ryo sho sho zengon. I nyakkan innen. Hiyu gonji. Shuju seppo. Shosa butsu-ji. Mi zo zan pai. (p. 221)

(19) Nyo ze ga jo-butsu irai. Jindai ku-on. Jumyo muryo. Asogi ko. Joju fu-metsu. Sho zen-nanshi. Ga hon gyo bo-satsu do. Sho jo jumyo. Kon yu mi jin. Bu bai jo shu. (p. 229)

(20) Nen kon hi jitsu metsu-do. Ni ben sho gon. To shu metsu-do. Nyorai i ze hoben. Kyoke shujo. Sho-i sha ga. Nyaku buk-ku-ju o se. Haku-toku shi nin. Fu shu zengon. Bingu gesen. Ton-jaku go-yoku. Nyu o oku-so. Moken mo chu. Nyakken nyorai. Jo zai fu-metsu. Ben ki kyoshi. Ni e endai. Fu no sho o. Nan-zo shi so. Kugyo shi shin. (p. 245)

(21) Ze ko nyorai. I hoben setsu. Bi-ku to chi. Sho-buś shus-se. Nan ka chigu. Sho-i sha ga. Sho haku-toku nin. Ka muryo. Hyaku sen man nok-ko. Waku u ken butsu. Waku fu ken sha. I shiji ko. Ga sa ze gon. Sho bi-ku. Nyorai nan ka tokken. Shi shujo to. Mon nyo ze go. Hit̂ to sho o. Nanzo shi so. Shin ne renbo. Katsu-go o butsu. Ben shu zengon. Ze ko nyorai. Sui fu jitsu metsu. Ni gon metsu-do. U zen-nanshi. Sho-butsu nyo-rai. Ho kai nyo ze. I do shu-jo. Kai jitsu fu ko. (p. 253)

(22) Hi nyo ro-i. Chi-e so-datsu. Myo ren ho-yaku. Zen ji shubyo. Go nin ta sho shi-soku. Nyaku ju niju. Nai-shi hyaku-shu. I u ji-en. On shi yo-koku. (p. 257)

(23) Sho shi o go. On ta doku-yaku. Yaku hotsu monran. Enden u ji. Zeji go bu. Gen rai ki ke. Sho shi on doku. Waku shitsu honshin. Waku fu shiŝ sha. Yo ken go bu. Kai dai kangi. Haiki monjin. Zen nan non ki. Gato guchi. Go buku doku-yaku. Gan ken kuryo. Kyo shi jumyo. (p. 261)

(24) Bu ken shi to. Kuno nyo ze. E sho kyobo. Gu ko yaku-so. Shiki ko mimi. Kai shitsu gu-soku. Toshi wago. Yo shi ryo buku. Ni sa ze gon. Shi dai ro-yaku. Shiki ko mimi. Kai shitsu gu-soku. Nyoto ka buku. Soku jo kuno. Mu bu shugen. (p. 267)

(25) Go sho shi chu. Fu shis͡shin ja. Ken shi ro yaku. Shiki ko gu
ko. Soku-ben buku shi. Byo jin jo yu. Yo shis-shin ja. Ken
go bu rai. Sui yak-kangi monjin. Gu-shaku ji byo. Nen yo go
yaku. Ni fu ko buku. Sho-i sha ga. Dokke jinnyu.
Ship͡ponshin ko. O shi ko shiki ko yaku. Ni i fu mi. (p. 275)

(26) Bu sa ze nen. Shi shi ka min. I doku sho chu. Shin kai ten-do.
Sui ken ga ki. Gushak͡ ku-ryo. Nyo ze ko yaku. Ni fu ko buku.
Ga kon to setsu hoben. Ryo buku shi yaku. Soku sa ze gon.
Nyoto to chi. Ga kon sui ro. Shi ji i shi. Ze ko ro-yaku. Kon ru
zai shi. Nyo ka shu buku. Mot͡ tsu fu sai. (p. 281)

(27) Sa ze kyo i. Bu shi ta-koku. Ken shi gen go. Nyo bu i shi. Zeji
sho shi. Mon bu haiso. Shin dai uno. Ni sa ze nen. Nyaku bu
zai sha. Jimin gato. No ken kugo. Konja sha ga. On so
ta-koku. Ji yui koro. Mu bu jiko. Jo e hikan. Shin zui shogo.
Nai chi shi yaku. Shiki ko mimi. Soku shu buku shi. Doku byo
kai yu. Go bu mon shi. Shi͡ chi toku sai. Jin ben rai ki.
Gen shi ken shi. (p. 285)

(28) Sho zen-nanshi. O i unga. Ha u nin no. Ses-shi ro-i. Komo zai
fu. Hot͡cha. Seson. Butsu gon. Ga yaku nyo ze. Jo-butsu irai.
Muryo muhen. Hyaku sen man noku. Nayuta. Asogi ko.
I shujo ko. I hoben-riki. Gon to metsu-do. Yaku mu u no.
Nyo ho setsu ga. Komo ka sha. Niji seson. Yoku ju sen shigi.
Ni setsu ge gon. (p. 291)

▪9▪

Niji butsu go. Sho bo-satsu gyu. Issai daishu. Sho zen-nanshi. Nyoto to
shinge. Nyorai jotai shi go. Bu go daishu. Nyoto to shinge. Nyorai jotai
shi go. U bu go. Sho daishu. Nyoto to shinge. Nyorai jotai shi go.
Zeji bo-satsu daishu. Mi-roku i shu. Gassho byaku butsu gon. Seson.
Yui gan ses̄hi. Gato to shinju butsu-go. Nyo ze san byaku i. Bu gon. Yui
gan ses̄hi. Gato to shinju butsu-go. Niji seson. Chi sho bo-satsu. San
sho fu shi. Ni go shi gon. Nyoto tai cho. Nyorai hi-mitsu. Jinzu shi riki.

At that time the Buddha spoke to the bodhisattvas and all the great assembly: "Good men, you must believe and understand the truthful words of the
Thus Come One." And again he said to the great assembly: "You must
believe and understand the truthful words of the Thus Come One." And
once more he said to the great assembly: "You must believe and understand the truthful words of the Thus Come One."

At that time the bodhisattvas and the great assembly, with Maitreya as
their leader, pressed their palms together and addressed the Buddha, saying: "World-Honored One, we beg you to explain. We will believe and
accept the Buddha's words." They spoke in this manner three times, and
then said once more: "We beg you to explain it. We will believe and accept
the Buddha's words."

At that time the World-Honored One, seeing that the bodhisattvas
repeated their request three times and more, spoke to them, saying: "You
must listen carefully and hear of the Thus Come One's secret and his transcendental powers." (LSOC, 265)

L ET US NOW begin our study of the "Life Span" chapter, the very foundation of the Buddha's teachings.

The chapter begins, "At that time . . ." The "Expedient Means" chapter also begins in this way. But in "Life Span," the words carry still greater significance.

Namely, they refer to the time when the Buddha finally will expound the fundamental Law of the essential teaching. In other words, the time has arrived when all people can eradicate from their lives fundamental darkness—the fundamental source of illusion that even highly advanced bodhisattvas such as Maitreya could not easily overcome.

Moreover, the expression "at that time" in "Life Span" points to the time after Shakyamuni's passing. It is for those living after the Buddha's passing that Maitreya beseeches Shakyamuni to expound his teaching.

The time has at last arrived when Shakyamuni will reveal the fundamental teaching that will illuminate the lives of all people in the world after his passing. It is the time to which the words "at that time" refer. That is why the chapter opens with a depiction of the solemn drama of the oneness of mentor and disciple.

At that time, the Buddha says, "You must believe and understand the truthful words of the Thus Come One" (LSOC, 265). He repeats this statement three times. "Truthful words" are those that directly express the truth to which the Buddha is enlightened. To put it another way, he says he will explain his enlightenment directly, abandoning all expedient means. Therefore, he urges that they receive this teaching with faith. This is a cry from the soul of the mentor, his wholehearted appeal to his disciples.

At that time, his disciples beg him to expound the teaching, saying, "We will believe and accept the Buddha's words" (LSOC, 265). The disciples thus earnestly entreat him three times to reveal it. Then they do so yet again. The Buddha understands that nothing can stand in the way of their earnest desire to know the truth.

At that time, the mentor begins expounding the teaching never before known, saying, "You must listen carefully and hear of the Thus Come One's secret and his transcendental powers" (LSOC, 265).

The Disciple Seeks the Mentor's Supreme Teaching

Many sutras describe the drama in which disciples entreat the Buddha three times to expound his teaching. Immediately after Shakyamuni attained the way, while he vacillated over whether he should begin preaching, Brahma implored him three times to expound the Law. Similarly, in "Expedient Means," he begins to teach the replacement of the three vehicles with the one vehicle only after Shariputra has made three sincere entreaties.

Traditionally, three rounds of entreaty indicate that an important teaching is about to be expounded and point to the Buddha's profound determination that this teaching should be spread. In the case of the "Life Span" chapter, however, it does not end with only three entreaties. The disciples' seeking spirit, like a torrent, truly knows no bounds. In response, the Buddha expounds the supreme teaching.

That the disciples entreat the Buddha to expound his teaching a fourth time indicates that the importance of the "Life Span" chapter far exceeds the Buddha's other teachings. It also suggests that the disciples' determination is so profound as to move the heart of the mentor.

The repetition of "at that time" to mark the developments in the exhortation and response between the Buddha and his disciples at the outset of "Life Span" also conveys a heightening spiritual unity of mentor and disciple. The time of the "Life Span" chapter is the moment when mentor and disciple become one in mind. It is the time of the oneness of mentor and disciple.

At that time, there is a perfect concordance between the compassion of the mentor and the determination of the disciples, the wisdom of the mentor and the earnestness of the disciples, the expectations of the mentor and the growth of the disciples. This time of perfect unity of mentor and disciple is the time when a broad path is opened for the salvation of all human beings into the limitless future.

In Nichiren's writing "The Object of Devotion for Observing the Mind," which is patterned on the question-and-answer format of "Life Span," it is only after the hypothetical questioner has persisted in asking the same key question four times that Nichiren Daishonin clarifies the nature of the true object of devotion for the entire world (see WND-I, 374–75).

Thus, from the standpoint of this passage's implicit meaning, it could be said that here the original Buddha, Nichiren Daishonin, is admonishing his disciples to believe in and accept and to practice the Buddha's "truthful words," Nam-myoho-renge-kyo.

When we recite this passage during our morning and evening recitation,[1] we are in effect vowing to advance kosen-rufu in accord with the spirit of the original Buddha. Every day we pledge to the Daishonin, "Without fail, I will believe in and spread the teaching of Nichiren Daishonin and help lead all people to enlightenment." A person of seeking spirit, of ardent vows, is a true disciple. Ours is a practice of boundless seeking spirit. We dedicate our lives to a vow to fulfill our missions in this lifetime.

The original Buddha solemnly watches over all our efforts in faith and actions for kosen-rufu. And he praises us most highly and protects us.

Those who live based on a boundless seeking spirit and resolute vows never become deadlocked. This is the path of infinite advancement. Always together with the Daishonin and always basing ourselves on the Gohonzon, we live out our lives along this path of absolute peace of mind.

The Thus Come One's Secret Indicates the Gohonzon's Power

At one point, Shakyamuni explains to his disciples that he is most earnest when it comes to pursuing the truth. Likewise, those who dedicate themselves to the Buddhist Law should possess the eye to strictly distinguish between true and false, good and evil, correct and erroneous. The Buddha is a person who clearly states the truth, a leader who wages a struggle using words of the utmost sincerity.

"The truthful words of the Thus Come One" are words that cause people to realize profound and enduring happiness. In this chapter, Shakyamuni finally reveals the eternal truth in accord with which he has lived, doing so for the sake of those in the world after his passing. And in the above passage, he specifically explains "truthful words" as meaning "the Thus Come One's secret and his transcendental powers."

"The Thus Come One's secret and his transcendental powers" indicates the great teaching to be expounded in "Life Span." Shakyamuni declares to Maitreya and the others that he is going to reveal at last the secret teaching and the powers and the functions of the Thus Come One.

Literally, in the context of the sutra, the secret of the Thus Come One is the revelation that Shakyamuni initially attained Buddhahood long ago in the remote past. This is called "attainment of Buddhahood in the remote past." In other words, Shakyamuni's true identity is that of the Buddha who attained enlightenment in the remote past. Since his true identity was not revealed anywhere in pre-Lotus Sutra teachings or in the theoretical teaching of the Lotus Sutra, it is called "hidden." And because it is known only to the Buddha, it is described as "intimate." This is the secret Shakyamuni finally clarifies and reveals in the "Life Span" chapter.

"His transcendental powers" refers to the various aspects and functions that this Buddha manifests in order to guide people and bring them benefit. In "Life Span," Shakyamuni explains that ever since he first attained Buddhahood, he has been appearing in various lands as different Buddhas, expounding a multiplicity of teachings and carrying out a variety of actions to lead people to enlightenment.

In other words, "the Thus Come One's secret" indicates the Buddha who attained enlightenment in the remote past, and "his transcendental powers" indicates his perpetual activities to lead people to happiness.

From this standpoint, all Buddhas are nothing but functions of the Buddha who attained enlightenment in the remote past. In the context of the sutra, therefore, the Buddha who attained enlightenment in the remote past is the true Buddha, while all other Buddhas, who are functions of this Buddha, are provisional Buddhas. "Provisional," here, means "shadow" or "vestige."

The Original Identity of All Buddhas

By contrast, the implicit meaning of "the Thus Come One's secret and his transcendental powers" alludes to the Law of Nam-myoho-renge-kyo, the ultimate cause behind the Buddha's enlightenment in the remote past. A state of life enlightened to Nam-myoho-renge-kyo is the true identity of all Buddhas. This state of life itself is both the essence of Buddhahood and the life of a true Buddha. From the deepest standpoint, the "true Buddha" is the Buddha of Nam-myoho-renge-kyo, that is, the "Nam-myoho-renge-kyo Thus Come One."

"The Thus Come One's secret," therefore, refers to the Nam-myoho-renge-kyo Thus Come One. And the functions of Shakyamuni to lead people to enlightenment are ultimately the functions of Nam-myoho-renge-kyo. This is the implicit, deepest meaning of "his transcendental powers."

Accordingly, Nam-myoho-renge-kyo is the true Buddha. And by contrast, Shakyamuni, Many Treasures and all other Buddhas are provisional Buddhas who manifest functions of Nam-myoho-renge-kyo.

Now, why is the interpretation of this passage important from the standpoint of Nichiren Buddhism?

The reason is that without clarifying what the Law is that originally enabled all Buddhas to attain enlightenment—that is, Nam-myoho-renge-kyo—the path for all people to attain Buddhahood could not be opened.

That ordinary people can attain Buddhahood is at the heart of the "Life Span" chapter. And "the Thus Come One's secret and his transcendental powers," the chapter's quintessence, points to the path by which they can do so.

"Life Span" clarifies that the true identity of all Buddhas is grounded in Shakyamuni's attainment of enlightenment in the remote past. Regarding "remote past" (*kuon*) Nichiren says, "This chapter ["Life Span"] as a whole deals with the true attainment in *kuon*. *Kuon* means something that was not worked for, that was not improved upon, but that exists just as it always has" (OTT, 141).

This is the implicit meaning of "remote past." As Nichiren says, remote past indicates that which "exists just as it always has." Life that exists just as it always has, life in its original state, is where the actual attainment of Buddhahood occurs. And this attainment of Buddhahood is itself "the secret of the Thus Come One." The Buddha's original state of life is identical with all people's original state of life. They could not be in any way different. Fundamentally, all people are Buddhas. The only difference is that the Buddha understands this while others are ignorant of it. Therefore, it is called "the Thus Come One's secret."

Life that exists just as it always has is the basis of the principle that ordinary people are Buddhas and the Buddha is an ordinary person; it is none other than Nam-myoho-renge-kyo. Nichiren Daishonin rcvcalcd this life of Nam-myoho-renge-kyo that exists just as it always has through his own existence as an ordinary person.

Therefore, when ordinary people such as ourselves believe in the Daishonin and chant Nam-myoho-renge-kyo, we can open up the life of beginningless time (*kuon-ganjo*) within our own lives. This is the meaning of "transcendental powers."

Eradicating Negative Causality

President Toda once said:

> It was Nichiren Daishonin who established the Law that enables ordinary people to break through the negative causality from the past that exists in their lives and return to beginningless time in the course of their day-to-day existence.
>
> To put it another way, believing wholeheartedly [in the Daishonin] and chanting Nam-myoho-renge-kyo is the method for transforming destiny for the better. Through following this method, the common mortal of beginningless time appears and the negative causes and effects formed in the interim all disappear.

"The common mortal of beginningless time appears," he says. What a wonderful way of putting it! Herein lies the heart of the Lotus Sutra. These words express the wisdom of President Toda, who read the Lotus Sutra with his life and attained the realization that the Buddha is life itself.

By "negative causality from the past" and "negative causes and effects formed in the interim," he refers to the countless causes and effects that bring people misfortune. However, just as the rising sun causes the stars to disappear from sight and brings on a fresh morning, through faith we can at once eradicate the countless negative causes and effects we have accumulated over countless eons. Just as we are, as ordinary people, we can return to the original life of the human being of beginningless time, which is totally free of karmic impurity. This is what he means by the "appearance of the common mortal of beginningless time."

Attaining Buddhahood does not entail the termination of the life of the ordinary person. One certainly does not become a being who is better than or superior to others.

Nichiren says:

> Living beings like ourselves have dwelt in the sea of the sufferings of birth and death since beginningless time. But they become votaries of the Lotus Sutra, and realize that their bodies and minds, which have existed since the beginningless past, are inherently endowed with the eternally unchanging nature; awaken to their mystic reality with their mystic wisdom; and attain the Buddha's body, which is as indestructible as a diamond. How then could they be different from that Buddha? Shakyamuni Buddha, the lord of teachings, who said numberless major world system dust particle kalpas ago, "I am the only person [who can rescue and protect others]," refers to living beings like ourselves. (WND-1, 36)

A State of Happiness as Indestructible as a Diamond

"Our bodies and minds that have existed since the beginningless past" means life that "exists just as it always has." This is what President Toda referred to as "the common mortal of beginningless time." We can establish a state of eternal happiness as indestructible as a diamond—that is, the true aspect of the Buddha—in our lives. This mystery of attaining Buddhahood is "the Thus Come One's secret and his transcendental powers."

In short, "the Thus Come One's secret and his transcendental powers" indicates the attainment of Buddhahood by ordinary people. Nichiren Daishonin says, "Outside of the attainment of Buddhahood, there is no 'secret' and no 'transcendental powers'" (OTT, 125).

The Buddha's secret and his transcendental powers do not in any way indicate supernatural or mystical abilities in the sense that these terms are commonly used.

President Toda remarked:

> People speak of transcendental powers as the ability to perform such fantastic feats as flying on a cloud. But the transcendental powers we speak of here are far greater. The secret and transcendental powers of the Nam-myoho-renge-kyo Thus Come One lead all people to happiness. We are concerned with the transcendental powers that enable ordinary people to become Buddhas.

Nichiren declares that we should not attach importance to supernatural or special powers. For example, in "On Reciting the Daimoku of the Lotus Sutra," he writes: "But whether they are correct or incorrect in their views is to be judged solely on the basis of the doctrines they expound. It is not to be decided on the basis of whether or not they have keen capacity or can display supernatural powers" (WND-2, 234).

Shakyamuni, too, when asked by King Ajatashatru about the difference between Buddhism and Brahmanism, said in the Samannaphala Sutta that the Buddhist practitioner gains virtue by abstaining from such questionable practices as offering fire to the gods or interpreting the calls of birds and animals.[2]

Nothing is as full of mystery as human life. Nothing is as respectable. Ordinary people, just as they are, can become Buddhas. While remaining ordinary persons, we can establish a state of happiness and total satisfaction arising from the very depths of our lives, the state of life of a Buddha.

There is no greater secret or transcendental power.

The Buddha's "secret and his transcendental powers" means the ability to enable all people to enjoy a life of supreme happiness. In other words, it is the power to elevate the lives of all people. And this is precisely the great beneficial power of the Gohonzon.

Nichiren Daishonin expressed his own life as the Nam-myoho-renge-kyo Thus Come One in the form of the Gohonzon. "The Thus Come One's secret and his transcendental powers" is nothing other than the Gohonzon.

Nichiren clearly says, "This object of devotion is based on the passage that reads, 'the Thus Come One's secret and his transcendental powers'" (OTT, 142).

Accordingly, from the standpoint of the implicit meaning, the passage "You must listen carefully and hear of the Thus Come One's secret and his transcendental powers" means, "Listen carefully, because the power of the Buddha and the power of the Law of the Gohonzon will now be expounded." Ultimately, the "Life Span" chapter explains and praises the power of the Gohonzon.

Our daily practice of gongyo and chanting Nam-myoho-renge-kyo is a struggle to break the chains of destiny and suffering and return to "the common mortal of beginningless time." And as a result of these efforts, the true path for attaining Buddhahood in this lifetime opens before us.

▪ 10 ▪

Issai seken. Tennin gyu. Ashu-ra. Kai i kon shaka-muni-butsu.
Shus̄ shaku-shi gu. Ko gayajo fu on. Za o dojo. Toku a-noku-ta-ra
san-myaku sanbodai. Nen zen-nanshi. Ga jitsu jo-butsu irai.
Muryo muhen. Hyaku sen man noku. Nayuta ko.

"In all the worlds the heavenly and human beings and asuras all believe that
the present Shakyamuni Buddha, after leaving the palace of the Shakyas,
seated himself in the place of enlightenment not far from the city of Gaya
and there attained supreme perfect enlightenment. But good men, it has
been immeasurable, boundless hundreds, thousands, ten thousands,
millions of nayutas of kalpas since I in fact attained Buddhahood."
(LSOC, 265–66)

IN THIS PASSAGE, Shakyamuni proclaims that he in fact attained
enlightenment in the remote past, numberless major world system
dust particle kalpas ago. This constitutes the core revelation of the
"Life Span of the Thus Come One" chapter.

Shakyamuni calls out to the countless multitudes at the Ceremony
in the Air, saying essentially: "Everyone supposes that, after abandoning my life at the palace and renouncing the world at the age of
nineteen, I attained the supreme enlightenment for the first time at
age thirty, near the city of Gaya beneath the bodhi tree."

People thought that Shakyamuni had initially attained Buddhahood in his present existence. This view is called his "attaining enlightenment for the first time in his present life." People believed this because, throughout the earlier sutras and in the Lotus Sutra's theoretical teaching, Shakyamuni consistently said so.

Here in the "Life Span" chapter, however, he refutes this view—which he himself had propounded—and proclaims, "It has been immeasurable, boundless hundreds, thousands, ten thousands, millions of nayutas of kalpas since I in fact attained Buddhahood" (LSOC, 265–66).

In other words, he reveals that he became a Buddha long ago in the inconceivably remote past. This is called his "attainment of Buddhahood in the remote past." Shakyamuni thus discards his provisional status as a Buddha who attained the way in his present lifetime and reveals his true identity as the Buddha who attained enlightenment in the remote past. This is called "casting off the transient and revealing the true."

To those disciples listening to him, it must have seemed as though heaven and earth had been reversed. For the view he now expounded was as different from the earlier view as water is from fire. Nichiren Daishonin says regarding this revelation, "But now all these passages have been exposed as gross falsehoods by this single pronouncement in the 'Life Span' chapter" (WND-1, 256).

"Falsehoods" means lies. Shakyamuni himself had propounded the view that he attained enlightenment for the first time only in this lifetime. If that was untrue, then the causes for attaining Buddhahood he expounded while propounding that view must also be untrue. This came as a great shock, because it meant the causes and effects of attaining Buddhahood that Shakyamuni had been preaching up to that time were false.

In "The Opening of the Eyes," Nichiren says:

When we come to the essential teaching of the Lotus Sutra, then the belief that Shakyamuni first obtained Buddhahood during his present lifetime is demolished, and the effects of the four teachings are likewise demolished. When the effects of the four teachings are demolished, the causes of the four teachings are likewise demolished. Thus the cause and effect of the Ten Worlds as expounded in the earlier sutras and the theoretical teaching of the Lotus Sutra are wiped out, and the cause and effect of the Ten Worlds in the essential teaching are revealed. (WND-1, 235)

The "four teachings," simply put, indicates the earlier sutras and the Lotus Sutra's theoretical teaching. In the pre-Lotus Sutra teachings, Shakyamuni explained that to become a Buddha, it was necessary to terminate the life of the nine worlds and that this served as the cause for attaining enlightenment.

And even in the Lotus Sutra's theoretical teaching, although it is revealed that Buddhahood exists within the beings of the nine worlds, the view of attaining Buddhahood taught in earlier sutras still had not substantially been rejected. This is because Shakyamuni himself was still preaching as a Buddha who had first attained enlightenment in his present existence. That is, he was preaching from the viewpoint that to become a Buddha, one first had to eradicate the nine worlds.

But in "Life Span," part of the essential teaching, he explains that he actually attained enlightenment in the remote past and so refutes the causes and effects pertaining to the attainment of Buddhahood as they were expounded in the earlier sutras and the theoretical teaching of the Lotus Sutra.

Buddhist scriptures explain that in previous existences, Shakyamuni had carried out virtuous practices as various figures, including the boy Snow Mountains, King Shibi and a deer king. Needless to say, each of these incarnations took place long after the time in the remote past when he first attained Buddhahood. The revelation that Shakyamuni attained enlightenment in the remote past means that, thereafter, when he practiced as a human, an animal or as a being of any of the nine worlds, he was taking on the appearance of a being of the nine worlds while in fact already possessing Buddhahood as his true identity.

This means that the life of the Buddha who attained enlightenment in the remote past is undeniably endowed with—and can freely move through and employ—the nine worlds.

The world of Buddhahood exists perpetually in life among the nine worlds, and the nine worlds exist perpetually in the life of the Buddha. "Attainment of Buddhahood in the remote past" indicates the view of life expressed by the principle of the mutual possession of the Ten Worlds. This is what "the cause and effect of the Ten Worlds in the essential teaching" in the above passage of Nichiren's writings indicates.

This cause and effect, which is the true cause and effect of attaining Buddhahood, can be clarified only by refuting the view that Shakyamuni first attained enlightenment during his present lifetime and revealing his actual enlightenment in the remote past.

Even though Shakyamuni talks about attaining Buddhahood in the earlier sutras and in the Lotus Sutra's theoretical teaching, since this discussion is based on the view that Shakyamuni first attained enlightenment during his present lifetime, it lacks a firm foundation.

In short, the Buddha who attained enlightenment in the remote past signifies life that exists eternally and is endowed with the Ten Worlds. In spatial terms, this is life as vast as the universe; in temporal terms, it is life that is eternal. This is, in fact, the ultimate nature of our own lives. "Attainment of Buddhahood in the remote past" indicates opening or gaining access to this boundless and immeasurable life, the cosmic and eternal life.

Beginningless Time Is the Original Moment of Life

In the context of the sutra, the "I" of "since I in fact attained Buddhahood" refers literally to Shakyamuni alone. It is his life that is said to be endowed with the Ten Worlds and to exist eternally.

However, from the standpoint of the implicit meaning of the passage, Nichiren says: "'I' represents the living beings of the Dharmarealm. 'I' here refers to each and every being in the Ten Worlds" (OTT, 126).

He clarifies that not only Shakyamuni but all people in the Ten Worlds are entities of the Buddha who attained enlightenment in the remote past. In essence, our own lives are endowed with the eternal life of the Buddha.

Only when this passage is read from the standpoint of its implicit meaning is there explicit assurance that all people can attain Buddhahood. Nichiren Buddhism, through what might be called a popular or humanist interpretation, opens the words of the "Life Span" chapter to all people.

Our lives are eternal entities endowed with the Ten Worlds. Because Buddhahood exists in our lives from the beginningless past through the infinite future, so long as we can encounter the right external factors, then we can open up and manifest the world of Buddhahood at any time and in any place.

Therefore, it is unnecessary for us to practice for countless eons to attain Buddhahood. We can become Buddhas in the course of this existence; we do not have to practice lifetime after lifetime without reaching our goal. Again, no matter how heavy our burden of karma, through tapping our inner life force, we can revolutionize our existence.

This represents a fundamental transformation in the view of attaining enlightenment, a great shift in perspective with regard to the causality for becoming a Buddha.

Nichiren Daishonin clearly explained that this cause for attaining Buddhahood is the Law of Nam-myoho-renge-kyo that his life embodied, which indicated he was the Nam-myoho-renge-kyo Thus Come One. And he manifested this great state of life in the form of the Gohonzon, which he bestowed upon all people of the Latter Day of the Law.

He says, "*Kuon* is Nam-myoho-renge-kyo, and 'true attainment' means awakening to the fact that one is eternally endowed with the three bodies" (OTT, 142). He also says: "'Attain' means to open or reveal. It is to reveal that the beings of the Dharma-realm are Buddhas eternally endowed with the three bodies" (OTT, 126).

Kuon refers to life that is endowed with the Ten Worlds and exists eternally; it indicates the Gohonzon of Nam-myoho-renge-kyo, which eternally embodies the Ten Worlds. "True attainment" refers to the manifestation of the Gohonzon within each of our lives and to gaining access to its benefit.

This is the implicit meaning of "attainment of Buddhahood in the remote past." To distinguish this meaning from the literal meaning of the phrase in the context of Shakyamuni's teaching, as I mentioned previously, it is called "beginningless time," or *kuon-ganjo*.

Beginningless time does not simply indicate a point in time even more distant than the remote past of numberless major world system dust particle kalpas ago; it means time without beginning or end. In light of its essential meaning, beginningless time could be said to represent the "original moment" of life. Once we awaken to the primal origin of life, every moment throughout past, present and future becomes for us the moment of beginningless time. In essence, Nichiren Buddhism teaches a way of life based on beginningless time. It enables us to address the reality of our situations with a fresh, forward-looking spirit, always basing ourselves on life's "original moment."

For us who accept and believe in the Gohonzon, and who carry out the practice of reciting the sutra and chanting Nam-myoho-renge-kyo, each day is beginningless time, the eternal origin of life. We can experience every moment as beginningless time.

The great author Romain Rolland writes: "Live in today. Be reverent towards each day. Love it, respect it."[3] Nichiren taught the great joy of living in the now—in the present moment, which contains both the eternal past and the infinite future.

President Toda said regarding beginningless time:

> When we observe our existence, we find that in the time before numberless major world system dust particle kalpas ago (i.e., in beginningless time) we lived with total freedom in a brilliant world of purity and joy. We were all beautiful in spirit and of like mind. We who once dwelled in such a sparkling world have now all emerged together in this saha world.
>
> Looking back, I feel as though it was only yesterday that we lived in that pure, pleasant world. How could we possibly forget the brilliant world where we then dwelled? How could we forget the friends with whom we then joyously lived in absolute freedom? And how could we forget the vows we made together at the assembly where the Lotus Sutra was expounded?
>
> Since this saha world is a world inhabited originally by friends who are all joyful and pure and bright and on good terms with one another, is it not most pitiful and sad that, having been forced to drink the poisons of greed, anger and jealousy by proponents of the provisional Mahayana, Hinayana and non-Buddhist teachings, we have become like crazed children and have all forgotten beginningless time?

Mr. Toda says that he recalls beginningless time as though it were only yesterday. Such was his immense state of life.

When we awaken to beginningless time, this saha world becomes one that is joyful, pure and bright. It becomes a world inhabited entirely by friends in harmony.

In reality, however, this is a world of ceaseless misery and strife. For precisely this reason, we who dwell in the moment of beginningless time are exerting ourselves to carry out the widespread propagation of the Mystic Law for people's happiness and for world peace.

Our daily activities, based on the prayer for the happiness of all people and realization of true world peace, represent a great movement to open up a new frontier of life.

Now Is the Time for the Essential Teaching, the Time to Cast Off the Transient and Reveal the True

The idea of the dignity of life is a familiar one. At the same time, everyone's confused about its essential meaning.

If the sanctity of life can become a solid touchstone of wisdom for all people, then humankind's destiny to repeatedly experience war and misery can be greatly transformed. It is toward this end that we are working.

From the twentieth century, a century of war, to a century of life—the crucial moment for this great transformation has arrived. This is the time of the essential teaching, the moment for "casting off the transient and revealing the true."

In any great transition, there is always an individual who stands up in response to the pressing needs of the time. As long as there is one such outstanding person, then two or three will follow. This is the principle of kosen-rufu.

The Lotus Sutra is the teaching that can enable all people to perceive life's sanctity unfailingly and to establish a dignified way of life. The lesson of the Lotus Sutra's theoretical teaching is that all people can uncover the wisdom of the Buddha inherent in their lives.

By contrast, the "Life Span" chapter of the Lotus Sutra's essential teaching reveals that Shakyamuni did not attain the Buddha wisdom initially in his present lifetime. Its lesson is that the eternal activities of life are fundamentally endowed with the Buddha wisdom and that Shakyamuni embodies that eternal life.

By casting off his transient status and revealing his true identity, Shakyamuni clarifies that each person embodies eternal life. The Lotus Sutra's teaching that all people can gain access to the wisdom of the Buddha and develop their state of life is thus substantiated.

Nichiren Daishonin actualized the principle of casting off the transient and revealing the true at the time of the Tatsunokuchi Persecution, which took place on the twelfth day of the ninth month of 1271.

In "The Opening of the Eyes," he says: "On the twelfth day of the ninth month of last year, between the hours of the rat and the ox [11:00 P.M. to 3:00 A.M.], this person named Nichiren was beheaded. It is his soul that has come to this island of Sado" (WND-1, 269).

Nichikan says regarding this passage:

> The fundamental meaning of this passage is as follows: the founder and great sage Nichiren speaks of the entity of the life of an ordinary person at the stage of hearing the name and words of the truth becoming the Buddha of limitless joy of beginningless time and attaining his true identity. He thus clearly indicates himself to be the original Buddha of the Buddhism of sowing [who makes his advent] in the Latter Day of the Law.

Nichiren manifested the life of the Buddha of limitless joy of beginningless time in the life of an ordinary person. This is how Nichiren actualized the principle of casting off the transient and revealing the true.

Nichiren's true identity is that of the Buddha of limitless joy of beginningless time. "Limitless joy" means "the body that is freely received and used" (OTT, 141). It indicates the life state of one who attains awareness that the entire universe is his or her own life and who freely receives and uses the power of the Mystic Law that is the wellspring of cosmic life.

"What Greater Joy Could There Be?"

To Shijo Kingo—who tearfully remarked when Nichiren Daishonin was about to be beheaded at Tatsunokuchi, "These are your last moments" (WND-1, 767)—Nichiren says, "What greater joy could there be?" (WND-1, 767).

Seen from the vast state of life of one who freely receives and uses the power of the world of Buddhahood pervading the universe, the schemes of Hei no Saemon and the priest Ryokan of Gokuraku-ji to destroy Nichiren must have seemed of very little consequence indeed. "I had long expected it to come to this" (WND-1, 764), the Daishonin says, reflecting dispassionately on the situation.

Even on Sado Island, he reveals his immense state of life: "I feel immeasurable delight even though I am now an exile" (WND-1, 386). Despite the severe conditions under which he lived, while in exile there he composed "The Opening of the Eyes" and "The Object of Devotion for Observing the Mind." These writings clarify the teaching that can lead all people to enlightenment during the ten thousand years of the Latter Day of the Law. It was also on Sado that he first began to inscribe the Gohonzon.

What a vast and boundless state of life Nichiren possessed! No persecution, no matter how severe, could destroy his spirit.

President Toda used to say: "There are those who say that the Daishonin was great because he endured such great persecutions. That may be so, but what makes him greater still is that, even while enduring all manner of great persecution, he continued struggling with immense compassion to lead all people to enlightenment."

Nichiren's casting off the transient and revealing the true should not be seen as putting him on a level inaccessible to ordinary people. What Nichiren in fact fully revealed at Tatsunokuchi is the ultimate potential human beings possess.

Through his own example, the Daishonin revealed the greatness and dignity of an individual human being. He certainly did not cease to be human. Rather, as a human being, he manifested a vast and unrestrained state of life in order to elevate the lives of all people.

The essence of Buddhism lies in the principle that ordinary people in their present form can manifest the supremely noble state of Buddhahood. The life of beginningless time can be manifested in the life of a common mortal. This is what Nichiren taught through his own example by casting off the transient and revealing the true.

Advance With a Great Awareness of Your Mission

We should each strive to manifest our own true identity through our faith and our practice for kosen-rufu. "Revealing the true" means to stand up based on the most profound awareness. By translating this awareness into action, we reveal our true identity.

President Toda said: "In terms of the surface meaning of the sutras, or in terms of our external function, we are Bodhisattvas of the Earth. But from the standpoint of faith, we are followers and later disciples of Nichiren Daishonin." This conviction, he went on to say, is the "central idea of the Soka Gakkai."

Because all members are standing up with the realization that they are children of the Buddha with a direct connection with Nichiren Daishonin, the SGI is casting off the transient and revealing the true as an organization.

We Each Possess an Important Mission for Kosen-rufu

The day of casting off the transient and revealing the true for the Soka Gakkai was May 3, 1951, when Josei Toda became the second Soka Gakkai president.

At that time, President Toda made his great declaration, vowing to achieve a membership of 750,000 households. In response to his impassioned call, the entire Soka Gakkai membership became filled with the great awareness: "We are Bodhisattvas of the Earth!" "We are the followers of the original Buddha!"

Around that time, President Toda often stated as follows: "Looking back, from around the spring of 1943, President Makiguchi would often say that the Soka Gakkai has to cast off the transient and reveal the true. If we did not actualize the principle of casting off the transient and revealing the true, he said, something was wrong with us. Hearing this, everyone just looked perplexed, not knowing what to do."

In the end, Mr. Toda fulfilled President Makiguchi's intent. The bond of mentor and disciple is the key to casting off the transient and revealing the true.

We are all children of the original Buddha. There is not one of us who does not have an important mission to fulfill. There are no SGI members whose true identity is other than a Bodhisattva of the Earth.

In his work *The Human Revolution*,[4] President Toda describes his attainment of enlightenment while in prison. Mr. Gan, the character representing him in the book, is an ordinary man who lives in a tenement. Why did he depict a story of enlightenment with a totally unexceptional person as the protagonist?

President Toda explained, "This is to make it clear that anyone at all can equally share in the mission to accomplish kosen-rufu."

"True identity" means true self. The life of the Buddha wells forth in those who awaken to their original mission. Whatever their personal or social situation, such people can realize victory in life with total composure. They can follow a joyful and meaningful path in life. Therefore, those who base themselves on the idea that kosen-rufu and their lives are inseparable will never become deadlocked.

Nichiren's life and the Gohonzon's power are as vast and boundless as the universe. Our own lives also contain infinite potential. Whether we actualize that potential depends entirely on the strength and depth of our determination in faith.

Rise With the Buddha Every Morning, Rest With the Buddha Every Night

Whenever we find ourselves in a deadlock, we need to challenge ourselves to offer sincere prayer and summon the great power of faith to resolve the situation. According to President Toda, this is what casting off the transient and revealing the true means for us. Faith means to struggle against deadlock. Faith is a struggle between the Buddha and devil forces. In Buddhism, victory or defeat in this struggle is the prime concern.

Every morning we start out from the origin of life. Every morning the sun of beginningless time rises in our hearts. *The Record of the Orally Transmitted Teachings* says, "Morning after morning we rise up with the Buddha, evening after evening we lie down with the Buddha. Moment by moment we attain the way, moment by moment we reveal our true identity" (p. 83). When we exert ourselves in chanting Nam-myoho-renge-kyo and carrying out activities for kosen-rufu, our true identity—the Buddha of limitless joy—appears in our lives. Our wisdom is activated, courage wells forth, and we can enjoy a state of life of total freedom. This is what casting off the transient and revealing the true means for us.

Nichiren explains the implicit meaning of the passage "it has been immeasurable, boundless hundreds, thousands, ten thousands, millions of nayutas of kalpas since I in fact attained Buddhahood," as follows: "The passage is thus saying that 'I [or the beings of the Dharma-realm] in fact revealed' the Buddhahood that is immeasurable and boundless in both past and future" (OTT, 126).

When through faith each of us realizes "Fundamentally, I am a Buddha," the true self in the present moment, which contains one's life over both the eternal past and the eternal future, becomes manifest. Then, the Daishonin teaches, we can engage ourselves freely on the great stage of eternal life.

The "Life Span" chapter reveals the cosmic life force we each originally possess.

▪ 11 ▪

Hi nyo go hyaku sen man noku. Nayuta. Asogi. Sanzen dai sen sekai. Ke shi u nin. Matchi mijin. Ka o tobo. Go hyaku sen man noku. Nayuta. Asogi koku. Nai ge ichi-jin. Nyo ze to gyo. Jin ze mijin. Sho zen-nanshi. O i unga. Ze sho sekai. Ka toku shiyui. Kyokei chi go. Shu fu. Mi-roku bo-satˆto. Ku byaku butsu gon. Seson. Ze sho sekai. Muryo muhen. Hi sanju sho chi. Yaku hi shin-riki sho gyu. Issai shomon. Hyaku-shi-butsu. I mu-rochi. Fu no shiyui. Chi go genshu. Gato ju. A-yui-ot-chi-ji. O ze ji chu. Yaku sho fu dasˆseson. Nyo ze sho sekai. Muryo muhen.

"Suppose a person were to take five hundred, a thousand, ten thousand, a million nayuta asamkhya major world systems and grind them to dust. Then, moving eastward, each time he passes five hundred, a thousand, ten thousand, a million nayuta asamkhya worlds he drops a particle of dust. He continues eastward in this way until he has finished dropping all the particles. Good men, what is your opinion? Can the total number of all these worlds be imagined or calculated?"

The bodhisattva Maitreya and the others said to the Buddha: "World-Honored One, these worlds are immeasurable, boundless— one cannot calculate their number, nor does the mind have the power to encompass them. Even all the voice-hearers and pratyekabuddhas with their wisdom free of outflows could not imagine or understand how many there are. Although we abide in the stage of non-regression, we cannot comprehend such a matter. World-Honored One, these worlds are immeasurable and boundless." (LSOC, 266)

HERE, SHAKYAMUNI dramatically describes just how long ago it was that he attained Buddhahood. The period he describes in this way is referred to as numberless major world system dust particle kalpas.

He starts out saying, "Suppose a person were to take five hundred, a thousand, ten thousand, a million nayuta asamkhya major world systems." In the expression "five hundred, a thousand, ten thousand, a million nayuta asamkhya," *nayuta* and *asamkhya* stand for incalculably large numbers. An infinite number multiplied by an infinite number certainly yields a product that no one could compute.

In the cosmology of ancient India, one major world system is itself an immense expanse. In a single world, there is a sun and a moon, and in the center, there is a Mount Sumeru, which towers unimaginably high. It might be compared to the concept of a solar system.

A major world system consists of one billion such worlds. In the "Life Span" chapter, however, Shakyamuni speaks of "five hundred, a thousand, ten thousand, a million nayuta asamkhya major world systems." This indicates a number of worlds so huge as to far exceed even the grand scale of the cosmos as we know it.

Shakyamuni then speaks of an immeasurable and boundless number of these worlds all being ground up into fine dust. The number of grains of dust thus produced would be even more incalculable. "Dust" means the smallest particle of substance to which matter can be broken down. In modern terms, it might correspond to atoms or elementary particles.

He then postulates someone taking this immeasurable quantity of dust particles and moving eastward, dropping a particle each time he passes five hundred, a thousand, ten thousand, a million nayuta asamkhya worlds.

The grains of dust must be dropped one at a time. If one continues in this manner until one runs out of dust, then how many worlds will one pass during this interval? This is what Shakyamuni asks Bodhisattva Maitreya and the others. It is clear that no one can answer him.

In response, Bodhisattva Maitreya, who in the "Life Span" chapter represents the assembly, replies, "These worlds are immeasurable, boundless—one cannot calculate their number, nor does the mind have the power to encompass them." "Nor does the mind have the power to encompass them" indicates that comprehension is beyond even the wisdom of voice-hearers and cause-awakened ones and great bodhisattvas who have attained the stage of non-regression. It is not simply a matter of magnitude of number or length of time; understanding in fact depends on one's state of life.

That it is unknowable to even great bodhisattvas at the stage of non-regression, who are said to have already extinguished a measure of darkness, means that one cannot grasp the remote past of the "Life Span" chapter without conquering the fundamental darkness from which all illusions and desires spring.

This is why Shakyamuni so strongly emphasized the need to "believe and understand" at the outset of the "Life Span" chapter. Nichiren Daishonin says, "The single word 'belief' is the sharp sword with which one confronts and overcomes fundamental darkness or ignorance" (OTT, 119–20).

The use of such astronomically large numbers can be found in the pre-Lotus Sutra teachings. In "Life Span," however, Shakyamuni does not explain "immeasurable" as simply an abstract number. He uses what on the surface seems a concrete example—saying that the worlds should be ground to dust and the particles of dust dropped one at a time. He thus causes his listeners to conjure up an image; it is as though he is progressively challenging them to change their way of thinking. While in both cases immeasurable numbers are employed, from the standpoint of Maitreya and the others, there is a different feeling, a different depth of spirit in the imagery of the "Life Span" chapter.

The description Shakyamuni uses here is not "according with other's minds" (i.e., according to the minds of beings of the nine worlds) such as are found in the pre-Lotus Sutra teachings. It is a description "according with the mind of the Buddha" whose purpose is to open up people's narrow lives and draw them into the vast state of life of the Buddha.

While listening to Shakyamuni's preaching, Maitreya and the others in the assembly no doubt felt as though they were being drawn powerfully into the great state of life of the Buddha who freely moves through the universe.

▪ 12 ▪

Niji butsu go. Dai bosas̄hu. Sho zen-nanshi. Konto funmyo.
Sengo nyoto. Ze sho sekai. Nyaku jaku mijin. Gyu fu jaku sha. Jin ni i jin.
Ichi-jin ikko. Ga jo-butsu irai. Bu ka o shi. Hyaku sen man noku.
Nayuta. Asogi ko.

At that time the Buddha said to the multitude of great bodhisattvas:
"Good men, now I will state this to you clearly. Suppose all these worlds,
whether they received a particle of dust or not, are once more reduced
to dust. Let one particle represent one kalpa. The time that has passed
since I attained Buddhahood surpasses this by a hundred, a thousand,
ten thousand, a million nayuta asamkhya kalpas." (LSOC, 266)

S HAKYAMUNI, saying he is going to make a clear proclamation,
reveals the remote past described as numberless major world system dust particle kalpas ago.

First, he says to take all the worlds passed so far, whether or not they
have received a particle of dust, and grind them into dust.

Then he associates this unfathomable number of particles of dust
with time, saying, "Let one particle represent one kalpa." A kalpa is
an extremely long period of time.

Finally Shakyamuni reveals that he attained Buddhahood at a time
in the past "a hundred, a thousand, ten thousand, a million nayuta
asamkhya kalpas" more distant than even this immeasurable number

of kalpas. This period is described as numberless major world system dust particle kalpas.

Numberless major world system dust particle kalpas ago indicates a point in the inconceivably remote past. Even so, the duration it represents is still finite. Because numberless major world system dust particle kalpas ago refers to the point in time at which Shakyamuni became a Buddha, it indicates a period with a definite beginning.

In essence, however, Shakyamuni's enlightenment is "without beginning." For Shakyamuni's purpose in explaining numberless major world system dust particle kalpas was to refute the view that he first became a Buddha in his present lifetime.

The central issue is the view of enlightenment. When inner darkness is dispelled, we find that life, fundamentally, is without beginning or end; to become a Buddha is to uncover and bring out that original life just as it is. In "The Object of Devotion for Observing the Mind," Nichiren says that the Shakyamuni present within the lives of us who embrace the Mystic Law is "the eternal Buddha since time without beginning" (WND-1, 365).

The principle of beginningless time (kuon-ganjo) clarifies the implicit meaning of this passage. Beginningless time means the wellspring of life and the wellspring of the universe. This primal life is the life of the Buddha of limitless joy of beginningless time; it is itself Nam-myoho-renge-kyo.

Nichiren states, "'Kuon is Nam-myoho-renge-kyo" (OTT, 142).

President Toda said:

> Nichiren Daishonin's life and our lives are without beginning or end. This is termed "beginningless time." They have neither beginning nor end. The universe itself is a great living entity. Since it is the universe, it has neither beginning nor end. This planet taken in isolation, however, has a beginning and an end.

Our lives are not creations of some author or artisan, such as a creating deity. We exist together with the universe, and together with the universe our existence continues infinitely. It could be said that life itself is both the creator and the creation.

From the deepest standpoint, all who heard Shakyamuni expound the "Life Span" chapter instantaneously changed their stance. They no longer gradually approached enlightenment by extinguishing earthly desires. Rather, they directly believed in and accepted the great life of Nam-myoho-renge-kyo. The span of time called numberless major world system dust particle kalpas is a skillful use of imagery for bringing people to base themselves on the great life of beginningless time originally inherent in themselves and the universe.

▪13▪

Ji ju ze rai. Ga jo zai shi. Shaba sekai. Seppo kyoke. Yaku o yosho. Hyaku sen man noku. Nayuta. Asogi koku. Dori shujo.

"Ever since then I have been constantly in this saha world, preaching the Law, teaching, and converting. And elsewhere I have led and benefited living beings in hundreds, thousands, ten thousands, millions of nayutas and asamkhyas of lands." (LSOC, 266)

SHAKYAMUNI FIRST SAYS that since attaining Buddhahood in the remote past, he has continually been preaching the Law and instructing people in this saha world.

In essence, he is saying that the saha world is the pure land where the Buddha dwells eternally. This is a revelation of truly immense significance. As President Toda put it, Shakyamuni "at this point turns Buddhism completely on its head."

In the pre-Lotus Sutra teachings, Shakyamuni had taught that this saha world was impure, a world defiled with earthly desires. He taught that the pure lands where the Buddhas dwelled lay elsewhere. For example, he taught that the Buddha Infinite Life, or Amida, dwelled in the western region of the universe, in the so-called pure land of Perfect Bliss. He also taught that the Thus Come One Medicine Master lived in the Pure Emerald World in the eastern region of the universe. These earlier teachings are still basically adhered to even in the Lotus Sutra's theoretical teaching.

Thus, in the earlier sutras, Shakyamuni distinguished between this impure saha world and other worlds that are pure. It is with this passage of the "Life Span" chapter that, for the first time, he clearly refutes this way of thinking.

The land where the Buddha dwells is called the Land of Eternally Tranquil Light. Therefore, this passage clarifies the principle that the saha world is itself the Land of Eternally Tranquil Light.

He then says, "And elsewhere I have led and benefited living beings in hundreds, thousands, ten thousands, millions of nayutas and asam-khyas of lands." In other words, Shakyamuni who attained enlightenment in the remote past has been guiding beings in countless other lands outside the saha world. This indicates that the Buddhas in other lands are transient projections, or emanations, of Shakyamuni.

In "The Opening of the Eyes," Nichiren says:

> When Shakyamuni Buddha revealed that he had gained enlightenment in the far distant past, it became apparent that all the other Buddhas were emanations of Shakyamuni. . . .
>
> In the earlier sutras and the theoretical teaching of the Lotus Sutra, he called the regions of the ten directions pure lands and spoke of the present world as an impure land. But now, in the "Life Span" chapter, he has reversed this, revealing that this world is the true land and that the so-called pure lands of the ten directions are impure lands, mere provisional lands. (WND-1, 256)

This saha world is the true land where the Buddha who attained enlightenment in the remote past carries out boundless activities and leads all people to happiness. Accordingly, if we were to seek a pure land apart from this saha world, then we would be seeking an ephemeral land outside of the true land. Our efforts would be in vain; it would be as though we were seeking a shadow or apparition.

Why in the earlier sutras did Shakyamuni discuss lands of tranquil light existing apart from the saha world? He did so to arouse a seeking mind in people caught up in the desires of secular life. The lands of tranquil light taught in the earlier sutras were no more than expedient pure lands.

It could be said that in "Life Span" Shakyamuni refutes the way of thinking that establishes ideal worlds apart from this real world. Human beings have a certain escapist tendency; we are inclined to believe that if we could just get away from reality and go to some different realm, then we could become happy. Illusory happiness can never become real. The "Life Span" chapter demolishes this illusory view.

Nichiren says, "It is not that he [the practitioner of the Lotus Sutra] leaves his present place and goes to some other place . . . Now the place where Nichiren and his followers chant Nam-myoho-renge-kyo, 'whether . . . in mountain valleys or the wide wilderness,' (chapter twenty-one, Supernatural Powers), these places are all the Land of Eternally Tranquil Light. This is what is meant by 'the place of practice'" (OTT, 192).

A place where people embrace the Mystic Law is the Land of Eternally Tranquil Light. The truth is that the saha world is the Land of Eternally Tranquil Light.

At the same time, however—as implied by the Sanskrit term "saha," meaning endurance—this is a world where people must continually endure various sorrows and sufferings. Just what does it mean to say that a world such as this is itself the Land of Eternally Tranquil Light?

This points to a great change in the meaning of saha world that occurs in "Life Span." Instead of a place of tragedy where people must continually endure suffering and sadness, it becomes a stage for people's liberation, where the Buddha continually saves the people while enduring all manner of hardships.

From the deepest standpoint, Shakyamuni who attained Buddhahood in the remote past is not the only one active on this stage. As I have already explained, the implicit meaning of "attainment of

Buddhahood in the remote past" is for us to return to the life of beginningless time.

Citing the sutra passage "Ever since then I have been constantly in this saha world, preaching the Law, teaching, and converting" (LSOC, 266), President Toda said: "This indicates that the great universe itself equals the Gohonzon. Since the beginningless past, the life of Nam-myoho-renge-kyo has existed together with the universe."

When we base ourselves on the life of beginningless time, the saha world becomes the universe. It becomes a great stage on which we can freely take action.

When we embrace the Mystic Law, we open up within ourselves the great life of beginningless time. Then we ordinary people can manifest our true identity as champions with a mission to dedicate our lives to the people's liberation while calmly enduring the difficulties of the saha world.

The way of life of a courageous Bodhisattva of the Earth lies in diving headlong into the most difficult situations, embracing those experiencing the greatest suffering, talking to and protecting friends. Through it all, we create a revolution of hope—a revolution toward the understanding that the saha world is itself the Land of Eternally Tranquil Light. When we lead such a way of life, our spirit shines.

Nichiren says: "The bodhisattvas of the essential teaching employing the power of great forbearance to proclaim and propagate Myoho-renge-kyo is known as saha. Forbearance is the Land of Eternally Tranquil Light. This mind of forbearance is called Shakyamuni Buddha" (OTT, 169).

To propagate the Mystic Law as Bodhisattvas of the Earth with the great power of forbearance based on the boundless life of Nam-myoho-renge-kyo is truly saha, or endurance. The Land of Eternally Tranquil Light exists in precisely such an attitude of forbearance.

By immersing ourselves in the reality of the saha world to help those suffering, while manifesting the original life of the universe within our own being through our daily gongyo and daimoku, we actualize the principle of the saha world is itself the Land of Eternally Tranquil Light. When we awaken to the supremely noble original life within ourselves, then the impure world of reality filled with suffering and fate turns into a pure land overflowing with joy and mission.

The True Heritage of Buddhism Lies in the Spirit to Transform the Land for the Better

There is an old Japanese saying: "Despise and abandon the impure world, and seek rebirth in the pure land." For a long time, Buddhism has been thought of as an escapist, passive and world-despising religion, as this saying epitomizes. This saying urges people to reject the real world so full of suffering and to yearn for rebirth in the Pure Land of Perfect Bliss after death.

But the concept of a pure land existing apart from reality is nothing more than an expedient means expounded in accordance with people's capacity. While such a teaching may give temporary consolation, it will not enable people to realize true happiness.

In his treatise "On the Protection of the Nation," Nichiren raises the question of whether those who practice the Lotus Sutra should pray to be reborn in a pure land. In answer, he first points out that in "Life Span," Shakyamuni says, "I have been constantly in this saha world." Based on this, he reasons, Shakyamuni, who revealed his identity as the Buddha who attained enlightenment in the remote past, is here in this saha world. Therefore, he concludes, there is no need to abandon this saha world and seek rebirth in some other land (see WND-2, 143). Rather, Nichiren teaches, we should seek the pure land in this saha world.

In essence, this world of reality is itself the pure land. And the spirit of Buddhism lies in working tenaciously to make that original pure land become manifest. Buddhism is certainly not a religion that encourages people to aim solely for personal enlightenment, secluding themselves away from others and society in mountains and forests. Nor is it a religion that urges people to give up on the present and place all their hopes in the promise of happiness after death.

"Pure land" has the active and practical meaning of "purifying the land of the Buddha." This is the original denotation of "pure land." In Japanese Buddhism, this original meaning has completely vanished, and the term has come to indicate a world after death, an afterworld. "Pure land," in other words, means to "purify the land." It indicates taking action to improve the environment and construct a better society.

The Buddhist scriptures go so far as to identify specific actions to be taken to transform the land. For example, Shakyamuni at one point says:

> Those who set up a park or a grove,
> The people who construct a bridge
> A place to drink and a well
> Those who give a residence:
>
> For them merit always increases,
> Both by day and by night,
> Those are the people going to heaven,
> Established in the Dhamma, endowed with virtue.[5]

King Ashoka (r.c. 268–232 BCE) of India put this spirit of Shakyamuni into practice as the governing ideal of his kingdom.

Nagarjuna, a great Buddhist scholar who lived around the third century, admonished a king of the time to "protect the sick, orphans and the poor"; to "carry out activities to aid those in areas ravaged by natural disasters, poor harvests and epidemics"; and to "not use his power to imprison people unjustly."

It must be said that the pure land, in terms of its original meaning in Buddhism, is alive and well only in the ideals and practice of Nichiren's teaching of "establishing the correct teaching for the peace of the land." The true heritage of Buddhism is found in the spirit to transform for the better the actual land in which we live.

President Toda once said: "We must make this saha world of ours a place of tranquillity and peace. Atomic weapons must not fly, and bombs must not rain down from airplanes. There must be no killing of people or death by starvation in the world where we are spreading the Mystic Law."

In gongyo, we offer prayers for world peace and for the happiness of all living beings. Every day, we listen to the worries of friends and exert ourselves in our practice for kosen-rufu. Truly this is the noble practice for purifying the land of the Buddha.

SGI members carry out their bodhisattva practice as emissaries of the Buddha. Let us make our communities, our countries and the entire world shine brightly as the Land of Eternally Tranquil Light.

When you advance with this determination, you are, in the words of the sutra, "in this saha world, preaching the Law, teaching, and converting."

▪14▪

Sho zen-nanshi. O ze chugen. Ga setsu nen-to-buʾto. U bu gon go. Nyu o nehan. Nyo ze kai i. Hoben fun-betsu. Sho zen-nanshi. Nyaku u shujo. Raishi ga sho. Ga i butsu-gen. Kan go shin to. Sho kon ridon. Zui sho o do. Shosho ji setsu. Myoji fudo. Nenki daisho. Yaku-bu gen gon. To nyu nehan. U i shuju hoben. Setsu mimyo ho. No ryo shujo. Hoʾkangi shin.

"Good men, during that time I have spoken about the Buddha Burning Torch and others, and described how they entered nirvana. All this I employed as an expedient means to make distinctions.

"Good men, if there are living beings who come to me, I employ my Buddha eye to observe whether their faith and other faculties are keen or dull, and then depending upon how receptive they are to salvation, I appear in different places and preach to them under different names, and describe my life span as long or short. Sometimes when I make my appearance I say that I am about to enter nirvana, and also employ different expedient means to preach the subtle and wonderful Law, thus causing living beings to awaken joyful minds." (LSOC, 266–67)

"DURING THAT TIME" refers to the period from when Shakyamuni attained Buddhahood in the remote past until his appearance as Shakyamuni in India. In this passage, Shakyamuni speaks in detail of his activities during that interval.

First, he clarifies that although in the past he had spoken of the appearance of the Buddha Burning Torch and other Buddhas, and described their entering nirvana, all these accounts of past Buddhas were merely expedients.

Shakyamuni had just explained that he dwells eternally in the saha world and continually takes action to lead people to enlightenment. Here he clarifies that his explanations of the appearance of past Buddhas and of their entering nirvana were merely expedient means to guide people. These past Buddhas were emanations that he, Shakyamuni, as the Buddha who attained enlightenment in the remote past, had manifested.

In an earlier sutra, Shakyamuni explained that in a previous existence he had practiced under Burning Torch as a bodhisattva named Learned Youth. As a result, Burning Torch predicted that Shakyamuni would definitely attain enlightenment in the future. Shakyamuni said that his practice at that time became the cause for his initial attainment of enlightenment in his current existence. The reason he mentions Buddha Burning Torch here is that, among all the Buddhas of the past, this name was best known to Shakyamuni's listeners.

But if the Buddha Burning Torch and the other Buddhas of the past are expedient means, then the Buddhist austerities Shakyamuni had practiced for countless eons under such Buddhas are also just expedients, as is the effect of his attaining enlightenment for the first time in his present existence.

In other words, with this statement Shakyamuni repudiates the causes for attaining Buddhahood accumulated during that time; and he repudiates the effect of his initial attainment of Buddhahood in his present existence. He identifies those causes and that effect as expedient means.

When these intermediary causes and effects are refuted, the true cause of Shakyamuni's attainment of Buddhahood is found to lie in his practice in the remote past; and the true effect is found to be his attainment of Buddhahood in the remote past. In this passage,

Shakyamuni clarifies that this true cause and true effect are the actual cause and effect of his enlightenment.

In raising the issue of entering nirvana, Shakyamuni is saying that the Buddha Burning Torch and other Buddhas entering nirvana were expedient means.

"Nirvana" indicates a state of life of peace and tranquillity attained through the extermination of earthly desires. The earlier sutras further teach that through exterminating the physical body as well, one could enter into a state of complete nirvana, or nirvana of no remainder. This understanding has come to inform the meaning of entering nirvana, which indicates the death of a Buddha.

Here, in "Life Span," Shakyamuni emphasizes that complete nirvana, in the sense of physical and spiritual extinction, is an expedient means. In the Lotus Sutra, true nirvana does not mean physical and spiritual extinction. Rather, it consists of the perfection of wisdom.

For this reason, Shakyamuni explains that even accounts of Buddhas entering nirvana are expedient means and that the perfected wisdom of the Buddha exists eternally as embodied in Shakyamuni, the Buddha who attained enlightenment in the remote past. Shakyamuni speaks to this matter in the passage of the verse section of the "Life Span" chapter, which reads, "as an expedient means I appear to enter nirvana" (LSOC, 271). So let us put off a detailed discussion of this matter until we come to that section.

Next, in the passage that begins, "Good men, if there are living beings who come to me," Shakyamuni reveals the nature of his activities "during that time" as the Buddha who attained enlightenment in the remote past.

Why did Shakyamuni, the Buddha who attained enlightenment in the remote past, appear during this interval in the guise of various Buddhas and bodhisattvas? The answer is that he was acting in accordance with the mystic principle of responsive communion, in which the Buddha appears in order to respond to the people's desire to seek him.

"If there are living beings who come to me" indicates the desire to seek. It describes the condition where people aspire to encounter and possess a seeking mind for the Buddha who attained enlightenment in the remote past.

"I employ my Buddha eye to observe whether their faith and other faculties are keen or dull" describes the response of the Buddha who attained enlightenment numberless major world system dust particle kalpas ago. In response to people's seeking minds, the Buddha who attained enlightenment in the remote past appears in the world as various Buddhas and bodhisattvas. The Buddha's appearance is motivated by compassion. Deep in their lives, those experiencing pain and suffering seek Buddhism; they aspire to encounter the Buddha. The Buddha, due to his power of compassion, hears their unvoiced cries and yearns to help them. And he responds by appearing in the world to lead all people to happiness. This is the mystic principle of responsive communion.

To act in response to seeing someone suffering is to manifest the compassion of the Buddha. This spirit of compassion, this spirit to sympathize with others' sufferings, underlies the practice of the SGI. Precisely because we base ourselves on such a spirit of compassion, earnestness is born, wisdom wells forth, ideas are quickly translated into action and there is development. We absolutely must never forget this.

President Toda once said, "People aspire for the Buddha and desire an outstanding leader, and in response the Buddha appears." The Buddha is a true leader who embodies a profound understanding of life.

We may encounter stalemates in life and society and as a civilization. Possessing a philosophy offering profound insight into life enables one to open the way forward through such deadlocks.

In an age lacking philosophy, people's hearts wander and drift. "Something seems wrong with how things are, but I don't know what to do," people say to themselves. "I want to become happy, but I don't know what real happiness is."

Broadly speaking, these unvoiced cries represent people's aspirations and their call to the Buddha for help. Following the example of the Buddha, let us stand up in response to people's cries and generate a current of dialogue for truth and justice.

Buddhas Yearn to Share Their Benefits With Others

Shakyamuni then details how he, as the Buddha who attained enlightenment in the remote past, has appeared in order to lead those seeking Buddhism to enlightenment.

First, he says that he uses his Buddha eye to determine whether their faculties are keen or dull and so gauges how it might be possible to lead them to enlightenment. And on that basis, Shakyamuni explains that he has appeared as various Buddhas and bodhisattvas of different names and different life spans.

He also says that at times he has announced that he would enter nirvana and then seemed to do so. The truth is that the life of the Buddha who attained enlightenment in the remote past is eternal. But to guide people, he has—as an expedient means—appeared under a variety of names and assumed various limited life spans and then pretended to enter nirvana.

The Buddhas and bodhisattvas of the past, as emanations of Shakyamuni who attained enlightenment in the remote past, appeared in order to guide people toward enlightenment. The Buddha thus freely shares his eternal life with his various emanations to teach and guide the people.

Eternal life is the Buddha's immeasurable benefit. T'ien-t'ai says, "'*Juryo*, or Life Span, refers to an overall reckoning. It indicates an overall reckoning of the benefits of the two Buddhas, the three Buddhas, and all the Buddhas of the ten directions and the three existences'" (OTT, 123). Allowing his life span to be fully consumed in the process, Shakyamuni bestowed his benefit upon people in countless places and ages. For the Buddha to save the people means for him to share his immense life force—his life span—with others. Fundamentally, the Buddha's benefit is life force; it is the power to thrive. In the "Life Span" chapter, Shakyamuni clarifies that the Buddha's life span is in fact immeasurable.

Each day, we receive this immeasurable life force, this immeasurable benefit, from the Gohonzon. Therefore, the more we praise the great beneficial power of the Gohonzon, the more our own lives increase in majesty and power and shine with brilliance.

With faith in the Gohonzon as the foundation, we pray, take action and speak out for the happiness of others. The maintenance of this correct rhythm directs one's entire being toward longevity, health and happiness.

To explain this rhythm of faith manifesting itself in daily life in practical terms, I once proposed the following four guidelines for leading a healthy life: (1) do an invigorating, daily gongyo; (2) conduct your daily life in a reasonable and productive manner; (3) be of service to others; and (4) maintain sound eating habits.

It might also be said that faith in the Mystic Law is the foremost catalyst of health and longevity.

Faith of Valiant Action Produces Great Joy

Let us now interpret the implicit meaning of this passage.

First, "if there are living beings who come to me" refers to our sitting upright before the Gohonzon.

In the Latter Day of the Law, the Buddha's act of employing the Buddha eye to observe people's capacity and preaching the Law in accordance with their circumstances indicates Nichiren's compassionate conduct in leading all people to enlightenment.

President Toda explained this passage as meaning that the Gohonzon perceives our faith and bestows upon us great compassion.

From our standpoint, "if their . . . faculties are keen or dull" could be said to indicate the strength or weakness of our faith. The deeper our faith becomes, the more we can manifest the immeasurable benefit of the Gohonzon.

In a lecture, President Toda said:

Before the Daishonin entered nirvana, he left the Gohonzon for us, the people of the Latter Day. While he was alive, he was respectfully called Nichiren Daishonin. After his passing, he is reverently called the Gohonzon bestowed upon all humankind. This is the meaning of "preach to them under different names" and "describe my life span as long or short." This Gohonzon is the true aspect of the Buddha.

Needless to say, Nichiren Buddhism is the great teaching for the limitless span of the Latter Day of the Law. It is the source of light illuminating all humankind throughout the eternal future. The length of time during which it will be effective is infinite.

"I . . . also employ different expedient means to preach the subtle and wonderful Law, thus causing living beings to awaken joyful minds" indicates none other than expounding the Law of Nam-myoho-renge-kyo and causing people to experience great joy through the power of the Gohonzon.

Those who earnestly embrace the Mystic Law will certainly never become miserable. This is true absolutely beyond any doubt.

President Toda went so far as to say that unless great joy wells forth when praying to the Gohonzon, then one's faith is not correct. When we experience such joy, a great flower of benefit blossoms in our lives.

But he qualified this, saying:

However, if knowing this you simply try to will yourself to be joyful, you won't experience true joy. If during your daily chanting your legs get numb and you find yourself thinking, "I can't wait until this is over . . . Oops, no, I have to be joyful," then you're not experiencing real joy.

Faith is taking spirited action. When we do so earnestly, our hearts become light and filled with momentum. Pessimism is alien to Buddhism.

Taking action on the side of justice brings joy. Let us cheerfully, joyfully and brightly advance along the path of our convictions.

▪15▪

Sho zen-nanshi. Nyorai ken sho shujo. Gyo o shobo. Toku hak̂ ku ju sha.
I ze nin setsu. Ga sho shukke. Toku a-noku-ta-ra san myaku sanbodai.
Nen ga jitsu jo-butsu irai. Ku-on nyaku shi. Tan ni hoben. Kyoke shujo.
Ryo nyu butsu-do. Sa nyo ze setsu.

"Good men, the Thus Come One observes how among living beings
there are those who delight in lesser teachings, meager in virtue and heavy
with defilement. For such persons I describe how in my youth I left my
household and attained supreme perfect enlightenment. But in truth the
time since I attained Buddhahood is extremely long, as I have told you.
It is simply that I use this expedient means to teach and convert living
beings and cause them to enter the Buddha way. That is why I speak in
this manner." (LSOC, 267)

T HE LIVES OF those who advance toward great ideals and dedicate themselves to continuous self-improvement are always
pervaded with hope, fulfillment and inspiration. They possess a brilliance of life that overflows from within and a kind of charm that
words cannot express.

The Lotus Sutra urges all people to proceed along the path of
continuous advancement. "Aim to realize the great state of life of the
Buddha!" "Cultivate the boundless universe within your heart!" The
Lotus Sutra expounds this supreme path.

To teach the Lotus Sutra, the Buddha first set forth various expedient teachings as a means to guide people.

Although Shakyamuni, in the earlier sutras and in the theoretical teaching, taught that he had renounced secular life at a young age and attained supreme enlightenment for the first time in his present existence, this was an expedient teaching. It was an expedient he expounded according to the understanding of "those who delight in lesser teachings, meager in virtue and heavy with defilement."

"Those who delight in lesser teachings" indicates persons who embrace the Hinayana or provisional Mahayana teachings or, more broadly, an inferior system of values or sense of purpose in life. As a result, they do not aspire to attain the great state of life of the Buddha. Regarding such people, T'ien-t'ai says: "Their hearts are tainted with worldly pleasures and attached to erroneous views"; and "They desire to turn their bodies to ashes and annihilate their consciousness."

"Meager in virtue and heavy with defilement" means that such people have accumulated few causes for attaining Buddhahood; their lives are defiled with earthly desires. "Defilement" indicates vices including greed, anger, foolishness, arrogance, doubt, mistaken views and jealousy.

Rather than trying to teach such persons about the eternal life of the Buddha who has been enlightened since numberless major world system dust particle kalpas ago, Shakyamuni told them that he attained enlightenment for the first time in this lifetime as a result of having carried out various practices in previous existences. By so doing, ultimately he was laying the groundwork for the revelation of the Buddha's eternal life span (that is, of his attainment of enlightenment in the remote past) here in the "Life Span" chapter.

Had he taught about the eternal Buddha from the outset, without employing such expedients, many would doubtless have slandered him, saying, "Who could believe this grandiose talk?" Or they might have given up hope entirely, convinced that they could not possibly attain such a great state of life. Either way, it would have led them to abandon their practice.

Because he started out by expounding the cause of his past practice and the effect of his attaining Buddhahood for the first time in his present life, people could accept what he said and therefore strive to attain their own enlightenment.

Moreover, with his teaching about the three vehicles being replaced by the one vehicle in "Expedient Means," Shakyamuni had indicated that all people inherently possess the world of Buddhahood. There he unequivocally declared: "The Thus Come Ones have only the single Buddha vehicle that they employ in order to preach the Law to living beings. They do not have any other vehicle, a second one or a third one" (LSOC, 64).

Because this foundation had already been laid, the disciples in the "Life Span" chapter caught a glimpse of their mentor's state of life, vast and boundless as the universe. Rather than being plagued by doubt, they could believe in the teaching of his attainment of Buddhahood in the remote past with a sense of excitement and joy.

It might be said that Shakyamuni's preaching of his initial attainment of enlightenment in this lifetime was part of a grand curriculum that the Buddha had conceived out of his profound determination not to allow even one person to regress in faith or fall away from the path to enlightenment. Such was the profound thought and tenacious effort required to enable people to believe in the eternal life of the Buddha.

Outside of Buddhism, as well, the eternity of life is a subject that many philosophers and religious thinkers have dedicated their lives to understanding. Ultimately, however, their insights have either not transcended the realm of ideas or have remained a matter of personal awakening. As such, these insights could not be practically communicated to people at large.

All this points to just how difficult it is to enable ordinary people "meager in virtue and heavy with defilement" to comprehend the vast life of the Buddha, which is without beginning or end. Herein lay the Buddha's heroic spiritual struggle.

For the people of the Latter Day, Nichiren manifested the great life of the Buddha in the form of the Gohonzon. Therefore, for us, faith in the Gohonzon becomes the path to life's eternity. Through believing in the Gohonzon, exerting ourselves in doing gongyo and chanting Nam-myoho-renge-kyo, and dedicating our lives to kosen-rufu, we can enter the path of eternal happiness of the Buddha.

Those who believe in and practice the Mystic Law are not people meager in virtue and heavy with defilement. They are people with "great roots of goodness" (WND-1, 385) who enjoy a status second to none.

This is truly an age that abounds with people meager in virtue and heavy with defilement who "delight in lesser teachings." It is regarded as natural to lead an inferior way of life dedicated only to the pursuit of pleasure or wealth. We may be living in an age devoid of values, when people simply find it extremely difficult to uphold great ideals.

In the very midst of this modern society, we are studying, believing in and practicing the great life philosophy of the supreme Law. With our gaze on eternity, we are taking action to lead all humanity to enlightenment. No other way of life is as noble or replete with good fortune. For precisely this reason, it is only natural that we should be envied. It would actually be quite strange if we did not encounter misunderstanding, prejudice or a certain amount of persecution.

Let us advance with dignity! Let us continue working with confidence and still greater joy to cultivate the hearts of others.

Regarding the significance of "Good men, the Thus Come One observes how among living beings . . ." T'ien-t'ai explains that it refers to Shakyamuni's determined and all-out struggle, like a bounding lion, to benefit the people of his day.

This sutra passage describes the Buddha's intensive struggle to lead the people to enlightenment. To practice for kosen-rufu with this same dedication and resolve is to read this passage with one's life.

▪ 16 ▪

Sho zen-nanshi. Nyorai sho en kyoden. Kai i dodas͡shujo.
Waku sek͡koshin. Waku set͡tashin. Waku ji koshin. Waku ji tashin. Waku
ji koji. Waku ji taji. Sho sho gon-setsu. Kai jitsu fu ko.

"Good men, the scriptures expounded by the Thus Come One are all
for the purpose of saving and emancipating living beings. Sometimes I
speak of myself, sometimes of others; sometimes I present myself,
sometimes others; sometimes I show my own actions, sometimes those
of others. All that I preach is true and not false." (LSOC, 267)

THE EARLIER SUTRAS Shakyamuni had expounded were all to
lead people to enlightenment. Here, Shakyamuni emphasizes
that these teachings, while expounded from a variety of different
viewpoints, all represent the truth, none are false.

In the passage that begins, "Sometimes I speak of myself, sometimes of others," "sometimes" appears six times. This is called the "six
modes of preaching."

Nichiren points to this passage as documentary proof of the principle that "the world of Buddhahood contains the Ten Worlds" (WND-1,
357). To explain, the words "myself" and "others" indicate the various states of life and activities of the beings of the Ten Worlds taught
by the Buddha who attained enlightenment in the remote past.

Nichiren, citing this passage, also says:

The Buddhas of the ten directions, the seven Buddhas of the past, the Buddhas of the three existences, Bodhisattva Superior Practices and the other bodhisattvas, Manjushri, Shariputra and the others, the great heavenly king Brahma, the devil king of the sixth heaven, the heavenly king Shakra Devanam Indra, the sun god, the moon god, the morning star god, the seven stars of the Big Dipper, the twenty-eight constellations, the five planets, the seven stars, the countless eighty-four thousand other stars, the asura kings, the heavenly gods, earthly gods, gods of the mountains, gods of the seas, household gods, village gods, and the rulers of all the various countries of the world—not one of these is other than [a provisional manifestation of] Shakyamuni Buddha, the lord of teachings! The Sun Goddess, Great Bodhisattva Hachiman—both these in their original form are Shakyamuni Buddha, the lord of teachings.

Shakyamuni Buddha is like the one moon in the sky, and the various other Buddhas, bodhisattvas, and beings are like the reflections floating on ten thousand different bodies of water. (WND-2, 811)

These manifestations of the Ten Worlds are all expedients Shakyamuni taught to free people from their sufferings.

These forms Shakyamuni assumed in order to bring real benefit to the people are expressions of the compassion of the Buddha who attained enlightenment in the remote past. Such descriptions are certainly not lies. Rather, they indicate just how grand is the state of life of Buddhahood.

In terms of the Latter Day of the Law, "the scriptures expounded by the Thus Come One" indicates Nichiren's writings. It seems to me that we can identify the same six modes of preaching in these writings, the scriptures of the Latter Day.

"Sometimes I speak of myself" indicates Nichiren speaking of the state of life of the original Buddha. "Sometimes of others" indicates Nichiren speaking of the state of life of beings of the nine worlds from hell to bodhisattva. "Sometimes I present myself" indicates Nichiren presenting the aspect of the original Buddha. "Sometimes others" indicates Nichiren presenting the aspect of ordinary persons of the nine worlds.

"Sometimes I show my own actions" indicates Nichiren showing the behavior of the original Buddha. In other words, it refers to Nichiren's struggles to perpetuate the Law and accomplish kosen-rufu. These struggles include his fierce propagation efforts while undergoing four great persecutions, including exiles to Izu and Sado, and his tireless efforts to encourage many disciples and set down his teachings in writing.

"Sometimes those of others" indicates the behavior of Nichiren's disciples who exert themselves to spread the teaching, make offerings to Nichiren and receive benefit.

The six modes of preaching of the original Buddha all refer to Nichiren's own conduct and his disciples' actions, based on faith, as related in his writings. The purpose of these various accounts is to save and emancipate the people. Not one of them is false.

The writings of Nichiren Daishonin express the great state of life of the original Buddha who yearns to save all people throughout the ten thousand years of the Latter Day of the Law. Every line of his writings explains one thing, the Law of Nam-myoho-renge-kyo. As President Toda said:

> All that the Daishonin saw and taught is Nam-myoho-renge-kyo. If someone were to come to the Daishonin and say, "Daishonin, please tell me what is your most essential teaching," he would tell the person: "OK, have a seat. It's Nam-myoho-renge-kyo. That's it in its entirety."

> The Daishonin's teaching over a period of thirty years all comes down to a single phrase. Therefore, if we believe in the Gohonzon, chant Nam-myoho-renge-kyo and propagate the teaching, then we are certain to attain enlightenment.

All of you are practicing this "most essential teaching" for the liberation of humankind.

The Daishonin writes: "I, Nichiren, have done nothing else, but have labored solely to put the five or seven characters of Myoho-renge-kyo into the mouths of all the living beings of the country of Japan. In doing so, I have shown the kind of compassion that a mother does when she labors to put milk into the mouth of her infant child" (WND-2, 931).

It may be that many of you who take compassionate action each day while striving to emulate Nichiren's spirit experience sufferings or hardships one after another. I make every effort to be aware of your noble and difficult struggles.

But through this faith, we can make all our actions shine as the conduct of Buddhas and bodhisattvas expressed by the passage "sometimes I present myself, sometimes others." To the extent that we worry, to the extent that we fight, all our efforts return to us as benefit.

"All that I preach is true and not false" (LSOC, 267), the sutra says. In Buddhism, no effort is ever wasted.

You may at times be fraught with worry, and at other times raise shouts of triumph, but I hope that you will join me in enacting a glorious drama on the stage of kosen-rufu.

▪17▪

Sho-i sha ga. Nyorai nyojit chi-ken. Sangai shi so. Mu u shoji.
Nyaku tai nyaku shutsu. Yaku mu zai-se. Gyu metsu-do sha.
Hi jitsu hi ko. Hi nyo hi i. Fu nyo san-gai. Ken no sangai.
Nyo shi shi ji. Nyorai myo ken. Mu u shaku-myo.

"Why do I do this? The Thus Come One perceives the true aspect of the
threefold world exactly as it is. There is no ebb or flow of birth and death,
and there is no existing in this world and later entering extinction. It is neither substantial nor empty, neither consistent nor diverse. Nor is it what
those who dwell in the threefold world perceive it to be. All such things the
Thus Come One sees clearly and without error." (LSOC, 267)

IN THIS PASSAGE, Shakyamuni clarifies the Buddha's magnificent
perspective on life, which could be said to represent the essence of
Buddhism. This passage, in other words, holds the key to elevating all
people's state of life.

Probably nothing is so remotely mysterious yet so close at hand as
birth and death. I am convinced that the "Life Span" chapter provides
at once the most fundamental and most convincing solution to this
enigma. And this passage contains an important part of that solution.

Nichiren Daishonin says, "First of all learn about death, and then
about other things" (WND-2, 759), thus indicating the centrality of the
issue of birth and death to Buddhism.

Josei Toda often said, "The final problem that Buddhism must solve is that of death."

How does one address the issue of birth and death? I think that offering a viable solution will be an important requisite for religions in the twenty-first century. It is partly with this in mind that we now study the profound teachings of "Life Span."

In this passage, Shakyamuni explains the Buddha's wisdom to perceive the true aspect of life in the threefold world exactly as it is. Previously, in "Expedient Means," he explained the Buddha's wisdom in terms of the "true aspect of all phenomena." Here he focuses on the life and death of living beings and explains the Buddha's wisdom to perceive the truth of the oneness of birth and death.

With his initial question, "Why do I do this?" he is asking why the Buddha, enlightened since the remote past, appears in various forms, appropriately expounds a variety of teachings, and can unerringly guide all people. To explain, he says, "The Thus Come One perceives the true aspect of the threefold world exactly as it is."

The threefold world refers to the world of unenlightened beings who transmigrate within the six paths (the first six of the Ten Worlds—from hell through the realm of heavenly beings). The threefold world comprises the world of desire, the world of form (or material world) and the world of formlessness (or world of the spirit). These are all worlds of illusion in which life is dominated by ignorance or darkness. This ignorance is itself the fundamental source of human misery and suffering.

The Buddha enlightened since the remote past is the Buddha who struggles perpetually to lead all people to happiness. This Buddha perceives the true aspect of the threefold world exactly as it is in order to liberate people from the suffering of birth and death.

The statement "The Thus Come One perceives the true aspect of the threefold world exactly as it is" indicates the Buddha's wisdom to lead all people to enlightenment.

Shakyamuni then clarifies the nature of the threefold world that he perceives with this wisdom, saying, "There is no ebb or flow of birth and death, and there is no existing in this world and later entering extinction." Here he indicates that in the threefold world there is neither birth nor death and that beings neither appear nor disappear. Accordingly, there is no distinction between those present in the world and those not.

That there is no birth and death strikes one at first as most surprising, for people generally regard birth and death as solemn facts of human existence. This sutra passage, however, is not denying the phenomena of birth and death. Rather, while recognizing their reality, it offers a reappraisal of birth and death from a more profound perspective on life.

Explained here is the true aspect of the life of the Buddha enlightened since the remote past. This Buddha is in fact an entity of life without beginning or end who dwells eternally in the saha world. As such, there is no fundamental distinction between birth and death, between existing in this world and later entering extinction. Even so, the Buddha appears in the world and then enters extinction as an expedient means to lead people to enlightenment.

Faith in the Gohonzon Leads to a Life Free of Error

In this passage, Shakyamuni directly applies the reality of the life of the Buddha enlightened since the remote past to the beings of the threefold world. And the comparison is entirely valid; there is in fact no difference between the true aspect of life of beings of the threefold world and that of the Buddha enlightened since the remote past. This, therefore, is an exact description of the true nature of the lives of all beings of the threefold world.

Nichiren Daishonin clarifies this in no uncertain terms:

The "Thus Come One" is the living beings of the threefold world. When we look at these living beings through the eyes of the "Life Span" chapter, we can see and understand the true aspect of these beings who in their original state possess the Ten Worlds. (OTT, 127)

The Thus Come One and the living beings of the threefold world are each an entity of life inherently possessing the Ten Worlds. Accordingly, the Thus Come One of the "Life Span" chapter represents none other than the living beings of the threefold world. Nichiren indicates that to view living beings in this way is to perceive them exactly as they are in their original state.

Needless to say, this original state of life is none other than Nam-myoho-renge-kyo, the state of the life of the Daishonin. The Daishonin manifested this state of life as the Gohonzon that is endowed with the Ten Worlds.

When we look at things in this way, we realize on a profound level that even our own birth and death are the birth and death of life in its "original state"—that is, our "greater life." Birth and death are simply alternating phases of this original state.

Therefore, Nichiren says, "*Myo* represents death, and *ho*, life" (WND-1, 216); and "Life and death are simply the two functions of Myoho-renge-kyo" (WND-1, 216). To put it another way, birth and death are part of the great rhythm of the Mystic Law, the very wellspring of cosmic life.

Nichiren says that all phenomena in the universe exhibit the phases of birth and death and perform to the rhythm of the Mystic Law. To see the universe exactly this way is to perceive the true aspect of the threefold world.

Our lives in their original state exist eternally together with the life of the universe; they are without beginning or end. When certain conditions are attained, we manifest birth. And, in time, we recede again into the universe, entering a state of rest. This is the nature of death. It is not the case that our lives are terminated through death. Rather, it could be said that death is an expedient means necessary for us to lead a fresh and vigorous existence in the future.

Fundamentally, there is no ebb or flow of birth and death; life, as thus conceived, embodies the oneness of birth and death. Our lives exist eternally and are inextinguishable. Those who thoroughly grasp this truth will neither take birth lightly nor needlessly fear death.

In other words, we can correctly fix our gaze on the present moment and advance along the path of continual self-improvement— succumbing neither to impatience nor to negligence. This is the way of life of one who "perceives the true aspect of the threefold world exactly as it is."

Ralph Waldo Emerson writes:

> It is the depth at which we live and not at all the surface extension that imports. We pierce to the eternity, . . . and, really, the least acceleration of thought and the least increase of power of thought, make life to seem and to be of vast duration.[6]

What matters is the "depth at which we live," the "power of thought" we manifest. A person who leads such a truly profound life can make each day worth ten days or even a month. In a year, he or she can create the value of ten or even a hundred years. This is the true measure of one's life span; it is not decided simply on the superficial basis of length of time.

I have lived my life and worked hard with this awareness, and I am determined to continue to do so. Therefore, no matter what happens, I have no fear. I can overcome anything with composure, with the spirit of a lion king.

When we base ourselves on the view that life spans past, present and future, we can overcome the sufferings of birth and death. We can manifest a state imbued with great peace of mind like that of the Buddha. Then we need fear nothing. We can wholeheartedly devote ourselves to the happiness of all people and the realization of world peace—to the eternal struggle to create value, which is the Buddha's will. Each of us is a child of the Buddha who can lead a dignified and noble existence.

In the sutra passage, Shakyamuni further explains the threefold world that the Buddha enlightened since the remote past correctly perceives, saying: "It is neither substantial nor empty, neither consistent nor diverse. Nor is it what those who dwell in the threefold world perceive it to be."

In short, the Buddha perceives the threefold world exactly as it is with his perfect wisdom of the Middle Way. His view is not biased as are the views of those dwelling in the threefold world.

Interpreting this passage in terms of its implicit meaning, the Thus Come One who "perceives the true aspect of the threefold world exactly as it is" is Nichiren. Nichiren embodies the life of compassion and wisdom existing eternally since beginningless time—the life of Nam-myoho-renge-kyo contained in the depths of "Life Span."

The Gohonzon we devote ourselves to is Nichiren's life of compassion and wisdom. In a lecture, President Toda said:

> When we reverently chant Nam-myoho-renge-kyo to the Gohonzon and feel the life of the Gohonzon in ourselves, the power of the Gohonzon wells forth abundantly in our lives, because our lives themselves are Nam-myoho-renge-kyo. When that happens, we will be free of great error in our judgment of the affairs of life or society.
>
> Through our faith, we feel the power of the Gohonzon, and this enables us to make our way unerringly through the

world. This is what we assert. Let's lead lives free of error through believing in the Gohonzon.

In the present age, surrounded by negative influences, nothing is more difficult than for us to lead lives free of error. At the same time, nothing is more important. Through faith in the Gohonzon, we feel the Buddha's heart of compassion and the Buddha's wisdom to perceive things exactly as they are, and as a result, we can advance correctly through life.

Wisdom Arises From Compassion

This is a time of change. The world and its individual nations are undergoing profound transformation. What is most needed at this time of great change? To give a single answer, it would have to be wisdom.

Individually or as a group, when people view the affairs of the age and society with a discerning eye and manifest fresh wisdom, they will not be dragged down by even the most tumultuous events. Instead, they can steer change toward development, toward victory and toward value creation.

By contrast, those who adhere to inflexible and outdated modes of thinking will be left behind. To respond incorrectly to change means defeat. Now is a time of such unforgiving strictness; we must not underestimate the challenge it represents. Therefore, for happiness and for victory, the wisdom of the Thus Come One who "perceives the true aspect of the threefold world exactly as it is" becomes increasingly important.

Simply put, knowledge corresponds to the past; it is technology. Wisdom is the future; it is philosophy. It is people's hearts that move the age. While knowledge may provide a useful point of reference, it cannot become a force to guide the future. By contrast, wisdom captivates people's hearts and has the power to open a new age. Wisdom is the key to understanding the age and creating the "time." Faith is a treasure house of infinite wisdom. Nichiren Daishonin says that faith is a "treasure chest of . . . three thousand realms in a single moment of life" (WND-1, 783). A mind that believes in the Mystic Law, in other words, is a treasure chest containing the Buddha's wisdom.

Therefore, we need not be surprised or taken aback by any changes or turmoil we encounter. We possess the Buddha's infinite wisdom in the treasure chest of faith in our lives. If we possess infinite wisdom, we can calmly take appropriate measures to surmount any and all difficulties that beset us with the rhythm of turning change into victory and turmoil into growth.

"The Thus Come One perceives the true aspect of the threefold world exactly as it is" describes the wisdom of the Buddha. The Buddha's wisdom is the ability to perceive "the true aspect of the threefold world," the true nature of reality, exactly as it is.

Why does the Buddha perceive the true aspect of the threefold world exactly as it is? It is to liberate the beings of the threefold world from suffering. The source of the Buddha's wisdom is compassion. The Buddha's wisdom arises from, and is one with, compassion.

The Buddha's wisdom to perceive the very core of the nature of reality arises from strong, single-minded, compassionate determination to save those who suffer. With such compassion, the Buddha can unerringly perceive in the world of suffering and divisiveness the world of the Mystic Law and harmony, which is indicated by the principle of three thousand realms in a single moment of life.

One of the Buddha's names is Endowed With Abundant Life Span. The Buddha's abundant life span is none other than eternal and universal wisdom. For this reason, the Buddha is also called One Who Subsists On Wisdom.

The "Life Span" chapter explains that the life span of One Who

Subsists On Wisdom is infinite. The Buddha enlightened since the remote past is essentially the embodiment of the wisdom to continue taking action to lead people to enlightenment.

Accordingly, the central significance of the Buddha of "Life Span" is that of wisdom. He is also the Thus Come One of the "reward body." The reward body, or attribute of wisdom, is the dignified virtue acquired by the Buddha as reward for his Buddhist practice. The core of this benefit is the Buddha's wisdom to perceive that the real world—just as it is—is the world of the Mystic Law. Through this wisdom, the Buddha can, of his own accord, freely receive, employ and enjoy a sense of profound comfort and ease derived from the Mystic Law. This Buddha is also called the Buddha of limitless joy, or the Buddha of absolute freedom.

In this sense, T'ien-t'ai designates the Buddha of "Life Span" as the "three bodies of the Buddha viewed in terms of the reward body, or attribute of wisdom." He says, in other words, that "Life Span" explains the three bodies—the Dharma body, the reward body and the manifested body—all from the standpoint of the Buddha's attribute of wisdom.

The Dharma Body Thus Come One signifies the Mystic Law, the central unchanging truth. The Buddha's wisdom is first and foremost the wisdom to perceive the Mystic Law. From the standpoint of the Buddha's enlightenment, wisdom and the Mystic Law are inseparable; apart from the Mystic Law, there is no wisdom. The Buddha embodying the Mystic Law, who is thus at one with wisdom, is called the Dharma Body Thus Come One.

From a temporal standpoint, the Mystic Law is eternal; from a spatial standpoint, it is boundless. As the rhythm of the universe, it continues to operate regardless of whether the Buddha is manifest in the world.

This is what is indicated by "There is no ebb or flow of birth and death . . ." There is neither birth nor death. There is neither substance nor void. Nor can it be said that there is either consistency or diversity among things. In short, the world of the Mystic Law cannot be wholly grasped with the ordinary wisdom of beings of the threefold world.

The Mystic Law is the very wellspring of cosmic life that encompasses all phenomena, including birth and death. The Buddha who perceives the Mystic Law exactly as it is and who embodies it—who, in other words, embodies the universe—is the Dharma Body Thus Come One.

However, unless the Buddha uses wisdom to expound the Mystic Law, others cannot freely employ its power, which is inherent in life. In actuality, therefore, the Mystic Law is at work only when the Buddha appears in the world and exercises wisdom to expound the Mystic Law. When people seek the Buddha, the Buddha's wisdom arises. The Buddha senses people's seeking spirit and appears in response.

The Buddha who appears in response to people's minds and their capacity is the Manifested Body Thus Come One. The Buddha's wisdom concretely manifests in the form of Buddhas and bodhisattvas and teaches and guides people. In "Life Span," these various forms are indicated by "Sometimes I speak of myself, sometimes of others" describing the six modes of preaching, which we studied earlier (see LSOC, 267).

The Buddha appears in a form people can most easily accept, behaves in a way that puts people's minds most at ease and guides them. Behind such appearance and action, the Buddha's wisdom is at work. Behind such appearance and action breathes the Thus Come One of the reward body.

The wisdom arising from the compassion to help others become happy is the underlying power that causes the Buddha to appear.

In this way, "Life Span" explains the nature of the Buddha enlightened since the remote past from the standpoint of the reward body. It clarifies that this Buddha is an entity endowed with the three bodies.

T'ien-t'ai says, "A single Buddha possesses all three bodies and the three bodies are all found within a single Buddha." The Buddha, as the unity of the three bodies, dwells in the world eternally. That is to say, the Buddha of the "Life Span" chapter eternally illuminates people's lives with the light of compassion and wisdom arising from a profound state of life. The profound light of the Buddha's character—that is, the Buddha's power to guide people—is inextinguishable.

The Ultimate Buddha Body

In terms of the implicit meaning of the sutra, the Buddha who possesses all three bodies and within whom the three bodies all exist is the Nam-myoho-renge-kyo Thus Come One, or Nichiren.

From the standpoint of the sutra's literal meaning, the Buddha enlightened since the remote past possesses the three bodies in the one reward body acquired as the result of the Buddha's practice.

By contrast, from the standpoint of implicit meaning, the one body of ordinary people is originally endowed with the three bodies. This is called "the Buddha originally endowed with the three bodies." These bodies are said to be originally endowed because the universe is inherently endowed with the virtues of the three bodies. There is no need for them to be created anew in each person. Accordingly, we can attain this Buddha body without changing our form as ordinary people.

The Buddha originally endowed with the three bodies is the ultimate Buddha body. The true intention of the "Life Span" chapter is to lead all people to enlightenment after Shakyamuni's passing. To make this universal salvation possible, Shakyamuni concealed in the chapter's depths the ultimate Buddha, the Buddha originally endowed with the three bodies.

Therefore, in clarifying exactly what "Life Span" teaches, Nichiren says:

> Common people like ourselves, who have been submerged
> in the sufferings of birth and death since time without begin-
> ning and who never so much as dreamed of reaching the
> shore of enlightenment, become the Thus Come Ones who
> are originally enlightened and endowed with the three bod-
> ies. That is, it [Shakyamuni's enlightenment in the remote
> past] reveals the ultimate principle of three thousand realms
> in a single moment of life. (WND-1, 479)

When we perceive the universe exactly as it is, we find it inherently endowed with the virtues of the three bodies. This is the true aspect of the world of living beings, which is steeped in the sufferings of birth and death. The universe—after giving rise to material substance, and the stars and the galaxies, and the mountains, rivers and oceans on Earth—eventually produced life. After producing a wide array of life forms over several hundred million years, it finally produced human-kind. It can be said that this is all the function of the Buddha originally endowed with the three bodies.

President Toda used to say that life and phenomena at each moment are the Thus Come One. Also, he discerned that the function to pro-duce and nurture life is the work of compassion with which the uni-verse is inherently endowed.

He taught that the universe, which continually seeks to carry for-ward this work of compassion, causes the latent world of Buddhahood to become manifest in response to the time. This is the mechanism whereby a Buddha appears.

What, then, can we do to perceive in our own lives the three bodies with which we are originally endowed? Nichiren says: "The eternally endowed three bodies mentioned here are gained through a single word. And that single word is 'faith' or 'to believe'" (OTT, 125). And, "If in a single moment of life we exhaust the pains and trials of mil-lions of kalpas, then instant after instant there will arise in us the three

Buddha bodies with which we are eternally endowed" (OTT, 214).

The three Buddha bodies with which our lives are inherently endowed become manifest through faith. The supremely noble Mystic Law, the Buddha's immeasurable wisdom and the function of compassion to lead all people to enlightenment are all contained in faith. Therefore, wisdom cannot fail to manifest in the lives of those who exert themselves in faith.

President Toda said:

> When we chant Nam-myoho-renge-kyo with faith in the Gohonzon, faith becomes the cause and our voice chanting becomes the effect. This faith and practice together form the simultaneity of cause and effect, and we instantly gain the effect of Buddhahood; the life of the Thus Come One of beginningless time, originally endowed with the three Buddha bodies, begins to flow abundantly in our being.

He also said:

> All benefits of the Gohonzon become manifest in the daily lives of us common mortals. Only through believing wholeheartedly in the original Buddha's great spirit of compassion and great power of wisdom can we ordinary people, as followers of the original Buddha, attain enlightenment in our present form. There are absolutely no other Buddhas.

Such is the greatness of the Gohonzon. Such is the great condition of happiness of those who thoroughly dedicate themselves to faith.

We are originally endowed with this state of life. We can develop it with total composure and in a manner true to ourselves, never needing to put on airs or become someone we're not. The important thing is to devote ourselves to faith.

The Buddha originally endowed with the three bodies is another name for those champions of faith who, while leading ordinary lives, attain greatness.

▪18▪

I sho shujo. U shu-ju sho. Shuju yoku. Shuju gyo. Shuju oku-so.
Fun-bek̂ ko. Yoku ryo sho sho zengon. I nyakkan innen. Hiyu gonji.
Shuju seppo. Shosa butsu-ji. Mi zo zan pai.

"Because living beings have different natures, different desires, different
actions, and different ways of thinking and making distinctions, and
because I want to enable them to put down good roots, I employ
a variety of causes and conditions, similes, parables, and phrases and
preach different doctrines. This, a Buddha's work, I have never for
a moment neglected." (LSOC, 267)

THIS PASSAGE EXPLAINS the Buddha's wisdom to benefit others
and the Buddha's compassionate vow not to allow even one
person to fall behind or slip by the wayside.

The wisdom of the Buddha who perfectly perceives the true aspect
of the threefold world is the "eye of compassion" to warmly watch
over all people in their infinite diversity. It is also the "eye of democ-
racy" that highly values each person's individuality.

The Buddha enlightened since the remote past conducts heart-to-
heart dialogue with individuals. Because the Buddha's life is eternal,
the Buddha may appear at any time or in any place.

Therefore, the Buddha's struggle to lead all people to happiness
never ends. Without rest, the Buddha continuously ponders and
works to relieve people of their sufferings. This passage clarifies that

the Buddha has ceaselessly continued such compassionate work since the remote past until the present.

Those needing to be saved are innumerable; they are rich in diversity and individuality. Because the Buddha is dedicated to saving them all, he possesses a long life span, deep wisdom and immeasurable benefit and virtue.

Because the Buddha's struggles for others are boundless, the resulting benefit is immeasurable. Tremendous life force—of a kind those who take action only for themselves can never understand—wells forth in the Buddha's being.

Living beings, Shakyamuni notes, have different natures, different desires, different actions, and different ways of thinking and making distinctions. In one scripture, he employs a beautiful metaphor to describe people's widely varying capacities: Some lotus flowers are blue, some are red and some are white. Some blossom under water, some reach the water's surface and some stand up out of the water.[7]

The Buddha Respects Differences Among People

People vary in capacity and temperament. This is natural; it is reality. Such variety is proof of life. If people were all the same, they would be like robots.

The Buddha highly respects these differences, this variety. A hundred people will have a hundred different joys, a thousand will have a thousand unique sufferings. The Buddha regards the various sufferings of all people as the Buddha's own. Therefore, the Buddha, possessing an accurate grasp of each person's unique disposition and desires, employs a variety of metaphors and words in expounding the Buddha's teaching and raises people so that, ultimately, they can all attain the capacity to hear the teaching of the one Buddha vehicle.

In Shakyamuni's day, there was a follower named Chudapanthaka. With his poor memory, he could not satisfactorily carry out the

Buddhist practice his peers did. In time, even his elder brother told him: "No matter how much you practice, it's of no use. You'd best go home!"

Thus rebuked and feeling dejected, Chudapanthaka left. But someone then approached him, gently took him by the hand and led him back: It was Shakyamuni. The Buddha handed him a dusty rag, which had been used to wipe the dust and dirt from feet. Chudapanthaka, too, was covered with dust. Shakyamuni told him, "Try to see this dusty rag as something clean."

There is in Buddhism a teaching that one should not be caught up with such external distinctions as "clean" or "unclean." True cleanliness, it teaches, exists only in the heart. Chudapanthaka could not understand Buddhism theoretically. He was so touched by Shakyamuni's compassion, however, that by merely looking upon the rag that he associated with his mentor's kindness, he could maintain the thought, "the dusty rag is pure." As a result, his practice became joyful, and he eventually became a leading disciple possessing the heavenly eye.

Though others may, the Buddha never abandons anyone, freely bringing forth the wisdom needed to save that person.

"I employ a variety of causes and conditions, similes, parables, and phrases and preach different doctrines" means that the Buddha is a master of dialogue, an expert at discussion. The German philosopher Karl Jaspers characterized Shakyamuni as one who makes free use of language. Indeed, the Buddha expounds teachings with perfect freedom and saves all people with the resonance of his conviction.

The objective of the Buddha's dialogue is to enable people to "put down good roots" in their lives. The ultimate cause that can enable all people equally to attain happiness, therefore, is none other than Nam-myoho-renge-kyo.

Faith in the Mystic Law is the greatest good cause. Teaching people about the Mystic Law constitutes the Buddha's supreme conduct. Accordingly, to teach friends about the Mystic Law is truly to carry out the Buddha's work.

A Person of Dynamic Action

In this passage, Shakyamuni says, "I have never for a moment neglected." In other words, he has continued carrying out the Buddha's work without a moment's pause. The Buddha is a stranger to rest. He will not desist until he has eradicated misery from the face of the earth.

Shakyamuni says: "Day and night, I have not a moment of regret. Even while sleeping, my heart is filled with the desire to save all people." Therefore, so long as one individual needs to be liberated from suffering—even if that person is at the farthest end of the earth—the Buddha will continue advancing. Shakyamuni visited countless towns and villages to spread his teaching. According to research, he visited the kingdom of Shravasti more than nine hundred times. Also, records of his travels indicate that he visited Rajagriha in the capital of the kingdom of Magadha more than one hundred twenty times; that he visited Vaishali, the capital of the kingdom of Vriji, forty-nine times; that he visited Kapilavastu, where he grew up, thirty-one times; and that he visited the kingdom of Kaushambi nineteen times.

Each site was separated by hundreds of miles. And, of course, walking was the only mode of transportation available. In his final propagation tour immediately before his death, he covered as many as four hundred miles. It seems to me likely that Shakyamuni's example in "never for a moment" neglecting the Buddha's work, as this record of his travels well illustrates, enabled his disciples to sense just how wonderful it is to be alive, to savor the magnificence of life itself.

In general, Buddhism is viewed as a static religion, epitomized by the image of a meditating or sitting Buddha. But the actual Shakyamuni was quite different. The true image of Shakyamuni is that of a dynamic, walking Buddha, an active Buddha.

The Buddha is another name for a person of unceasing effort. The Buddha continuously takes action to create happiness for people and to liberate them from any kind of authoritarianism. "I have never for a moment neglected" describes this aspect of dynamic action and struggle.

Nichiren, too, led a life of "never for a moment" neglecting the Buddha's work. He surpassed even Shakyamuni in his capacity to propagate the teaching while enduring difficulties. From the time he boldly proclaimed Nam-myoho-renge-kyo in 1253, Nichiren struggled without rest for the happiness and peace of all people. His persecution at the hands of the authorities grew particularly severe after he produced his letter of remonstration "On Establishing the Correct Teaching for the Peace of the Land" in 1260.

Nichiren was assailed by repeated storms of persecution. These included the Matsubagayatsu Persecution (1260), the Izu Exile (1261–63), the Komatsubara Persecution (1264), the Tatsunokuchi Persecution (1271) and the Sado Exile (1271–74). Yet, no matter how great the difficulties, Nichiren says, "Not once have I thought of retreat" (WND-2, 465). "The battle goes on even today" (WND-1, 392), he calmly states.

Even in his later years at Mount Minobu, his life was anything but suggestive of retirement. While dwelling in a crude hut, he continued energetically to lecture to his disciples on the Lotus Sutra and other teachings.

With fiery words, he took on the arrogant authorities and religious figures who were leading the people astray. At the same time, he continued to send a stream of warm encouragement to those plunged in suffering. Even if we consider only his extant letters, the sheer volume is unrivaled.

Nichiren, without question, carried out the Buddha's work unceasingly, never neglecting it even for a moment. "From the time that I was born until today," he says, "I have never known a moment's ease" (WND-1, 965).

That is not all. Nichiren inscribed the Gohonzon and eternalized the practice of immense compassion. He opened the path for the salvation of all people of the Latter Day of the Law. He writes, "If Nichiren's compassion is truly great and encompassing, Nam-myoho-renge-kyo will spread for ten thousand years and more, for all eternity" (WND-1, 736). There is no greater example of someone never for a moment neglecting the Buddha's work. How fortunate we are, indeed!

Regarding "I have never for a moment neglected," President Toda once said humorously:

> While we have our Sundays, there is no such thing as a Sunday for the Gohonzon. It would be really inconvenient if the Gohonzon were to say to us, "I'm taking today off." Or if we were to develop a stomachache at night and go to chant to the Gohonzon but found that it was sleeping and would not wake up.

He also remarked:

> It is only natural that people such as us should spend an hour or two working for others. Even so, our efforts amount to no more than a hundred-millionth or a quadrillionth of the work of the Buddha. Looking at things in this light we cannot help trying harder.

Setting off to attend a meeting or give guidance, President Toda often repeated to himself, "I have never for a moment neglected." Even if he was tired or physically weak, he would go out all the same, saying, "The Buddha never for a moment neglected his work. Since I have dedicated my life to this mission, I must also do my best." His words still reverberate in my heart.

My attitude is the same. As a follower of Nichiren Daishonin and as a disciple of Josei Toda, I have prayed and taken action for kosen-rufu without rest.

Buddhism is a practice of assiduity. Because this spirit of never for a moment neglecting the Buddha's work exists in the SGI, we have realized our present great development. For leaders of kosen-rufu, there is no standing still.

That said, leaders should not push members unreasonably when they are fatigued or in need of rest. The secret of never for a moment neglecting the Buddha's work is to help people conduct themselves in a value-creating, rhythmical and joyful manner. Again, leaders should always think about and earnestly consider what they can do to help everyone advance with burning hope. This single-minded determination is comparable to the Buddha's attitude in never for a moment neglecting the Buddha's work.

Let us struggle forward, not anxiously but with composure. What does "I have never for a moment neglected" mean for us? It is to always struggle courageously and in high spirits. No matter the waves or adverse winds we encounter, we should stand up and face them with a fighting spirit. Doing so accords with this passage.

Having such a spirit directs our lives toward health and longevity. "I will fulfill my mission for the sake of others and for society." When we so determine, we are living the eternal way of the Buddha as characterized by "I have never for a moment neglected" in the "Life Span" chapter.

▪ 19 ▪

Nyo ze ga jo-butsu irai. Jindai ku-on. Jumyo muryo. Asogi ko. Joju
fu-metsu. Sho zen-nanshi. Ga hon gyo bo-satsu do. Sho jo jumyo.
Kon yu mi jin. Bu bai jo shu.

"Thus, since I attained Buddhahood, an extremely long period of time
has passed. My life span is an immeasurable number of asamkhya kalpas,
and during that time I have constantly abided here without ever entering
extinction. Good men, originally I practiced the bodhisattva way, and the
life span that I acquired then has yet to come to an end but will last twice
the number of years that have already passed." (LSOC, 267–68)

THE TEXT, from this point on, is directed primarily to future
generations.

On the surface, "Life Span" would appear to be explaining the
remote past of numberless major world system dust particle kalpas
ago. In actuality, however, the concern of the chapter lies with the
future.

Nichiren says that the "Life Span" chapter was "preached entirely
for the people who live in the world after the passing of the Buddha.
And among such people, it was preached for Nichiren and his followers, who are living today in the Latter Day of the Law" (WND-2,
487). He also says: "Although the Buddha seems to have preached
his original enlightenment here for the people of his lifetime, when

we examine this sutra passage we can see that he in fact intended it primarily for the people after his passing" (WND-2, 487).

In *Words and Phrases of the Lotus Sutra*, T'ien-t'ai comments that this passage of the Lotus Sutra clarifies that throughout the future the Buddha's great power of benefit will always exist in the world and benefit living beings.

Thus, the true intention of "Life Span" is the salvation of people in the future. Let us try to confirm this based on the passage itself.

It begins, "Thus, since I attained Buddhahood, an extremely long period of time has passed. My life span is an immeasurable number of asamkhya kalpas" (LSOC, 267).

This summarizes the gist of what has been taught in "Life Span" up to this point. Namely, an inconceivably long period of time, known as numberless major world system dust particle kalpas, has elapsed since Shakyamuni became a Buddha. Furthermore, the passage clarifies that the Buddha enlightened since the remote past has "constantly abided here without ever entering extinction." This is certainly directed toward the future. Precisely because the Buddha abides in this world continuously, throughout past, present and future, the Buddha can appear in any time or place where there are people of seeking spirit. The Buddha's activities to lead people to enlightenment continue unabated from the remote past, through the present of Shakyamuni's lifetime [in India], and on into the future after his passing. They continue eternally over the three existences.

"Life Span" identifies the actual Buddha who constantly abides in this world throughout past, present and future to save all people of the Latter Day of the Law. This Buddha dwells even in the world of the Latter Day—a world held to have no Buddha and in which, it was thought, the Law would become extinct.

In view of this, it is clear that the concept of the Latter Day of the Law in Buddhism is not describing the end of the world. Actually, nothing could be more antithetical to Buddhism than an apocalyptic doctrine designed to stir up feelings of unease. Buddhism exists to allow people to have peace of mind arising from the very depths of their being.

Next, Shakyamuni says, "Originally I practiced the bodhisattva way, and the life span that I acquired then has yet to come to an end but will last twice the number of years that have already passed." With this, it becomes still clearer that "Life Span" is a teaching for the future.

Shakyamuni explains that the life span he attained as a result of his bodhisattva practice in the remote past not only encompasses the interval since numberless major world system dust particle kalpas in the past but will continue in the future for an interval twice as long.

In other words, the Buddha enlightened since the remote past continues taking action to lead people to enlightenment over an incredibly long period equal to twice the length of time described as numberless major world system dust particle kalpas. This clarifies that the true intention of the "Life Span" chapter is to enable future generations to attain enlightenment.

The Buddhism of the True Cause

These sutra passages directed toward the future reveal the crucial doctrine of the mystic principles of true cause and true effect.

True cause and true effect are the cause and effect of Shakyamuni's attainment of enlightenment in the remote past. Shakyamuni's bodhisattva practice in the remote past is the true cause. The result, his attaining Buddhahood, is the true effect.

The true cause is the fundamental cause for attaining Buddhahood. It is the source of happiness. This cause lies in the practice Shakyamuni carried out in the remote past. Because it is mystic and beyond comprehension, it is called the "mystic principle of the true cause."

From the standpoint of the sutra's literal meaning, the mystic principle of the true cause is indicated by the statement "originally I practiced the bodhisattva way, and the life span that I acquired then has yet to come to an end but will last twice the number of years that have already passed."

"The life span that I acquired then has yet to come to an end" indicates that Shakyamuni's wisdom, cultivated by his carrying out bodhisattva practices in the remote past, is immeasurable and inexhaustible.

The bodhisattva path, that is, the practice to benefit others, is the very path for polishing wisdom and developing good fortune. A richness of heart, a dedication to the happiness of others, is the key to cultivating inexhaustible wisdom.

If we juxtapose the nine worlds with the world of Buddhahood, the Shakyamuni who carries out bodhisattva practice represents ordinary beings of the nine worlds. The lives of beings of the nine worlds are endowed with the life span of immeasurable wisdom; it is their ultimate reality. That's another reason why the true cause of enlightenment is called "mystic." Buddhism's purpose is to enable people to develop the original mystic life that all possess.

The true effect is the actual state of Buddhahood that the Buddha enlightened since the remote past attained as a result of practicing the true cause. Because this state of life is difficult to understand and, hence, mystic, it is called the "mystic principle of the true effect." According to T'ien-t'ai, the true effect is to attain a state of life pervaded with the four virtues: eternity, happiness, true self and purity.

This state of life is as expansive and pure as a cloudless sky. Moreover, it is a state of indestructible and unshakable happiness.

In terms of the sutra's literal meaning, the passage "since I attained Buddhahood, an extremely long period of time has passed. My life span is an immeasurable number of asamkhya kalpas, and during that time I have constantly abided here without ever entering extinction" clarifies the mystic principle of the true effect. It explains that the Buddha who attained the true effect of enlightenment in the remote past constantly abides here in this world without ever entering extinction. In short, the doctrine of true cause and true effect in "Life Span" reveals that not only is the life of the world of Buddhahood—the true effect—eternal, but so is the life of the nine worlds—the true cause.

Because the life of the nine worlds also constantly exists in the Buddha's life, the Buddha can continue, even after attaining enlightenment, to carry out bodhisattva practices to lead beings of the nine worlds to enlightenment. Actual enlightenment in the remote past does not mean that the Buddha, having gained the "true effect," ceases to carry out the bodhisattva practices that are the "true cause." Nor does it mean that the Buddha extinguishes the life of the nine worlds within his being and departs for another world, a world of Buddhas.

Both the nine worlds and the world of Buddhahood are eternally present. This is the true aspect of life revealed in the Buddha's having actually attained enlightenment in the remote past. In this way, Shakyamuni clarified for the happiness of the people in the future the fundamental principles for attaining Buddhahood—the principle of the mutual possession of the Ten Worlds and the principle of three thousand realms in a single moment of life. That is the crucial point.

In "The Opening of the Eyes," Nichiren says that the doctrine of true cause and true effect "reveals that the nine worlds are all present in beginningless Buddhahood and that Buddhahood is inherent in the beginningless nine worlds. This is the true mutual possession of the Ten Worlds, the true hundred worlds and thousand factors, the true three thousand realms in a single moment of life" (WND-1, 235).

"The beginningless nine worlds" and "beginningless Buddhahood" indicate true cause and true effect, respectively. Both exist in the single entity of the Buddha who attained enlightenment in the remote past. This entity of the mutual possession of the Ten Worlds and of three thousand realms in a single moment of life constantly abides in this world without entering extinction.

From a literal standpoint, however, the sutra indicates that the life of the Buddha enlightened since the remote past (i.e., the true effect) encompasses not only the true effect but also the true cause. In other words, in Shakyamuni's Buddhism, emphasis is placed on the true effect.

By contrast, Nichiren Buddhism emphasizes the true cause. The ordinary beings of the nine worlds are seen as central and not subsidiary. This is because those who need liberation in the Latter Day are ordinary people. For this reason, we need to look again at the passage expressing the mystic principle of the true cause, "originally I practiced the bodhisattva way."

Just what, ultimately, is the driving force that enabled Shakyamuni the common mortal to attain a life span of immeasurable wisdom as a result of carrying out bodhisattva practices in the remote past? It is none other than Nam-myoho-renge-kyo. Nam-myoho-renge-kyo is hidden in the depths of the statement "originally I practiced the bodhisattva way."

In "The Opening of the Eyes," Nichiren says, "The doctrine of three thousand realms in a single moment of life is found in only one place, hidden in the depths of the 'Life Span' chapter of the essential teaching of the Lotus Sutra" (WND-1, 224). "The depths of the 'Life Span' chapter," more precisely, means the depths of the phrase "originally I practiced the bodhisattva way."

Shakyamuni the common mortal of the remote past attained Buddhahood as a result of practicing Nam-myoho-renge-kyo. As the Daishonin indicates when he refers to "this wonderful single Law [*myoho*] that simultaneously possesses both cause and effect [*renge*]" (WND-1, 421), both the true cause and the true effect are contained in Nam-myoho-renge-kyo.

And, as suggested by the principle of the simultaneity of cause and effect, both the true cause and the true effect exist in each moment of resolute faith in the single Law of Nam-myoho-renge-kyo.

This mystic moment of life is the ultimate meaning of Nichiren's teaching of the mystic principle of the true cause; it's the culmination of the doctrine of three thousand realms in a single moment of life. Both the true cause and the true effect exist in the lives of ordinary people. A change in a person's moment of life fundamentally changes everything.

Nichiren Buddhism, based on this deepest perspective of the Lotus Sutra, recognizes the existence of true cause and true effect in a single moment, thereby teaching us a vitally essential way of living. Namely, it shows us how to base ourselves always on the source of life itself and from there initiate fresh progress.

From moment to moment, we experience happiness and sadness, suffering and joy. The condition we experience in the present moment of life is an effect produced by causes we created in past moments. This is relatively easy to grasp. But at the same time, our lives at the present moment are also the cause for future effects. While this makes sense theoretically, it is difficult to actually live with this awareness.

What will come about in the future depends on our present moment of life.

President Toda said:

We who practice the Buddhism of the mystic principle of the true cause view the continuous stream of reality occurring in our lives at each instant as the cause for the future. To put it another way, we determine to make the present reality the cause for the future.

He also said:

In the daily life of someone who firmly believes in the Gohonzon, daily events are activated as the pure causes rooted in the remote past. Boundless life force wells forth in such a person due to the benefit of the Gohonzon.

Therefore, when this cause is translated into effect, the person is sure to experience good results.

True cause and true effect are both contained in our lives at each instant. This is the simultaneity of cause and effect. Through our single-minded faith, therefore, we can turn everything that arises in the course of our daily lives—even misfortune—into a true cause grounded in the remote past, a fundamental cause for our happiness. We can set out in all endeavors based on the pure wellspring of life. And as a result, we can direct our entire selves toward establishing a state of life of unshakable happiness. This is what it means to "live based on the mystic principle of the true cause."

The Importance of the Present Moment

The spirit of the Buddhism of the true cause finds expression in the practice of cultivating respect for the dignity of life.

It is the passage "originally I practiced the bodhisattva way" that directly indicates this. As I've said, "I" indicates Shakyamuni the ordinary human being—just like us—who carried out bodhisattva practices in the remote past. He was by no means superhuman. "Remote past" means the source or wellspring of life. Shakyamuni the practitioner of the true cause represents the ordinary people of beginningless time who base themselves on the wellspring of life.

Nichiren Buddhism takes Shakyamuni the practitioner of the true cause as the object of devotion.

This Shakyamuni is identified with Nichiren, the original Buddha of the Latter Day of the Law. This is the principle of the remote past is itself the Latter Day of the Law. This is clear from such statements by Nichiren as: "The practice that Nichiren now carries out does not differ in the least from the conduct of the [common mortal Shakyamuni] at the stage of hearing the name and words of the truth in the remote past" (GZ, 863); and "There is no difference of superior and inferior between Shakyamuni's practices in the remote past and Nichiren's practices today" (GZ, 864).

The stage of hearing the name and words of the truth refers to someone who has embraced faith in the Mystic Law. Nichikan explains that we identify Shakyamuni the practitioner of the true cause with the Daishonin, and the remote past with the Latter Day, because there is absolutely no difference in the practices or stages of the two.

In either case, "practice" means the practice of embracing the Mystic Law. And "stage" means the stage of practice of an ordinary person at the stage of hearing the name and words of the truth, that is, one who has taken faith in the Mystic Law.

The statement that Nichiren and Shakyamuni are the same in their practice and stage means that the practice of thoroughly embracing the Mystic Law as a human being is the same, whether in the remote past or in the Latter Day.

The practice of upholding the Mystic Law is mystic and incomprehensible. That's because it contains both the true cause and the true effect of attaining Buddhahood—that is to say, the fundamental principle for becoming happy. This is the mystic principle of the true cause.

In the Latter Day of the Law, therefore, Nichiren, who is identical with Shakyamuni the practitioner of the true cause, should be revered as the object of devotion.

The Practice of Respecting Others

What is the bodhisattva way that Shakyamuni practiced in the remote past? It is indicated in part by the practice of Bodhisattva Never Disparaging. Bodhisattva Never Disparaging was Shakyamuni's name in a previous existence, when he carried out bodhisattva practices during a decadent age following the death of the Buddha Awesome Sound King. This story is described in the Lotus Sutra.

Regarding Bodhisattva Never Disparaging, Nichiren says: "The word 'I' here refers to Shakyamuni Buddha when he was carrying out the true cause of his original enlightenment. This passage concerning how the Buddha 'originally practiced the bodhisattva way' refers to the practice of the bodhisattva Never Disparaging" (OTT, 161).

In other words, the practice of Bodhisattva Never Disparaging corresponds to the bodhisattva way of Shakyamuni the practitioner of the true cause.

Whenever he met someone, Bodhisattva Never Disparaging would make a gesture of reverence to the person and exclaim, "I have profound reverence for you." This was because he recognized that everyone could become a Buddha. His practice was based on feelings of the most profound sympathy for his fellow human beings.

Respecting others is the supreme practice for cultivating appreciation for life's dignity, and it was an important part of the bodhisattva way Shakyamuni practiced in the remote past. Bodhisattva Never Disparaging single-mindedly persevered in his practice of respecting the dignity of life.

But he lived in a corrupt and impure age. People couldn't understand the nobility of his actions. A defiled age is one in which the arrogant sneer at the truly great and shamelessly flaunt their own paltry wisdom to make themselves appear greater than they are. Such foolish people persecute a person of justice, who refuses to compromise his convictions.

People beat Bodhisattva Never Disparaging with staves and drove him away with stones. Under such circumstances, he adopted an interesting strategy. When he was driven off, he would retreat a little way but would not leave. When he was out of reach of the sticks and rocks, he would turn around and return to his practice of veneration, saying, "I have profound reverence for you."

Bodhisattva Never Disparaging was very flexible in his actions. He was neither submissive nor confrontational. He was not in the least cowardly, nor was he zealously heroic or motivated by a tragic spirit.

Within his flexibility, he possessed great strength. No matter how great the persecutions he encountered, he absolutely never wavered in his conviction. He never abandoned the philosophy in which he believed. He never backslid in his faith.

In a sense, upholding the Mystic Law means to put one's conviction into practice. This became the cause for Bodhisattva Never Disparaging to attain Buddhahood, and he was later reborn as Shakyamuni Buddha.

This practice of Bodhisattva Never Disparaging—gentle, persistent and among the people—is the true cause for attaining Buddhahood. It seems to me that his practice must typify Shakyamuni's original practice of the bodhisattva way in the remote past.

The practice of discussing and praising the Mystic Law among people deepens an individual's own faith in the Law and ultimately enables him or her to attain the true effect of Buddhahood. Practice is itself mystic.

President Makiguchi said: "Just as people who don't have daily lives won't understand the principles of daily life, those who lead lives of medium or minor good cannot possibly understand the way of life of great good. Unless people practice, they cannot possibly cherish true faith."

Only when we carry out bodhisattva practice can we understand true faith. Only if we practice can we comprehend the profound significance and manifest the immeasurable benefit of faith.

A way of life based on the principle of the true cause is to practice among the people without putting on airs. There is no need whatsoever for such people to get all dressed up, as it were. Honest and straightforward, they give others peace of mind and plant the seeds of happiness in others' hearts through their unaffected actions. This is the bodhisattva practice of the true cause.

Nichiren is the Buddha of the mystic principle of the true cause. Even though he was the original Buddha, he always practiced the bodhisattva way as an ordinary person. From start to finish, he struggled as a common mortal. The ordinary person is supreme. This is the essence of Nichiren Buddhism.

After he had cast aside his transient role as Bodhisattva Superior Practices and, during the Tatsunokuchi Persecution, revealed his true identity as the original Buddha, Nichiren did not manifest any special physical characteristics, such as the thirty-two features. Nonetheless, the Law of beginningless time shone brightly in his heart. And he carried out the actions of the original Buddha for the people of the Latter Day. Nichiren manifested ultimate humanity. This was his "casting off the transient and revealing the true."

Our Buddhist practice is not one of revering the true effect. Since embracing the Mystic Law is in itself enlightenment, when we embrace the Gohonzon we can immediately manifest the world of Buddhahood in our lives. The bodhisattva practice of the Buddhism of the true cause is to direct ourselves toward the nine worlds while basing ourselves on the life of Buddhahood. It is, it might be said, to dive headlong into the mundane reality of society dominated by the nine worlds, while basing ourselves on the life of Buddhahood.

Our practice entails constantly going back and forth between the practice for oneself of doing gongyo and chanting Nam-myoho-renge-kyo and the practice for others of spreading the Mystic Law. The key to manifesting the world of Buddhahood lies in this continuing activity.

Accordingly, the Buddhism of the true cause exists in the way of life, the practice, of ceaselessly striving to improve one's immediate, everyday surroundings and carry the age and society forward. The principles that faith equals daily life and Buddhism manifests itself in society are thus central to Nichiren Buddhism.

Now Is the Time to Take Action

Nichijun, the sixty-fifth chief priest of Taiseki-ji, as I have mentioned many times, discussed the spirit of the Buddhism of the true cause as follows: "If people think of it merely as characterizing the Buddha's aspect in teaching others and fail to realize that it is the model for their own lives, then the teaching of the Buddhism of sowing of the true cause is dead."

These are my sentiments exactly. Discussion of Buddhism divorced from real life destroys the spirit of the original Buddha.

Nichijun also remarked, "It could be said that the Buddhism of sowing of the true cause means to always have a forward-looking spirit." This, too, I have said repeatedly. The spirit of the Buddhism of the true cause exists in a heart brimming with hope for the future.

When we have the sense that "Now is the time!" or "It's my efforts from now on that count!" we can continually challenge our present circumstances with a forward-looking attitude. This is what it means to live based on the "mystic principle of the true cause." I hope all of you will attain such a way of life.

Once the brilliant sun of the "mystic principle of the true cause" rises in our hearts, the causality of fate or karma originating in the past rapidly loses its glow, like the stars and other celestial bodies at daybreak.

Time and again, President Toda explained that when we dedicate ourselves to the Mystic Law, the causes and effects created in the interim all disappear and the "common mortal of beginningless time" appears.

The common mortal of beginningless time is another name for the

Bodhisattvas of the Earth. The Bodhisattvas of the Earth are born of their own volition in this corrupt world to lead suffering people to happiness. Of their own free will, they position themselves where they can practice to make good causes, and they are born with a karmic destiny that they themselves have chosen. They do this to enact the drama of transforming destiny and proving the greatness of Buddhism.

Therefore, while we each have unique destinies, by exerting ourselves for kosen-rufu based on faith, we can use all the circumstances we encounter to lessen karmic retribution and transform destiny. Nichiren says, "The sufferings of hell will vanish instantly" (WND-1, 199). When we embrace the Mystic Law, our karmic impediments cease to be karmic impediments.

When we embrace the Gohonzon, we can acquire in our lives both the Buddha's practices (causes) and benefits (effects). Karmic impediments originating in the past all become the key for us to open the great state of life of Buddhahood. Earthly desires themselves become enlightenment, and we can create comfort and tranquillity in suffering and hardship.

The world of Buddhahood contains the nine worlds of suffering, and the world of Buddhahood can only become manifest in concert with the reality of the nine worlds. Only thus does the true aspect of life that is the mutual possession of the Ten Worlds become apparent.

The important thing is to not shrink back in the face of hardship. We must not have a weak spirit full of lamentation or doubt. When we have a powerful, forward-looking inner resolve, we can change all aspects of our existence and manifest a wonderful state of life of indestructible happiness. This is based on the principle of three thousand realms in a single moment of life.

Whether experiencing suffering or joy, we need to continue chanting the Mystic Law with the prayer in our hearts to attain Buddhahood in this lifetime. No matter what happens, we need to continue advancing a step at a time toward kosen-rufu, in high spirits and with robust hearts. Those who maintain such a strong mind of faith moment by moment will be embraced by the original Buddha's immense and boundless compassion. This is the wonderful essence of the Buddhism of the "mystic principle of the true cause."

Shakyamuni tells us:

> The past should not be followed after, the future not desired.
> What is past is got rid of and the future has not come.
> But whoever has vision now here, now there, of a present thing,
> Knowing that it is immovable, unshakable, let him cultivate it.
> Swelter at the task this very day.[8]

Most important is right now—the present moment. Our present inner resolve, our determination, enables us to sever the bonds of karmic causality with the strength arising from within and enter the sure path of happiness.

Faith grounded in the true cause always emerges from the source of life itself while aiming toward a state of eternal happiness and a supreme way of life. The spirit of the Buddhism of the true cause is the spirit of limitless hope and eternal progress.

Therefore, each day we return to the original source of life, and from there we begin to advance anew. Reciting the sutra and chanting Nam-myoho-renge-kyo is the secret teaching for returning to the state of beginningless time. Every day, we set forth from that eternal origin. What enables us to continually do so is faith of the Buddhism of the true cause.

·20·

Nen kon hi jitsu metsu-do. Ni ben sho gon. To shu metsu-do.
Nyorai i ze hoben. Kyoke shujo. Sho-i sha ga. Nyaku buk-ku-ju
o se. Haku-toku shi nin. Fu shu zengon. Bingu gesen. Ton-jaku
go-yoku. Nyu o oku-so. Moken mo chu. Nyakken nyorai. Jo zai
fu-metsu. Ben ki kyoshi. Ni e endai. Fu no sho o. Nan-zo shi so.
Kugyo shi shin.

"Now, however, although in fact I do not actually enter extinction,
I announce that I am going to adopt the course of extinction. This is
an expedient means that the Thus Come One uses to teach and
convert living beings.

"Why do I do this? Because if the Buddha remains in the world for
a long time, those persons with shallow virtue will fail to plant good roots
but, living in poverty and lowliness, will become attached to the five
desires and be caught in the net of deluded thoughts and imaginings.
If they see that the Thus Come One is constantly in the world and never
enters extinction, they will grow arrogant and selfish, or become
discouraged and neglectful. They will fail to realize how difficult it is to
encounter the Buddha and will not approach him with a respectful
and reverent mind." (LSOC, 268)

THIS PASSAGE EXPLAINS why the Buddha enters nirvana even
though his life span is in fact eternal. This is thematically related
to the passage "as an expedient means I appear to enter nirvana"

(LSOC, 271), which we will study later in the verse section of the chapter.

Entering nirvana was the ultimate expedient means Shakyamuni employed to guide people to attain the supreme state of Buddhahood. The teaching of the "Life Span" chapter is the crystallization of Shakyamuni's spiritual battle to engrave the Buddha's wisdom, the Buddha's compassion and the Buddha's struggle in the lives of his disciples and cause them to advance along the same path as he.

If the Buddha were to remain in the world forever, then people of shallow virtue would likely be content to lead spiritually impoverished and craven lives, abandon any attempt to accumulate good causes and become ensnared in mistaken beliefs. They would undoubtedly succumb to arrogance and indolence, unable to "realize how difficult it is to encounter the Buddha" and to "approach him with a respectful and reverent mind."

Therefore, the Buddha enters nirvana as an expedient to cause people to arouse a seeking mind. The Buddha is the teacher of the supreme path. He appears and then enters nirvana to arouse in people a seeking spirit for this supreme path, a desire to advance and improve themselves.

If the Buddha were always in the world, then disciples, thinking, "The World-Honored One will always be here," would relax, become lazy and forget the path of self-improvement. Under such circumstances, they could not possibly attain Buddhahood.

Although at first they would revere the Buddha and exert themselves in their practice, in time they would become used to having the Buddha always in their environment, succumb to inertia and lose their sense of excitement and appreciation in being able to advance with the Buddha. Increasingly, they would give in to small-mindedness and neglect their Buddhist practice. Such is the tendency of the human heart. It may well be that Shakyamuni sensed this in the attitude of his disciples.

And so, to cause his disciples to "realize how difficult it is to encounter the Buddha" and to "approach him with a respectful and reverent mind," Shakyamuni taught, as an expedient means, that the Buddha enters nirvana. To realize how difficult it is to encounter the Buddha and to possess a spirit of respect and reverence is the true wellspring of faith. This means having a sense of joy, excitement and appreciation in having met the Buddha and a spirit of veneration toward the Buddha.

From one standpoint, Buddhism is a philosophy for helping people become self-sufficient; it explains how people can develop themselves through their own effort. We cannot develop a truly profound state of life if we have to always depend on the mentor.

At the same time, Buddhism is a teaching of respect for human beings. Through our spirit and actions to seek the Buddha who—as a human being—attained the supreme state, we can develop in ourselves the same vast state of life. This is the principle of the oneness of mentor and disciple in Buddhism.

It is extremely difficult for human beings to be both self-reliant and truly respectful of others. Those with a strong independent spirit often have an equally strong tendency to look down on others. And those who can respect others may tend to depend on them to such an extent that they lack self-reliance. It must be said that both cases represent a lack of maturity.

The scholars and leaders from throughout the world with whom I have formed friendships are highly independent and make tremendous efforts in their respective fields. Moreover, when you meet them, you find them humble with a refreshing character filled with respect for others. In people of the highest caliber, self-sufficiency and respect for others are perfectly combined.

Buddhism is the path that enables people to develop the supreme character of a Buddha. It could be said that many concerns of modern society come down to issues of humanistic education and the cultivation of character as expounded in Buddhism.

The sutra passage we are studying here speaks of people being "attached to the five desires" (LSOC, 268). It seems to me that this accurately describes our situation today. We live in a society of desire, as it were.

A society that does not seek lofty ideals and a noble way of life will gradually be undermined by base desires. This lack of rectitude in adult society directly and negatively impacts children. It would seem that "attached to the five desires and . . . caught in the net of deluded thoughts and imaginings" sums up the ills of people today.

The fundamental cause of society's various problems, including the impoverishment of education, lies in the lack of a philosophy and principles for correctly controlling and guiding the five desires.

Shakyamuni taught that he would enter nirvana to cure people of these ills. He fully grasped the human heart's tendency to be inevitably drawn toward the shallow. So he expounded his teaching to guide people's hearts toward the life state of the Buddha, which towers as high as the magnificent Himalayas.

The great mission of Buddhism lies in this: cultivating and developing character.

In light of this passage's spirit, to desire only to be constantly together with the mentor is not the way of a disciple. The way of a disciple lies rather in embracing the mentor's teaching and struggling with all one's might as a self-sufficient practitioner. This is the path of a true disciple.

Among Josei Toda's disciples, some merely indulged themselves in his vast mercy. Some, because they were close to him, misused his influence and behaved arrogantly. Some left when things got difficult, scurrilously mocking him for his business failure or on some other account.

These were all people who, in the words of the sutra, had become "arrogant and selfish." They had little appreciation for having encountered such a rare mentor. They did not "realize how difficult it is to encounter" such a person, nor did they possess "respectful and reverent minds."

President Toda was the greatest mentor a person could have. Realizing this most profoundly, I have lived up to the strict spirit of the oneness of mentor and disciple. As a result, today nothing and no one can defeat me. And the Soka Gakkai has greatly developed just as President Toda envisioned—no, to an even greater extent. I want my friends in the youth division in particular to deeply engrave in their lives this history of solemn struggle and triumph.

The crucial point is our determination to inherit, completely, the mentor's spirit. This is our prayer: to wage a great struggle to succeed with this spirit. This is the spirit Shakyamuni tries to explain in this sutra passage.

Shakyamuni's teaching to not depend on others and to maintain a seeking mind might well be characterized as strict. At the same time, we cannot help being profoundly moved by Shakyamuni's mercy, deep as the ocean, to elevate everyone to his own state of life, that of the Buddha.

"My disciples, develop a dignified self." This is the spiritual cry of Shakyamuni, the great leader of humankind.

Our Purpose Is to Lead Wonderful Lives

Expanding on this idea of entering nirvana, of dying, we can say that death, in enabling us to sense life's wonder, is an expedient means for us to lead a rich and fulfilled existence.

President Toda lectured on this passage of the sutra:

> Nothing would be more fearful than to not die. It would be one thing if this concerned only human beings. But if all living beings were to not die, the consequences would be truly calamitous.
>
> Suppose that cats and dogs and mice and even octopuses all were to not die. This would create great problems. If nothing were to die, then what would happen? Even if

someone or something were beaten or killed or run over by a train or deprived of food, it would not die. The result would be pandemonium . . .

Thus, for people to not die would be problematic. On the other hand, it would also be problematic if we knew when we were going to die. If we knew, for example, that we had only three days left, then we would not have time, for example, to sit around like this listening to a lecture.

Death is necessary. And the fact that we are not aware of when we will die with any precision makes life interesting. This is mystic. And it is because of the mystic nature of our existence that we come to take faith in the Gohonzon. Life is, in fact, very interesting.

These words reveal President Toda's great and profound insight into the nature of life and death.

Because we die, we can appreciate the wonder of life. We can savor the great joy of being alive. This is truly one of life's essential truths.

It would be pointless to be so filled with the fear of death that, upon falling sick or being injured, we immediately despair and become depressed. At the same time, however, I can't believe those who claim they don't mind risking their lives or who say they are not in the least afraid of dying. This is nothing more than bravado.

The most fearful thing of all is inner, or spiritual, death—losing the desire to lead a truly fulfilled and meaningful life. Norman Cousins, who was dubbed the "conscience of America," came to the following conclusion based on his experiences of overcoming a number of grave illnesses: "Death is not the ultimate tragedy of life. The ultimate tragedy is depersonalization."[9]

No one can escape death. Precisely because of this, when people resolve to live each instant with all their might, to make the present moment shine by living true to themselves and leading genuinely humane existences, they can summon immense strength. At the same time, they can display a considerate spirit toward others.

Herein lies the wondrous nature of life and the Middle Way. Buddhism is the philosophy that teaches this essential way of life.

▪ 21 ▪

Ze ko nyorai. I hoben setsu. Bi-ku to chi. Sho-bus͡shus-se. Nan ka
chigu. Sho-i sha ga. Sho haku-toku nin. Ka muryo. Hyaku sen man
nok-ko. Waku u ken butsu. Waku fu ken sha. I shiji ko. Ga sa ze gon.
Sho bi-ku. Nyorai nan ka tokken. Shi shujo to. Mon nyo ze go. Hit͡ to
sho o. Nanzo shi so. Shin ne renbo. Katsu-go o butsu. Ben shu zengon.
Ze ko nyorai. Sui fu jitsu metsu. Ni gon metsu-do. U zen-nanshi.
Sho-butsu nyo-rai. Ho kai nyo ze. I do shu-jo. Kai jitsu fu ko.

"Therefore as an expedient means the Thus Come One says: 'Monks,
you should know that it is a rare thing to live at a time when one of the
Buddhas appears in the world.' Why does he do this? Because persons
of shallow virtue may pass immeasurable hundreds, thousands, ten
thousands, millions of kalpas with some of them chancing to see a Buddha
and others never seeing one at all. For this reason I say to them: 'Monks,
the Thus Come One is hard to get to see.' When living beings hear these
words, they are certain to realize how difficult it is to encounter a Buddha.
In their minds they will harbor a longing and will thirst to gaze upon the
Buddha, and then they will work to plant good roots. Therefore the
Thus Come One, though in truth he does not enter extinction, speaks
of passing into extinction.

   "Good men, the Buddhas, the Thus Come Ones, all act in such a
manner. They act in order to save living beings, so what they say is true
and not false." (LSOC, 268)

THIS PASSAGE EXPLAINS how irreplaceable and supremely worthy is a life that forms a connection with the Buddha. It is most rare to live when a Buddha is in the world. People with little accumulated merit may fail to see a Buddha, the passage says, even with the passing of "immeasurable hundreds, thousands, ten thousands, millions of kalpas." This suggests just how difficult it is to form a connection with Buddhism.

Shakyamuni says, "Monks, the Thus Come One is hard to get to see"—can we not envision Shakyamuni boldly conveying these words as his will for the future?

Buddhism teaches the importance of one's debt to the mentor, who literally channels every ounce of energy into training disciples to enable them to overcome arrogance and dependency and advance along the correct and grand path of faith equals daily life. This passage brings home the disciples' immense debt of gratitude to the Buddha.

Upon hearing these words, Shakyamuni's disciples no doubt aroused a genuine seeking spirit, solemnly determining to rectify their attitude in Buddhist practice and to receive with their entire being the teaching of the mentor so rarely encountered.

Possessing such a seeking spirit produces "good roots" in our lives and enables us to establish a state of indestructible happiness. By manifesting such a seeking mind, "persons of shallow virtue" become persons of merit and virtue. This is thanks to the Buddha's great compassion and constitutes "salvation" in the truest sense. If the Buddha raised people to be dependent on him, it would not contribute in the least to their actual liberation from suffering. Genuine salvation is accomplished only by raising people of correct faith, that is, people possessing both self-reliance and an earnest mind to seek the way. Only thus can the Buddha's desire to liberate all people from suffering be fulfilled.

Chanting Nam-myoho-renge-kyo Is the Greatest Good Cause

In terms of the teaching hidden in the depths, the Buddha is the Nam-myoho-renge-kyo Thus Come One, or Nichiren Daishonin himself. And "persons of shallow virtue" indicates the people of the Latter Day of the Law.

Nichiren prayed for all people of the Latter Day to become people of merit and virtue, and he entered extinction as an expedient means to guide them along this path. Through his passing, he taught the people of the Latter Day the truth that "the Thus Come One is hard to get to see."

And for all those who could not meet him, Nichiren manifested the great life of Nam-myoho-renge-kyo—his true identity—in the form of the Gohonzon, which he bestowed upon all people of the Latter Day. How vast, indeed, is the mercy of the original Buddha!

Accordingly, we should read the passage "In their minds they will harbor a longing and will thirst to gaze upon the Buddha, and then they will work to plant good roots" as describing us, the people of the Latter Day. A mind that harbors a longing for the Buddha and thirsts to gaze upon the Buddha is a mind of strong faith in the Gohonzon. And to plant good roots is to chant the Mystic Law, as indicated in *The Record of the Orally Transmitted Teachings*, "The term 'good roots' refers to the daimoku" (p. 129).

Encountering the Gohonzon is tantamount to meeting the original Buddha. Our having met the Gohonzon is due to a profound and mystic relationship.

Nichiren says:

It is extremely rare to be born as a human being. Not only are you endowed with human form, but you have had the rare fortune to encounter Buddhism. Moreover, out of the Buddha's many teachings, you have encountered the daimoku, or the title, of the Lotus Sutra and become its votary. Truly you are a person who has offered alms to a hundred thousand million Buddhas in his past existences! (WND-I, 993)

We who have encountered the Gohonzon are no longer people of shallow virtue. The original Buddha declares that we are people of great merit and virtue who have formed connections with an incalculable number of Buddhas in the past.

How mystic, indeed, are our lives! What a profound mission we possess! To teach us this, Nichiren Daishonin led a life of great struggle and died as a truly exemplary human being. He conducted himself as he did in order to guide all people; his conduct in every respect qualifies, in the words of the sutra, as "true and not false." SGI members are proving this through their faith.

President Toda once remarked:

> We should deeply appreciate and take pride in our being able to spend the remaining twenty or thirty years, or perhaps forty or fifty years, of our lives filled with joy in having met the Gohonzon, which is rarely encountered even once in millions or tens of millions of years.

Throughout our lives, let us advance with dignity along the path of the Bodhisattvas of the Earth, further deepening our unique relationship with the Buddha and working to accomplish the Buddha's decree.

▪22▪

Hi nyo ro-i. Chi-e so-datsu. Myo ren ho-yaku. Zen ji shubyo. Go nin ta sho shi-soku. Nyaku ju niju. Nai-shi hyaku-shu. I u ji-en. On shi yo-koku.

"Suppose, for example, that there is a skilled physician who is wise and understanding and knows how to compound medicines to effectively cure all kinds of diseases. He has many sons, perhaps ten, twenty, or even a hundred. He goes off to some other land far away to see about a certain affair." (LSOC, 268–69)

THIS IS THE beginning of the famous parable of the Skilled Physician and His Sick Children.

In "Expedient Means," Shakyamuni says, "I have through various causes and various similes widely expounded my teachings" (LSOC, 56). The Buddhist scriptures are indeed replete with parable, allegory and metaphor. To enable people to grasp his profound teaching and make it readily accessible, the Buddha explained it using a variety of brilliantly conceived illustrations and comparisons.

The Greek philosopher Aristotle said: "The greatest thing by far is to be a master of metaphor. It is the one thing that cannot be learnt from others; and it is also a sign of genius, since a good metaphor implies an intuitive perception of the similarity in dissimilars."[10] The Buddha was truly a genius at discourse.

Using common sense illustrations and metaphors to explain things makes it possible to move people's hearts. When people are moved, they can change their state of life. The Buddha's parables are expressions of his compassionate desire to try, by any means available, to help people change themselves and become happy. They are also the crystallization of his wisdom.

In the Lotus Sutra, Shakyamuni's skill as a master at dialogue is fully displayed. There are in fact a great many parables in the Lotus Sutra. Among these, seven are particularly important: These are known as "the seven parables."

Along with the parable of the Skilled Physician and His Sick Children that we are about to study, the seven include: the parable of the Three Carts and the Burning House; the parable of the Wealthy Man and His Poor Son; the parable of the Three Kinds of Medicinal Herbs and Two Kinds of Trees; the parable of the Phantom City and the Treasure Land; the parable of the Jewel in the Robe; and the parable of the Bright Jewel in the Topknot.

Of these seven, only the parable of the Skilled Physician and His Sick Children is expounded in the sutra's essential teaching, or second half. The rest are all contained in the earlier, theoretical teachings.

At this point in "Life Span," the ultimate teaching of the Buddha's eternal life has already been expounded. But that is not in itself sufficient. As I said earlier, the Buddha's true objective is to enable people to practice this supreme teaching themselves and come to fully embody its truth.

As the ultimate expedient he employs toward this end, the Buddha appears to enter extinction. The story of the Skilled Physician and His Sick Children expresses "as an expedient means I appear to enter nirvana" (LSOC, 271) in the form of a parable.

This parable also indicates how, at the time of his extinction, the Buddha expounds the Mystic Law to save the people of later ages. Its aim is to help people in the Latter Day, after the Buddha's passing, understand that it was for them that the Buddha preached the Mystic Law.

The parable begins by introducing the principal characters. There is a great physician who possesses brilliant wisdom and excels in compounding medicines and curing people's illnesses. He has many children, who are said to number "ten, twenty, or even a hundred." Shakyamuni then indicates that the physician goes elsewhere to attend to some matter.

The skilled physician represents Shakyamuni, who attained enlightenment in the remote past. He is a Buddha endowed with infinite wisdom. Compounding medicines symbolizes expounding teachings.

While it seems extraordinary that the physician should have a hundred children, they are meant to represent all people, who are like children to the Buddha.

The physician's journey is a metaphorical description of how Shakyamuni, following his attainment of Buddhahood in the remote past, left this world for an interval in order to appear in other worlds.

The Buddha is often described as the "king of physicians," a physician of unparalleled skill. Just as a physician provides appropriate curative methods according to the condition of the patient, the Buddha understands the most appropriate means for curing people of their sufferings. That is why the Buddha is represented as a physician.

There are various kinds of illnesses. Taking cold medicine for a toothache won't do you any good, nor will taking eye drops to treat a stomachache. A skilled physician thoroughly understands the relationships between medicine and disease.

Some people may feel that all religions are the same, so whichever one they want to practice will be OK. But this would be like saying it's fine to take any medicine to treat any ailment. Wouldn't this be to treat one's life irresponsibly? I believe people should closely examine how their religion affects how it is they lead their lives.

Moreover, the Buddha is not simply a skilled physician; he is the king of physicians. He understands the wonderful medicine for curing fundamental darkness, which is the root cause of all suffering. And this ultimate teaching he left behind for future generations is the Mystic Law hidden in the depths of the "Life Span" chapter.

▪23▪

Sho shi o go. On ta doku-yaku. Yaku hotsu monran. Enden u ji.
Zeji go bu. Gen rai ki ke. Sho shi on doku. Waku shitsu honshin. Waku
fu shis̄ha. Yo ken go bu. Kai dai kangi. Haiki monjin. Zen nan non ki.
Gato guchi. Go buku doku-yaku. Gan ken kuryo. Kyo shi jumyo.

"After he has gone, the children drink some kind of poison that makes
them distraught with pain and they fall writhing to the ground.

"At that time the father returns to his home and finds that his children
have drunk poison. Some are completely out of their minds, while others
are not. Seeing their father from far off, all are overjoyed and kneel down
and entreat him, saying: 'How fine that you have returned safely. We were
foolish and by mistake drank some poison. We beg you to cure us and
let us live out our lives!'" (LSOC, 269)

AFTER THE SKILLED physician departs, his children mistakenly
drink not the medicine prepared by their father but poison produced by someone else. The poison enters their systems and, writhing
in pain, the children fall to the ground.

The father then returns home. Those children who drank only a
small amount of the poison still have their wits about them. But others
who drank a lot already have completely lost their minds.

Even so, amid their pain, the children rejoice to see that their father
has come back. His return must have put their hearts at ease and given
them a profound reassurance.

As I discussed previously, the physician represents the Buddha, and his children, the people. The poison the children drink indicates mistaken teachings that were not expounded by the Buddha.

T'ien-t'ai explains, "Drinking poison means believing in the mistaken teachings of an erroneous teacher." Such a teacher, he says, "is like a physician who claims that he will cure someone's disease while in fact he only makes it worse" and thus robs people of the strength to do good.

"Distraught with pain" and "fall writhing to the ground" describe those who labor under sufferings and agonize because of their belief in such erroneous teachings.

Providing the Power to Live Amid an Age of Illness

Nichiren says, "They have become distraught because they lack the life force of the 'Life Span' chapter" (OTT, 130).

The "life force of the 'Life Span' chapter" is the Buddha's great life force to challenge any difficulty and his wisdom to overcome all sufferings by discerning their fundamental nature.

"Distraught" describes the state of those who, confused by mistaken teachings, lose sight of the life force of the "Life Span" chapter and, as a result, lose the hope to live and the courage to survive. Nichiren also says, "'They fall writhing to the ground' indicates that they fall into the Avichi hell" (OTT, 130). "Ground" means the world of hell or, more broadly, the sufferings of the three or the four evil paths. "They fall writhing to the ground" indicates tumbling down the slope of the evil paths of existence.

In this present age, people have ceased to live with powerful conviction based on sound philosophy. People's life forces are waning and their spirits are ill. All humankind is in danger of falling "writhing to the ground." As a result, deep in their hearts, people are searching for a philosophy that is based on the human being, a system of thought that thoroughly explains the potential and supreme worth of each person.

The Buddha gives people the strength to live and is therefore likened to a "great king of physicians." T'ien-t'ai compares the Buddha to a physician of unparalleled skill who not only cures people's illnesses but enables them to become even healthier and more vigorous than before they got sick.

No matter what sufferings people may be experiencing, through the Mystic Law's beneficial medicine, they can turn things around and become happier than they have ever been, realizing a truly vibrant state of life. Buddhism teaches how we can change poison into medicine and transform our destiny for the better.

The Mystic Law, the essence of Buddhism, embodies the meanings "to open," "to be fully endowed" and "to revive." The Mystic Law elucidates the treasure house of wisdom and life force inherent in our lives, and it enables us to open up this treasure house so we can lead fresh and revitalized existences. The SGI has protected and spread this ultimate teaching of the sanctity of life.

"Minds" in the above passage, or more literally "original minds," refers to the "original mind of faith" in the Mystic Law. Nichiren says, "'Original minds' refers to the seeds of enlightenment sown by the Buddha" (OTT, 130). All people are connected with the Mystic Law since beginningless time. All people originally are entities of the Mystic Law. To be awakened to this reality is to manifest one's original mind of faith.

The Gohonzon of Nam-myoho-renge-kyo expresses the Buddha's life, which is pervaded with wisdom, just as it is. To believe in and uphold this Gohonzon is to plant the seed of happiness, or perceive the Mystic Law, in one's life.

Nichiren says, "The fact that now Nichiren and his followers chant Nam-myoho-renge-kyo is an indication that they have not lost their original minds" (OTT, 130). Nichiren guarantees that all who believe in the Gohonzon and exert themselves in practice for themselves and others are, without exception, people who "have not lost their senses" (LSOC, 269).

Not losing our original mind or our senses means to possess great confidence that, no matter what happens, things will work out for the best—as long as we continue advancing with the Gohonzon and faith as our basis. Benefit is sure to bloom magnificently in the lives of those who stand up with this great conviction.

Through Faith We Can Extend Our Life Span

The children who have drunk the poison entreat their father: "Let us live out our lives!" President Toda explained these words as meaning "please give us the strong vitality we need to succeed in all areas of our lives and the benefit of resolving all sufferings." He cited this passage as documentary proof of the tenet that if you practice faith things will improve.

Also, depending on one's sense of mission, faith in the Mystic Law can in fact lead to the extension of one's life span. It is said that when Shakyamuni was on the verge of death, he extended his life by three months to lead Subhadra and other itinerant practitioners to enlightenment.

Buddhism traditionally teaches that life span is a matter of destiny. It is held to be immutable karma determined by a person's merit and virtue. But Nichiren says that the Mystic Law has the power to change even immutable karma.

Nichiren Daishonin, to encourage someone suffering from illness, related his own experience of having extended his mother's life through prayer, "When I prayed for my mother, not only was her illness cured, but her life was prolonged by four years" (WND-1, 955). The recipient of this letter was so heartened by the Daishonin's encouragement that she aroused strong faith and extended her life by more than twenty years.

Toward the end of 1957, President Toda was extremely weak due to his experience in prison and his difficulties following the war. Yet he cheerfully told a doctor examining him: "If it's a matter of life force, then I have absolute confidence [in my ability to recover]. As expressed by 'Let us live out our lives!' the power of Buddhism makes it possible to extend even one's predetermined span of life."

Just as he said, he made an astonishing recovery. And after successfully completing the ceremony on March 16,[11] he died when the cherry trees were in full bloom.

I myself was so weak and sickly as a youth that I was once told I would not reach thirty. But I met President Toda and, devoting my entire life to the mission of kosen-rufu, I have continued to charge ahead all these years. I have lived far longer than my mentor. I cannot help feeling that my mentor, through his intensive struggles, purposely shortened his own life and gave those years to me. How fortunate it is to have such a mentor!

"Distinctions in Benefits," the seventeenth chapter of the Lotus Sutra, says that those who hear the Buddha expound his eternal life span (i.e., those who hear the "Life Span" chapter) and who believe in and accept it will use their long lives to save others in the future (see LSOC, 280).

Nichiren says, "The votary of the Lotus Sutra is the Thus Come One whose life span is immeasurable" (WND-1, 471). Those who determine to spread the correct teaching, those who awaken to the mission to accomplish kosen-rufu, are Buddhas of eternal life.

Through our personal connections, each of us can lead to the Mystic Law any number of people whom no one else can reach. Everyone, therefore, has an irreplaceable mission. Please lead long lives until each of you has fully accomplished your unique mission. Let us have the spirit to introduce even one person to the Mystic Law, to help even one person become happy and, toward that end, to live even one day longer. Such an earnest attitude extends our lives; such a sense of mission increases our vitality.

Those who wholeheartedly dedicate themselves to kosen-rufu shine from the depths of their beings. They are vigorous and high-spirited. While others may live a comparable number of years, those who dedicate their lives to kosen-rufu can create many tens, hundreds or even thousands of times more value. The amount of value we create is the true measure of our life span.

Those now deceased who dedicated their lives to kosen-rufu have undoubtedly already begun new lives of mission.

Each of you has a noble mission. Every morning and evening, I pray that each of you will live up to the spirit of the passage "Let us live out our lives!"—always in high spirits, always youthful and always filled with hope.

▪24▪

Bu ken shi to. Kuno nyo ze. E sho kyobo. Gu ko yaku-so. Shiki ko mimi. Kai shitsu gu-soku. Toshi wago. Yo shi ryo buku. Ni sa ze gon. Shi dai ro-yaku. Shiki ko mimi. Kai shitsu gu-soku. Nyoto ka buku. Soku jo kuno. Mu bu shugen.

"The father, seeing his children suffering like this, follows various prescriptions. Gathering fine medicinal herbs that meet all the requirements of color, fragrance, and flavor, he grinds, sifts, and mixes them together. Giving a dose of these to his children, he tells them: 'This is a highly effective medicine, meeting all the requirements of color, fragrance, and flavor. Take it and you will quickly be relieved of your sufferings and will be free of all illness.'" (LSOC, 269)

WHAT parent, seeing his or her children suffer, would not try to relieve their pain? The image comes to mind of a father desperately hurrying to grind down medicinal herbs in a mortar to quickly prepare the medicine and saying: "I know you're suffering. Just hang in there a little longer. I'm going to give you some medicine to drink."

The Buddha, similarly, shares the sufferings of all people as though they were his own.

True compassion means to relieve people of their suffering and give them joy, not simply to pity them. The Buddha joins with people in their worries, struggles until he has actually eliminated their suffering and gives them true happiness and peace of mind.

At one point in the Lotus Sutra, Shakyamuni says, "I am the father of living beings and I should rescue them from their sufferings and give them the joy of the measureless and boundless Buddha wisdom . . ." (LSOC, 95).

Shakyamuni's compassion is like the unconditional love of a merciful mother who sympathizes with people in their suffering. At the same time, it is also the strict love of a merciful father who wages a thorough struggle to actually remove that suffering and impart true peace and comfort.

The Lotus Sutra reveals the Buddha's strict, fatherly love. The pre-Lotus Sutra teachings present only fragmentary glimpses of the "motherly love" of the Buddha's compassion. The Great Teacher Dengyo says: "The pre-Lotus Sutra teachings preach only love. While they contain a little of the teaching of the Buddha's motherly aspect, they lack the teaching of strictness." It is important to understand that the fundamental causes of suffering cannot be eliminated with merciful motherly love alone.

The Buddha can save all people precisely because he possesses the virtues of both a strict father and a merciful mother.

This is particularly true now in the Latter Day of the Law, which is much more impure than Shakyamuni's age. Today, the three poisons—greed, anger and foolishness—are ingrained in people's lives much more deeply. It is no easy matter to remove such suffering. Therefore, as the strict father of the Latter Day, Nichiren Daishonin resolutely conducted dialogue to move people at the depths of their lives.

President Toda explained:

This teaching of Nam-myoho-renge-kyo is the love of a strict father. Reward and punishment are very strict in this Buddhism.[12] Since it is not motherly love alone, there is both scolding and love, each where it is due, each with the aim of steadfastly leading people to happiness. This is fatherly love.

"Strict father" and "loving mother" are of course metaphors for the Buddha's virtues. They are not, by any means, attempts to make hard and fast claims about the roles of mothers and fathers in the home. In many cases, in fact, the mother is much stronger than the father.

We Originally Possess the Highly Effective Medicine

In the parable, the father combines the medicinal herbs he has selected and makes a highly effective medicine that is outstanding in color, fragrance and flavor and gives this to his children. This refers to the principle of "freeing one from suffering and bringing one joy" (OTT, 173).

The teaching that meets "all the requirements of color, fragrance, and flavor" that the Buddha has given people is the wisdom of the Lotus Sutra. The Buddha's teaching does not merely relieve suffering. Like a father who bestows his entire estate upon his children, the Buddha imparts his wisdom—which is the seed of happiness—upon all people.

The ultimate expression of this teaching is Nam-myoho-renge-kyo. Nichiren Daishonin left behind Nam-myoho-renge-kyo as the effective teaching that meets all requirements of color, fragrance and flavor.

People can take this medicine with peace of mind because it is excellent in color, fragrance and flavor. T'ien-t'ai indicates that color, fragrance and flavor correspond to the three types of learning, which are three disciplines Buddhist practitioners seek to master. They are precepts, meditation and wisdom. T'ien-t'ai explains that color corresponds to precepts, fragrance to meditation and flavor to wisdom.

In terms of Nichiren Daishonin's Three Great Secret Laws, color corresponds to the sanctuary of the essential teaching (the place where people practice), fragrance to the object of devotion of the essential teaching (Gohonzon) and flavor to the daimoku of the essential teaching (Nam-myoho-renge-kyo).

"He grinds, sifts, and mixes them together" might be likened to the process of producing pure extract. Shakyamuni concentrated the essence of all his teachings in the Lotus Sutra. Nichiren "grinds, sifts, and mixes" the causes (practices) and virtues (effects) of all Buddhas and expresses the result as the Three Great Secret Laws listed above.

Regarding "meeting all the requirements," Nichiren says, "'All' here means that it is the highly effective medicine of Nam-myoho-renge-kyo that includes the ten thousand practices, ten thousand good acts, and the various paramitas" (OTT, 131). And, "Showing profound compassion for those unable to comprehend the gem of the doctrine of three thousand realms in a single moment of life, the Buddha wrapped it within the five characters [of Myoho-renge-kyo], with which he then adorned the necks of the ignorant people of the latter age" (WND-1, 376).

Medicine produces its effect only if ingested. In metaphorical terms, the doctrine of the three thousand realms in a single moment of life established by T'ien-t'ai is not the medicine for the people of the Latter Day—the people of this age cannot ingest it as it is. How can it be made simpler and clearer, so that anyone can ingest (i.e., practice) it? It is the Buddha's work, as an excellent physician, to find a solution to this problem.

Encouraging the children to drink the medicine, the father tells them: "This is a highly effective medicine, meeting all the requirements of color, fragrance, and flavor. Take it and you will quickly be relieved of your sufferings and will be free of all illness."

From the standpoint of Nichiren Buddhism, this passage indicates the benefit of the Gohonzon. The Gohonzon is the highly effective medicine for those who are suffering. Its great benefit is such that, in the words of Nichikan, "No prayer will go unanswered, no offense will remain unforgiven, all good fortune will be bestowed and all righteousness proven." It truly "meets all the requirements." As for those who embrace the Gohonzon, not only will their sufferings quickly vanish, but they also will realize a state of life that is happy and free of ailment.

President Toda characterized the father's words here as the "Buddha's promise." From the standpoint of its implicit meaning, this sutra passage represents Nichiren Daishonin's declaration that all people of the Latter Day of the Law can definitely become happy.

The Daishonin says: "In the five characters of the daimoku there is not a single thing that is not included. Therefore, if we take a dose of it, we will 'quickly be relieved of our sufferings'" (OTT, 131).

Everyone is entitled to become happy. It is the prerogative of those experiencing the greatest suffering to become the happiest. Those who work the hardest can develop their lives far more than others. This is the mystic nature of faith. People who advance together with those experiencing the greatest suffering are genuine Buddhists.

Suffering Is Necessary to Bring Out the Full Flavor of Joy

In any age, ordinary people suffer the most under the weight of society's strains and distortions. None are more miserable than those who follow foolish leaders.

Individuals of genuine greatness never forget that the people are the true treasures of society. In his preface to *Les Misérables*, Victor Hugo wrote, "So long as ignorance and poverty exist on earth, books of the nature of *Les Miserables* cannot fail to be of use."[13]

"I want to rid the world of misery"—this was President Toda's heartfelt proclamation. He was an unparalleled leader who always advanced together with the people.

When lecturing on the passage of the "Life Span" chapter we are studying, Mr. Toda, with characteristic humor, once remarked: "We have come to this saha world to enjoy ourselves. But without a dash of suffering, we couldn't savor the full flavor of joy. The fact is that the world, far from being a place of amusement, is full of suffering."

Those listening to him learned that as long as they possessed the "highly effective medicine" of the Mystic Law, they each could cross the raging seas of society and establish a state of profound calm and composure. How such broad-minded words of a true spiritual leader dispelled the dark clouds of unease and shed light into the hearts of people living amid the confusion of the postwar era!

This is the way of a true leader. No matter how exhausted President Toda was, whenever he found members who were suffering or worn out, he poured his entire being into encouraging them. With the same spirit and immense life force, SGI members today embrace those who are struggling or sick.

All of you have been taking action with this spirit. Even with your own pressing concerns, you drive yourselves to try your best to encourage those in dire need. When you hear reports about how people have become happy or gained benefit through faith, it dispels all sense of fatigue. The SGI has created such a network of people helping one another become happy. It is a great castle of happiness created by the hearts of ordinary people. No one can destroy this noble solidarity of the Bodhisattvas of the Earth.

Nichiren Daishonin observes that even though people of power can destroy Buddha images or temples, they are powerless to destroy Buddhism itself (see WND-2, 388). And it is impossible for someone's spirit to be destroyed from the outside. As long as we have beautiful unity, the world of the Mystic Law is absolutely indestructible.

We live in a time when the three poisons are particularly strong, and we suffer just as the children in the parable suffered from the poison they drank. The deadlock of the present age is due to people having forgotten their inner revolution. This is the lesson of the twentieth century. In every field, people search for a philosophy to remove the poisons in their hearts. All humankind thirsts for the "highly effective medicine" of the Mystic Law.

Nichiren says that followers who practice the Mystic Law are the "original possessors of this highly effective medicine" (OTT, 132). Our compassionate practice to relieve others of suffering and give them joy will doubtless spearhead the revival of the heart and the revival of humanism in the twenty-first century.

·25·

Go sho shi chu. Fu shis̄hin ja. Ken shi ro yaku. Shiki ko gu ko. Soku-
ben buku shi. Byo jin jo yu. Yo shis-shin ja. Ken go bu rai. Sui yak-kangi
monjin. Gu-shaku ji byo. Nen yo go yaku. Ni fu ko buku. Sho-i sha ga.
Dokke jinnyu. Ship̄ponshin ko. O shi ko shiki ko yaku. Ni i fu mi.

"Those children who have not lost their senses can see that this is good
medicine, outstanding in both color and fragrance, so they take it immediately and are completely cured of their sickness. Those who are out of their
minds are equally delighted to see their father return and beg him to cure
their sickness, but when they are given the medicine, they refuse to take it.
Why? Because the poison has penetrated deeply and their minds no longer
function as before. So although the medicine is of excellent color and
fragrance, they do not perceive it as good." (LSOC, 269)

EVERYONE WANTS to become happy and get along with others.
No one starts out wanting to be miserable or to live with others
in a state of mutual hatred and contempt.

In reality, however, we find people living under just such conditions.
Often people tumble down the slope of misfortune due to errors in
judgment that result from their preoccupation with trivialities. They
may come into conflict or even start wars with one another over issues
that, in the larger scheme of things, are truly insignificant.

Nichiren says: "Fish want to survive; they deplore their pond's shal-
lowness and dig holes in the bottom to hide in, yet tricked by bait, they

take the hook. Birds in a tree fear that they are too low and perch in the top branches, yet bewitched by bait, they too are caught in snares" (WND-I, 301).

Although in their hearts people desperately seek happiness, at crucial junctures they in fact move in the opposite direction. The sick children in the above passage represent people with distorted lives and foolish minds who are unable to judge things correctly.

The Buddha uses the light of wisdom to guide distorted lives in the correct direction, the direction of happiness. This is the lesson of the parable of the Skilled Physician and His Sick Children.

"True Mind" Means a Mind of Belief in the Mystic Law

Among the children who drank poison, some have not yet lost their minds, or more literally, their true or original minds.[14] These children, perceiving the medicine prepared by their father to be excellent in color and fragrance, drink it without hesitation. Their sickness is immediately cured.

Nichiren says, "'True mind' means the mind that believes in the Lotus Sutra" (WND-I, 495), and he speaks of "the true mind of the Buddha nature" (WND-I, 495). "True mind" is nothing other than the Buddha nature. People, even while laboring under various illusions, can believe in the Lotus Sutra precisely because they possess the Buddha nature in the depths of their lives.

The parable then goes on to explain about the children who have lost their minds. They, too, rejoice upon seeing their father return and beseech him to cure them. But when the essential medicine is given to them, they cannot bring themselves to drink it. That's because the poison has penetrated them deeply, and they are no longer lucid.

In other words, deep-seated illusions prevent the power of the Buddha nature from emerging. Although such people seek happiness—and although the fundamental cause for becoming happy is right before their eyes—they fail to realize it.

Unable to recognize the medicine "of excellent color and fragrance" for what it is, they suspect that it is bad. Not only do they fail to believe in the Mystic Law, they actively reject it. They suffer from delusion to the extent that they cannot distinguish between good and bad, true and false. Nichiren says:

> The words "the poison has penetrated deeply" refer to persons who have become deeply committed to the provisional teachings, an action that constitutes slander of the Law. For that reason, they do not believe or accept the highly effective medicine of the Lotus Sutra. (OTT, 132)

"Deeply committed to the provisional teachings" indicates the distorted judgment and attitude of those who criticize superior teachings out of attachment to inferior teachings.

Broadly speaking, this might be said to describe the attitude of those who forget the spirit of self-improvement and advancement. Such people instead become attached to a shallow way of life and, moreover, criticize those who live earnestly and with a lofty spirit.

Regarding the parable of the Skilled Physician and His Sick Children, President Toda said: "When we first read these passages, they seem to describe Shakyamuni's time. But when we examine them carefully, we find that they are prophetic words pointing to this age of the Latter Day of the Law."

This sutra passage certainly sheds light on the absurd conditions of society today. Although people seek care, ultimately they refuse to drink the medicine. In the depths of their hearts all people desire to live in earnest. But the power of good in the human spirit—that of dedication, courage, benevolence and wisdom—has grown weak. That's because society lacks a firm philosophy or set of ideals. As a result, people's sense of values is unstable; they confuse good and evil, truth and falsehood, selflessness and selfishness, the lofty and the base.

Buddhism characterizes the illusion that pleasurable circumstances can continue indefinitely as the "four inverted views." This describes the mistaken views of the qualities of eternity, happiness, true self and purity held by someone who lives only for the pursuit of pleasure. This shallow outlook stems from the assumption that such momentary pleasures as money and worldly fame will continue forever, that they are pleasurable, that pursuing them is being true to oneself and achieving them a wonderful thing.

For the sake of those caught up in such thinking, Shakyamuni first expounded the principles of impermanence, suffering, non-self and non-substantiality and severely criticized attachment to pleasure. After he had raised the state of life of these people through such expedient teachings, he expounded the Lotus Sutra, which finally revealed the true aspect of the indestructible virtues of eternity, happiness, true self and purity.

To illustrate, let us consider happiness. The happiness of the four inverted views may be expressed as "If I'm happy now, nothing else matters." Such a sentiment can produce no vital force or true brilliance in one's life.

But the happiness that may be gained by carrying out activities for kosen-rufu comprises true comfort and joy that wells forth from the very depths of one's being. It is happiness of a completely different kind.

Constantly going out to offer people encouragement, thinking, "I wonder how that person is doing," or "Is that person in high spirits?" is certainly a laborious undertaking. But in the course of such continual dialogue, we see smiles return to the faces of friends formerly mired in suffering, and we see people overcome the turbulent waves of destiny and become revitalized.

The joy and sense of reward we feel at such times far surpasses what we might experience from watching a great drama. This is a way of life genuinely based on eternity, happiness, true self and purity.

With pride as SGI members, let us lead lives richly imbued with the virtues of eternity, happiness, true self and purity. Let us create in our environments a fresh brilliance of life and a correct sense of values. Let us dauntlessly spread the philosophy of the dignity of life and let us carry out the actions of bodhisattvas. The path to transforming a society of distorted values lies in carrying out such efforts.

·26·

Bu sa ze nen. Shi shi ka min. I doku sho chu. Shin kai ten-do.
Sui ken ga ki. Gushak̂ ku-ryo. Nyo ze ko yaku. Ni fu ko buku.
Ga kon to setsu hoben. Ryo buku shi yaku. Soku sa ze gon. Nyoto
to chi. Ga kon sui ro. Shi ji i shi. Ze ko ro-yaku. Kon ru zai shi.
Nyo ka shu buku. Mot̂ tsu fu sai.

"The father thinks to himself: My poor children! Because of the poison
in them, their minds are completely befuddled. Although they are happy
to see me and ask me to cure them, they refuse to take this excellent
medicine. I must now resort to some expedient means to induce them
to take the medicine. So he says to them: 'You should know that I am
now old and worn out, and the time of my death has come. I will leave
this good medicine here. You should take it and not worry that it will
not cure you.'" (LSOC, 269–70)

SEEING THE CHILDREN who adamantly refuse to drink the medicine, the father thinks, "My poor children!"

These words are tremendously moving. They convey the immense
mercy of the Buddha, who seeks to lead everyone, without exception,
to happiness. Still, the father does not attempt to force the children to
drink the medicine.

Compulsion cannot change the distortions lurking in the depths of
people's hearts. It is important that people take up the medicine and

drink it of their own accord. Only by doing so can you say that you have the perception to see your life clearly and without distortion.

Out of his compassionate concern for the children and his desire for them to display true self-motivation, the father, rather than compel them, uses his wisdom to get them to take the medicine of their own accord.

"How can I prompt them to decide to drink the medicine?" he wonders. "I'll use an expedient means to cause them to drink it."

As his expedient, he chooses to announce that he will soon die. The father tells them: "I have grown old and weak, and it appears that I will soon die. I will leave the medicine here for you to drink. You need not worry that your sufferings will not be cured, for they will be cured without fail." He then sets out and sends someone back to announce that he has died.

The father has not actually died; he merely causes the children to think that he has. In this way, he seeks to purge them of their tendency to depend on him and in so doing dispel their delusions.

An expedient means, as I have said many times, is an expression of the Buddha's compassion. If the Buddha were always present in the world, people would become dependent. Under such circumstances, the Buddha could not attain the objective of raising people to the same state of life as his own. So the Buddha arouses immense compassion and, as the ultimate expedient means, appears to enter extinction.

On one level "I leave this good medicine here for you now" refers to Shakyamuni leaving the Lotus Sutra for those in the world after his death. What is the meaning hidden in the depths of this passage?

Nichiren says, "'I will leave this' indicates that it is for the Latter Day of the Law. 'Here' means the country of Japan in the continent of Jambudvipa" (OTT, 133). He characterizes Japan as a country filled with "persons of incorrigible disbelief" (WND-1, 304). The Daishonin appeared in a land of people of incorrigible disbelief, and he left behind the great Law of Nam-myoho-renge-kyo for the people of the Latter Day.

Regarding the passage "You should take it and not worry that it will not cure you," Nichiren says that "you" indicates all people of the Latter Day, and "take" means embracing and chanting Nam-myoho-renge-kyo. He says: "From the time we swallow it, we become eternally endowed with the three bodies. Thus we are cured of the sickness of attachment to the Buddha who first attained enlightenment under the bodhi tree" (OTT, 133).

"The sickness of attachment to the Buddha who first attained enlightenment under the bodhi tree" reminds us that as long as we suppose there is a separation between the Buddha and other people, we cannot recognize the tremendous life that exists within us.

The Mystic Law is the great teaching that enables all of us to realize that we are originally Buddhas. When the immense life of the Buddha manifests within our being, all our sufferings disappear like dew in the morning rays of the sun.

When that happens, we are in the state in which we will "not worry that it will not cure" us. We need not worry about anything. We will definitely become happy. This is what the Buddha declares.

·27·

Sa ze kyo i. Bu shi ta-koku. Ken shi gen go. Nyo bu i shi. Zeji sho shi.
Mon bu haiso. Shin dai uno. Ni sa ze nen. Nyaku bu zai sha. Jimin gato.
No ken kugo. Konja sha ga. On so ta-koku. Ji yui koro. Mu bu jiko.
Jo e hikan. Shin zui shogo. Nai chi shi yaku. Shiki ko mimi. Soku shu
buku shi. Doku byo kai yu. Go bu mon shi. Shī chi toku sai. Jin ben
rai ki. Gen shi ken shi.

"Having given these instructions, he then goes off to another land, where
he sends a messenger home to announce, 'Your father is dead.'

"At that time the children, hearing that their father has deserted them
and died, are filled with great grief and consternation and think to themselves: If our father were alive he would have pity on us and see that we are
protected. But now he has abandoned us and died in some other country
far away. We are shelterless orphans with no one to rely on!

"Constantly harboring such feelings of grief, they at last come to their
senses and realize that the medicine is in fact excellent in color and fragrance and flavor, and so they take it and are healed of all the effects of the
poison. The father, hearing that his children are all cured, immediately
returns home and appears to them all once more." (LSOC, 270)

"WHAT WILL become of things after I am gone?" This is the constant thought of a genuine leader. That a leader should attend
to the present goes without saying. But it is constantly thinking about

the future and setting the stage for future generations that distinguish an outstanding leader.

This may be harsh, but leaders concerned only with their own age are egoists. Society and the people who come in the wake of such leaders will suffer. This is an essential leadership principle, and it holds true in all areas.

Moreover, the Buddha is a great leader among leaders, who has stood up for the eternal happiness of all beings. "How can I save people after my passing?" This is the Buddha's greatest concern; therein lies his true mission and his will for the future.

The statement "he sends a messenger home to announce" and other statements in this passage clarify this point.

The skilled physician, after preparing the effective medicine and setting out on a journey, sends home a messenger who announces to the children that their father has died in the course of his travels.

The children are thunderstruck. Filled with grief, they finally open their eyes and realize that the effective medicine their father left behind is in fact excellent in color and fragrance and flavor, and they take it. As a result, they are completely cured of their sickness.

The important point here is that the father induces the children to take the effective medicine by concealing himself. As long as he remained at their side, the children refused to take the medicine and simply sank deeper into suffering. Under these circumstances, the father used the expedient means of having someone inform the children that he had died in another land. He could thus finally cause his beloved children to take the medicine and so lead them to happiness.

The skilled physician, needless to say, is Shakyamuni himself, and the children are the people in the world after Shakyamuni's passing. The children's grief upon hearing the sad news of their father's death—"We are shelterless orphans with no one to rely on!"—is the heartfelt cry of people who have lost the Buddha. It could also be said to represent the cry of people today whose lives, cut off from the cool, fresh waters of a reliable philosophy, have become parched and dry.

What, then, is the effective medicine? It is the teaching left behind by the Buddha. It is the Law. According to T'ien-t'ai, "highly effective medicine" means the sutras and teachings of the Buddha.

In summation, the parable of the Skilled Physician and His Sick Children indicates how the Buddha (the skilled physician) uses the expedient means of his death to enable the people in the world after his passing (the children) to believe in the teaching (the effective medicine) he has left behind. This is a restatement of the principal theme of the entire "Life Span" chapter.

The passage "he sends a messenger home to announce" begs the question: Just who exactly is the messenger sent by the skilled physician?

The messenger communicates the news of the father's death to the children. Entrusted with the father's spirit to somehow lead the children to happiness, the messenger fulfills a vital role in enabling them to take the medicine.

Perhaps without this messenger the children would have died from the illness. In fact, the messenger represents people with the most important mission in Buddhism. The "messenger [sent] home to announce" represents those who can communicate the correct Buddhist teaching to people after the Buddha's passing; it indicates the Thus Come One's messengers, who can spread Buddhism's hopeful teaching in an age bereft of hope.

Regarding this point, Nichiren clearly states, "When the sutra says, 'he sends a messenger home to announce,' it refers to the Bodhisattvas of the Earth" (WND-1, 372).

The Bodhisattvas of the Earth will shoulder the task of propagation after Shakyamuni's death. That these bodhisattvas will gallantly appear in the evil world of the Latter Day, when Shakyamuni's teaching has lost its power to lead people to enlightenment, and spread the

effective medicine of the Mystic Law that the Buddha left behind—
this indeed is a message of hope.

On one level, Nichiren struggled to spread the Mystic Law as Bodhisattva Superior Practices, leader of the Bodhisattvas of the Earth. On
the level of the Lotus Sutra's implicit teaching, he is the original Buddha, who left behind the great beneficial medicine of Nam-myoho-
renge-kyo, which can lead all people throughout the Latter Day to
enlightenment. The Daishonin is himself the skilled physician and the
"father" of all people.

Accordingly, from this standpoint, the messenger is none other
than those who advance kosen-rufu in strict accord with the Daishonin's teachings.

On one level as Bodhisattvas of the Earth, and on another as followers of the original Buddha, we are emissaries of the Thus Come
One who tell others about the supreme teaching of the Mystic Law
and show actual proof of its greatness. This is the honorable status
we all enjoy.

Never before in the history of Buddhism has there been a popular
movement like ours that has spread the correct Buddhist teaching to
such an extent or led so many people to happiness. More than anything else, this reality, this role we have played, attests to the fact that
we are the noble emissaries of the Buddha.

Nichiren calls out to his disciples:

> Now, at the beginning of the Latter Day of the Law, I,
> Nichiren, am the first to embark on propagating, through-
> out Jambudvipa, the five characters of Myoho-renge-kyo,
> which are the heart of the Lotus Sutra and the eye of all
> Buddhas. . . . My disciples, form your ranks and follow me,
> and surpass even Mahakashyapa or Ananda, T'ien-t'ai or
> Dengyo! (WND-1, 764–65)

"I have opened the way to world kosen-rufu," Nichiren says. "My disciples, follow me! And accomplish a great mission!"

As messengers "sent to announce," our mission is to carry out the original Buddha's spirit and spread the Mystic Law throughout the entire world.

Even the skilled physician could not have saved his children without a messenger. Similarly, without the popular movement of Bodhisattvas of the Earth who embrace the great effective medicine of the Mystic Law, the people of the ailing present age cannot be saved.

Together, let us proudly advance along the glorious path of life of Bodhisattvas of the Earth.

28

Sho zen-nanshi. O i unga. Ha u nin no. Ses-shi ro-i. Komo zai fu. Hot̄ cha. Seson. Butsu gon. Ga yaku nyo ze. Jo-butsu irai. Muryo muhen. Hyaku sen man noku. Nayuta. Asogi ko. I shujo ko. I hoben-riki. Gon to metsu-do. Yaku mu u no. Nyo ho setsu ga. Komo ka sha. Niji seson. Yoku ju sen shigi. Ni setsu ge gon.

"Good men, what is your opinion? Can anyone say that this skilled physician is guilty of lying?"

"No, World-Honored One."

The Buddha said: "It is the same with me. It has been immeasurable, boundless hundreds, thousands, ten thousands, millions of nayuta asam-khya kalpas since I attained Buddhahood. But for the sake of living beings I employ the power of expedient means and say that I am about to pass into extinction. In view of the circumstances, however, no one can say that I have been guilty of lies or falsehoods."

At that time the World-Honored One, wishing to state his meaning once more, spoke in verse form, saying: . . . (LSOC, 270)

AFTER CONCLUDING the parable of the Skilled Physician and His Sick Children, Shakyamuni puts the question to his disciples: "Can anyone say that this skilled physician is guilty of lying?"

"What do you think?" he asks them. "You certainly wouldn't say that he is lying, would you?"

He waits for the disciples to indicate their assent and then says, "It is the same with me," and goes on to explain his spirit by way of analogy to the skilled physician.

This is another passage conveying the atmosphere of the heartfelt give-and-take Shakyamuni cultivated with his disciples. It certainly was not one-way communication. Shakyamuni was not arbitrary or dogmatic. It is indeed difficult to find leaders with such magnanimity in society today.

Shakyamuni's spirit in expounding his death as an expedient means comes down to the one passage "for the sake of living beings." While possessing an immeasurable span of life, to save others he used the power of expedient means to announce his own extinction.

This compassionate spirit no doubt deeply penetrated the lives of those gathered when he expounded the Law. For those who open-mindedly and wholeheartedly caught the mentor's spirit, Shakyamuni could hardly have appeared guilty of lies or falsehoods. As we learned before, all that the Buddha preaches "is true and not false."

This points to the fundamental difference between an expedient means and a lie. The distinguishing characteristic of an expedient means in Buddhism is that it arises from profound compassion for others and contributes to improvement in their lives. This is the essential point.

In a general discussion of leadership in society, the German philosopher Karl Jaspers argues: "Both of them, democrat and tyrant, address themselves to the people . . . Which of them will meet with success can be decided in each instance only by the people themselves; the decision they reach is a decision over themselves."[15]

Outwardly, democratic leaders and dictators appear similar in that they both appeal to the people.

In every case, it is ultimately the people themselves who must determine whether leaders' words are true or false. It is the people's choice in which direction they will advance. Therefore, the only way is for the people themselves to become wise.

Thus, Buddhists have to speak the truth and spare nothing of themselves in taking resolute action for the people (i.e., "for the sake of living beings").

In an age rife with pretension and vanity, SGI members have steadfastly taken action for the sake of living beings. Confident in this fact, let us advance joyfully as we splendidly prove the value of this way of life.

THE "LIFE SPAN" CHAPTER
VERSE SECTION

A Song in Praise of the Greater Self

THE MORNING SUN of the new century has arisen—in the sky above the world and in the great sky of our hearts.

The SGI is the sun of the world. Each of us, therefore, is a sunlike existence. The brilliance of our lives illuminates our homes, our communities and society at large.

The sun burns on its own. It is a scorching ball of fire. Nichiren Daishonin says, "In the breast of the Buddha is a great fire" (WND-1, 509). It is the flame of great compassion that impels the Buddha to go into the midst of those burdened with suffering and thoroughly burn away their misery. It is the light of the Buddha's great wisdom to lead all people to enlightenment.

The fire of the Buddha continues to burn eternally. It never goes out. The Daishonin says that even if the entire world were under water and about to be washed away, still this great fire could not be extinguished (see WND-1, 509).

The Buddha continues to illuminate people's lives perpetually. The source of this light is the "Life Span" chapter of the Lotus Sutra. The verse section that concludes the chapter contains the inextinguishable flame of the Buddha's immense compassion and the light of the Buddha's great wisdom.

What Is the Verse Section?

The verse section of the "Life Span" chapter is also referred to as the *jigage*. What does *ge* in *jigage* mean? It is a transliteration of the

Sanskrit term *gatha,* which is also sometimes rendered as *keta* or *kada.* In short, it means "verse."

To put it another way, a *gatha* or *ge* is a text that relates the Buddha's teaching or that praises the virtues of the Buddha and bodhisattvas through verse. They are Buddhist scriptures that are easily recited and memorized. Since this *ge* begins with the words pronounced in Japanese *ji ga,* it is called the *jigage.*

The English poet Percy Bysshe Shelley remarks, "A great poem is a fountain forever overflowing with the waters of wisdom and delight."[1] The verse section of the "Life Span" chapter is an inexhaustible well-spring of wisdom and delight. It is a true paean to freedom.

The benefit that accrues to those who read and recite this verse is vast and immeasurable.

Nichiren Daishonin says that the *jigage,* or verse section, "represents the soul of the twenty-eight chapters of the sutra" (WND-1, 516). He also states:

> The Buddhas throughout the ten directions looked up to the verse section of the "Life Span" chapter as their teacher and attained Buddhahood. This verse section is like a father and a mother to the people of the world.
>
> A person who embraces the "Life Span" chapter of the Lotus Sutra is sustaining the life of the Buddhas. (WND-1, 517)

He teaches that the lives of all Buddhas of the past, present and future, as well as in the ten directions, flow inexhaustibly through each of our lives. Accordingly, he says that to become the enemy of one who embraces the verse section is tantamount to becoming an enemy of all Buddhas throughout the past, present and future (see WND-1, 517).

Just what is the life of the Buddha contained in the verse section that Nichiren praises so highly? The prose section we studied concludes with the words, "At that time the World-Honored One, wishing to state his meaning once more, spoke in verse form, saying . . ." (LSOC, 270).

The teaching that the Buddha expounds in the prose section of "Life Span" is indeed repeated in the verse section, which, it might be said, was born of the Buddha's determined spirit to convey and enable all people to understand this teaching.

But the verse section does not simply repeat the teaching of the chapter's prose section. It is all the more clearly intended for the future and more strongly imbued with the Buddha's compassion.

Toward the Future, Toward Humankind

The prose section of "Life Span" reveals Shakyamuni's eternal life. It clarifies that he attained the way long ago, in the remote past, and reveals that he has ceaselessly continued to instruct people in this saha world since his enlightenment. For the benefit of future generations, it explains that the Buddha's life span is such that he has "constantly abided here without ever entering extinction" (LSOC, 267–68).

However, the verse section expands further upon these words and lauds still more highly the Buddha's inextinguishable life. This is T'ien-t'ai's interpretation in the tenth volume of *Words and Phrases of the Lotus Sutra*.

The verse section explains that whenever people seek the Buddha, the Buddha appears in the world, and the land where the Buddha appears becomes a Buddha land of peace and tranquillity.

But if the Buddha constantly abides in this world without ever entering extinction, then why can't people see him? And what can they do to gain the ability to see him? This, too, is explained in the verse section. It might be said that the verse section reveals the key to forming the profound bond between the Buddha and disciples of seeking mind, the eternal bond of the oneness of mentor and disciple existing throughout past, present and future.

As I mentioned previously, Shakyamuni starts preaching the "Life Span" chapter in response to a question put to him by Bodhisattva Maitreya. But "Life Span" taken as a whole was not expounded merely for the benefit of Maitreya and the others assembled there. Rather, it is a teaching clearly intended for the people of later ages, for us.

The true audience of the "Life Span" chapter comprises all people in the world after Shakyamuni's passing and, in particular, those of the Latter Day of the Law. The verse section is in truth a message for future generations of humankind.

Also, the final line of the verse section explains the Buddha's constant wish: "How can I cause living beings to gain entry into the unsurpassed way and quickly acquire the body of a Buddha?" (LSOC, 273). The verse section in its entirety exudes the Buddha's compassionate desire to enable all people to establish in their hearts a state of true happiness.

Each word of the verse section is imbued with the Buddha's compassion to enable all people to become Buddhas. From the standpoint of Nichiren Buddhism, everyone is an entity of the Mystic Law; all people are Buddhas. And the verse section of the "Life Span" chapter praises the benefit we attain when we open our eyes to this truth. It profoundly calls out to each of us to advance along the path of truth and genuine happiness open to all people, as clarified in the chapter's prose section.

Nichiren says that each character of the Lotus Sutra is a "golden Shakyamuni" (WND-1, 486). And he explains that when we read or recite the verse section of the "Life Span" chapter, whose golden characters number 510, each of these characters becomes a sun and a Buddha, illuminating all worlds and the entire universe and leading all people to happiness (see WND-1, 517–18).

The verse section illuminates the lives of all people. Every day in the morning and evening, we recite this scripture, the ultimate treasure of humankind. Therefore, our benefit is great beyond measure.

Not only do we recite the verse section, we also practice it and prove its truth. We are communicating and spreading its benefit to all people. Nichiren Daishonin and all Buddhas of the three existences and the ten directions no doubt praise our efforts. How wonderful! How truly fortunate we are!

The Verse Section Represents Oneself

To say each character is a Buddha means that the verse section expresses the life of the Buddha in its totality.

Nichiren says:

> The word "Since" (*ji* [which also means self or freely]) marks the beginning of the verse section, and the words "quickly acquire the body *(shin)* of a Buddha" mark the end. The beginning and end are "since" and "body," which make up *ji-shin* (oneself). (OTT, 140)

Here Nichiren teaches that the verse section from beginning to end explains the Buddha's self or life.

Nichiren indicates that the body of the verse section in its entirety, coming between the words *ji* (self) and *shin* (body), signifies the actions and conduct of oneself. Thus it says in *The Record of the Orally Transmitted Teachings*, "The *Jigage* section represents 'the body [inherently endowed with boundless benefits] that is freely received and used' *(ji-ju-yu-shin)*, or the Buddha of limitless joy" (p. 141).

The body or self that "is freely received and used" means to realize that the entire universe is in fact oneself and to freely receive and use the power of the Mystic Law, which is the wellspring of universal life.

Nichiren here indicates that the verse section expresses the state of life of absolute freedom of the original Buddha.

The verse section elucidates the vast and eternal state of life of indestructible happiness that is free of all hindrance and, moreover, that exists forever, freely and joyously acting throughout the universe.

The "body that is freely received and used" also refers to the ordinary outward appearance of the Buddha. It indicates the form of ordinary people as distinguished from that of a Buddha assuming august attributes.

President Toda said that the verse section "is the scripture of the Buddha himself and the scripture of us ourselves." It might be said that the verse section is a poem praising the "greater self" and sings of the totally free state of life of this self.

Nichiren says, "A single individual has been used as an example, but the same thing applies equally to all living beings" (WND-2, 844). The verse section celebrates the self of the original Buddha of beginningless time and at the same time praises our own selves.

"One's-self I sing."² With these words, Walt Whitman begins his paean to humankind, *Leaves of Grass*. Whitman, his words full of strength and conviction, sings:

> *In all people I see myself, none more and not one*
> *a barley-corn less . . .*
> *I know I am solid and sound . . .*
> *I know I am deathless . . .*
> *I know I am august . . .*
> *I exist as I am, that is enough.*³

Whitman, too, perceived a holy and most noble light within the human being, within the self. His spirit truly resonates with that of the verse section of the "Life Span" chapter. Buddhism teaches the path whereby all people can become aware of this original greater self.

Shortly after he began his journey of propagation, Shakyamuni called out to a youth whom he met in the forest: "Seek out your self!" "Seek out your self!" "Know your true self!" "Start digging right at your feet!" Herein lies the source of happiness and the path of hope.

Therefore, President Toda always encouraged people to "live your own life," to "live true to yourself":

Whether you suffer from poverty or failure in business, are miserable because of marital discord or suffer injury from a fall or other accident, ultimately all such sufferings are your own life. They are manifestations of the living phenomenon that is your self. When we view things this way, we see that all occurrences in our daily existence involve changes in our lives themselves. The important thing, therefore, is to try to cause more positive changes and ceaselessly make efforts to secure happiness.

The key is to live true to yourself. You have to realize that living true to yourself is the only way. To live based on other people or circumstances, always thinking, "Things would be fine if that person would only do such-and-such" or "If the world were only like this, then I could be happy," is a mistake, is it not?

No matter where we go, we can never escape ourselves. Happiness and misery, everything in life, are contained in the single word "self." Ultimately, victory or defeat in life comes down to a matter of disciplining and dignifying this inescapable thing that is the self.

One must not have a weak self that's easily blown this way and that depending on the wind's direction. One who can profoundly distinguish between true and false and who possesses a solid self will not be swayed by rumors and hearsay.

We have to develop a towering self. The verse section of the "Life

Span" chapter praises the wonder and greatness of the true self, of the self that basks in the realization: "I am originally a Buddha!"

Be as Majestic as the Himalayas

When I visited Nepal, I spoke with some children of a local village near Katmandu on a hill commanding a fine view of the Himalayas. They were all intelligent and charming. Their faces were radiant, and their eyes shone. I said to them: "The Buddha was raised in view of the great Himalayas. He strove to become as great as these mountains. He cultivated himself to become a person of victory and towering majesty."

"Construct a self that is as majestic as the Himalayas!" This is the spirit of Buddhism. We can all develop a self that is crowned with such victory.

While joyously singing a song of life, let's advance with composure and dignity for the betterment of ourselves, for the happiness of others and for world peace.

Our conduct is a great poem in praise of the self that shines eternally throughout past, present and future.

🍁 The "Life Span" Chapter Verse Section

The following are the passages from the "Life Span" chapter verse section that SGI members recite during gongyo. The numbers next to each passage correspond to the numbered lectures that follow; page numbers where the lecture for each passage can be found also appear here. The appendix on p. 387 contains the full English translation.

(**29**) Ji ga toku bur̂rai.
Sho kyo sho kosshu.
Muryo hyaku sen man.
Oku sai asogi.
Jo seppo kyoke.
Mushu oku shujo.
Ryo nyu o butsu-do.
Nirai muryo ko. (**p. 309**)

(**30**) I do shujo ko.
Hoben gen nehan.
Ni jitsu fu metsu-do.
Jo ju shi seppo.
Ga jo ju o shi.
I sho jin-zu-riki.
Ryo tendo shujo.
Sui gon ni fu ken. (**p. 317**)

(**31**) Shu ken ga metsu-do.
Ko kuyo shari.
Gen kai e renbo.
Ni sho katsu-go shin.
Shujo ki shin-buku.
Shichi-jiki i nyunan.
Isshin yok̂ ken butsu.
Fu ji shaku shinmyo.
Ji ga gyu shuso.
Ku shutsu ryojusen. (**p. 325**)

(32) Ga ji go shujo.
Jo zai shi fu-metsu.
I ho-ben-rik̂ ko.
Gen u metsu fu-metsu.
Yo-koku u shujo.
Kugyo shingyo sha.
Ga bu o hi chu.
I setsu mujo ho.
Nyoto fu mon shi.
Tan ni ga metsu-do.
Ga ken sho shujo.
Motsu-zai o kukai.
Ko fu i gen shin.
Ryo go sho katsu-go.
In go shin renbo.
Nai shutsu i seppo. (p. 339)

(33) Jin-zu-riki nyo ze.
O asogi ko.
Jo zai ryojusen.
Gyu yo sho jusho.
Shujo ken ko jin.
Dai ka sho sho ji.
Ga shi do annon.
Tennin jo juman.
Onrin sho do-kaku.
Shuju ho shogon.
Hoju ta keka.
Shujo sho yu-raku.
Shoten gyaku tenku.
Jo saŝ shu gi-gaku.
U mandara ke.
San butsu gyu daishu. (p. 343)

(34) Ga jodo fu ki.
Ni shu ken sho jin.

Ufu sho kuno.
Nyo ze shitsu juman.
Ze sho zai shujo.
I aku-go innen.
Ka asogi ko.
Fu mon sanbo myo. (p. 355)

(35) Sho u shu ku-doku.
Nyuwa shichi-jiki sha.
Sokkai ken gashin.
Zai shi ni seppo.
Waku-ji i shi shu.
Setsu butsu-ju muryo.
Ku nai ken bussha.
I setsu butsu nan chi. (p. 361)

(36) Ga chi-riki nyo ze.
Eko sho muryo.
Jumyo mushu ko.
Ku shugo sho toku.
Nyoto u chi sha.
Mot̑ to shi sho gi.
To dan ryo yo jin.
Butsu-go jip̑ puko. (p. 367)

(37) Nyo i zen hoben.
I ji o shi ko.
Jitsu zai ni gon shi.
Mu no sek̑ komo.
Ga yaku i se bu.
Ku sho kugen sha. (p. 371)

(38) I bonbu tendo.
Jitsu zai ni gon metsu.
I joken ga ko.
Ni sho kyoshi shin.
Ho-itsu jaku go-yoku.

Da o aku-do chu.
Go jo chi shujo.
Gyo do fu gyo do.
Zui o sho ka do.
I ses shuju ho. (p. 375)

(39) Mai ji sa ze nen.
I ga ryo shujo.
Toku nyu mu-jo do.
Soku joju busshin. (p. 379)

▪ 29 ▪

Ji ga toku bur͡rai.
Sho kyo sho kosshu.
Muryo hyaku sen man.
Oku sai asogi.
Jo seppo kyoke.
Mushu oku shujo.
Ryo nyu o butsu-do.
Nirai muryo ko.

"Since I attained Buddhahood
the number of kalpas that have passed
is an immeasurable hundreds, thousands, ten thousands
millions, trillions, asamkhyas.
Constantly I have preached the Law, teaching, converting
countless millions of living beings,
causing them to enter the Buddha way,
all this for immeasurable kalpas."
(LSOC, 270)

As I HAVE MENTIONED, the verse section of the "Life Span" chapter explains matters pertaining to the Buddha himself. However, President Toda made it a point to stress that the text can be read in two ways.

From a literal standpoint, "Since I attained Buddhahood" means since Shakyamuni became a Buddha. But a more profound meaning is found hidden in the depths of the text.

Regarding "attained Buddhahood," my mentor taught: "The state of Buddhahood is not something that comes to us from without. Rather, this passage clearly describes the function of the Buddha that bounds forth from within our own lives."

In other words, this passage's literal meaning refutes the view that Shakyamuni first attained enlightenment during his lifetime in India. It clarifies that he in fact attained Buddhahood in the remote past, reiterating the teaching articulated earlier in the chapter that the Buddha's life is eternal.

But from the standpoint of its implicit meaning, this passage teaches that all people's lives are eternally endowed with the Buddha's three bodies.

Nichiren indicates that this passage refers to the three bodies of a Buddha (see OTT, 133). This passage elucidates the three bodies that are the fundamental life of the Buddha, and it indicates that since the beginningless past, our lives, too, have been endowed with these three bodies. This is the meaning of the passage in Nichiren Buddhism.

As expounded in the "Life Span" chapter, both the world of Buddhahood and the nine worlds are inherent and simultaneously present in life. Nichiren interprets "Since I attained Buddhahood" as meaning, "It is saying that these Ten Worlds are part of the makeup of a Buddha with his eternally endowed three bodies" (OTT, 133).

From the standpoint of the passage's implicit meaning, the Buddha who attained enlightenment in the remote past did not "become" a Buddha by having eradicated the nine worlds. Rather the Buddha simultaneously possesses both the nine worlds and the world of Buddhahood. This is called being "eternally endowed with the Ten Worlds."

"Eternally endowed with" means originally or inherently possessing. It describes the original essence of life that "was not worked for, that was not improved upon, but that exists just as it always has" (OTT, 141). This is also termed beginningless time, or "uncreated." It is the original and true aspect of life just as it is.

To manifest the essence of life that exists just as it is means to develop and use fully the power inherent in our lives.

To illustrate, soon after a severe winter, fresh young shoots emerge. The tender new sprouts grow at a frantic pace and glisten in the morning sunlight. There is nothing the least bit tentative in their appearance. They're not timid; they're not playing around. Each moment, they live life to the fullest. They certainly aren't stubborn or inflexible. Through and through, they live true to themselves. As a result, they shine and achieve a marvelous harmony with everything around them.

This is the condition of life that the French author Romain Rolland describes when he writes: "I have gained my own fulfillment! I have won mastery over myself! What possession could compare to this."[4]

What's more, we who have encountered the Mystic Law can open up our original selves and make our lives shine eternally. What a tremendous privilege this is! How truly fortunate we are!

I will never forget President Toda lecturing on this passage. It was a truly great lecture.

"All of you, circle the characters *ji* (self) and *toku* (attained),"[5] Mr. Toda said, his slightly hoarse voice resounding through the room. Everyone circled the two characters with their pencils. Some had looks of fascination, and others looked perplexed, their expressions seeming to say, "Why are you having us do this?" President Toda gazed about the room, taking in everyone's reaction.

Then he continued:

When we put these two words together, we get "self-attained" (*jitoku*), and what is left over is "I, the Buddha, come" (*ga burrai*). "I" (*ga*) indicates the Dharma body;

"Buddha," the reward body; and "come," the manifested body. In other words, these stand for the Buddha's three bodies. So the implicit meaning of *ji ga toku bur͡rai* is to attain, on one's own, the three bodies of the Buddha.

"We attain, on our own, the Buddha's three bodies." When we heard this, everyone was taken aback. In the phrase *ji ga toku bur͡rai*, which we had read many times without clearly understanding, the two characters *ji* and *toku* now stood out conspicuously. He thus taught that Buddhahood is a state of life we achieve from within, that Buddhahood inherently exists within our own lives. And the participants could fully grasp his meaning.

Pervading President Toda's lecture was his sincere wish to teach us that all people are originally Buddhas, that ordinary people who chant the Mystic Law are Buddhas.

This was also Nichiren's spirit. His free and nondogmatic interpretation of the Lotus Sutra in *The Record of the Orally Transmitted Teachings*, from the standpoint of the revitalization of the human being, is truly the crystallization of his immense compassion.

Let us now turn once again to the three bodies.

The Dharma body is the Mystic Law itself, the eternal and unchanging truth. Since this is the true essence of the self, it corresponds to *ga* (self or I) in *ga bur͡rai*.

The reward body is the Buddha's wisdom to awaken to the Mystic Law, and the benefit and virtue with which a Buddha is endowed in reward for awakening to the Law. Since a Buddha is someone awakened to his or her original self, the reward body corresponds to *butsu* (Buddha) [which, in combination with *rai*, meaning here "to come" from a place of origin, contracts to form *bur͡rai*].

The manifested body indicates the physical form a Buddha assumes in order to save the people. Fundamentally, such actions arise from the Buddha's compassion. Since the Buddha appears where there are people, this body corresponds to *rai* (come).

These three bodies are the inherent properties of Shakyamuni who attained enlightenment in the remote past.

Living at one with the eternal Law, the Buddha employs boundless wisdom and manifests immeasurable benefit to eternally lead all people to happiness. This Buddha who eternally leads people to enlightenment is Shakyamuni who attained enlightenment in the remote past. Nichiren Daishonin is the Buddha who attained on his own the inherent and uncreated three bodies of the Buddha.

The three bodies represent the inherent power to enjoy one's existence to the fullest and lead others to happiness through the Mystic Law. To awaken to the true self that yearns for the happiness of oneself and others is the greatest of all joys and the greatest peace of mind.

The Record of the Orally Transmitted Teachings explains that we who follow the Daishonin are Buddhas originally possessing the three bodies: "Now when Nichiren and his followers chant Nam-myoho-renge-kyo, they are acting as votaries of these words, 'since I attained Buddhahood'" (p. 134).

When we chant daimoku and practice for ourselves and others, we can attain the three bodies inherent in our lives. We can realize the same state of life as Nichiren. The three bodies become manifest in the lives of those who fight against adversity and struggle for kosen-rufu as Bodhisattvas of the Earth.

When friends suffer, we cannot stand by doing nothing. We cannot pretend not to notice. We take action for those around us—even to the point of forgetting about our own immediate difficulties. The SGI is a gathering of such heroes of the people.

This was certainly evident in our fellow members' actions in Kansai at the time of the Great Hanshin Earthquake [1995]. "Defeat is unthinkable!"—this was their spirit. Everyone was faced with calamitous circumstances, but they took action, wringing out every ounce of strength. Their actions, words and gestures of encouragement brought hope and courage to countless others.

Members sincerely turned to the Gohonzon to chant Nam-myoho-renge-kyo for suffering friends, even forgetting the passage of time. And, on seeing friends' agonized faces, they offered them words imbued with confidence and courage: "It's going to be all right. We can definitely overcome this!" The members were not directed to do this by anyone. Nor, for that matter, on the orders of someone else could people be expected to exert themselves so tirelessly.

When we are caught up in what others think, in formality or appearances, we cannot manifest the power eternally inherent in our lives. But we can manifest such power when we earnestly dedicate ourselves to others and to kosen-rufu. The Buddha originally endowed with the three bodies—the limitless power inherent in life—vibrantly manifests in a person of such spirit, single-minded determination and action.

In whom could the Buddha possibly appear, if not in such a person? Just whom could the "Buddha endowed with the three bodies" possibly indicate? It is our lives that the passage in *The Record of the Orally Transmitted Teachings* describes:

> If in a single moment of life we exhaust the pains and trials of millions of kalpas, then instant after instant there will arise in us the three Buddha bodies with which we are eternally endowed. (p. 214)

We ourselves can manifest the eternally inherent three bodies, the vast state of life of the Buddha. This is a state of life seldom attained even when sought, a state of life so grand that the very idea of seeking it rarely even occurs to people. Through the single word "faith," through steadfastly embracing the Mystic Law, we can attain Buddhahood on our own, the Buddhahood with which we are inherently endowed. As the sutra says, "This cluster of unsurpassed jewels has come to us unsought" (LSOC, 124).

In our hearts we possess the supreme treasure. The courage to face any difficulty, boundless hope, burning passion and inexhaustible wisdom—all of these are facets of the originally inherent jewel of our lives. Those who forge ahead in faith with this confidence are Buddhas. Their lives turn into clusters of "unsurpassed jewels." In lifetime after lifetime and world after world, they are people of wealth and influence, leading lives of great fulfillment.

Ultimately, Buddhahood is attained on one's own, not through someone else. It is something we achieve through our own efforts. Through faith in the Mystic Law, we can definitely manifest the great state of absolute freedom of the eternal and undying self. This is the essence of the verse section and the conclusion the "Life Span" chapter puts forth.

▪30▪

I do shujo ko.
Hoben gen nehan.
Ni jitsu fu metsu-do.
Jo ju shi seppo.
Ga jo ju o shi.
I sho jin-zu-riki.
Ryo tendo shujo.
Sui gon ni fu ken.

"In order to save living beings,
as an expedient means I appear to enter nirvana
but in truth I do not pass into extinction.
I am always here, preaching the Law.
I am always here,
but through my transcendental powers
I make it so that living beings in their befuddlement
do not see me even when close by."
(LSOC, 270–71)

SHAKYAMUNI, who attained Buddhahood in the remote past, numberless major world system dust particle kalpas ago, is the Buddha who eternally leads people to enlightenment throughout the past, present and future. Why does a Buddha, whose life is eternal, pass into extinction?

The answer is that he does so as an expedient means "to save living beings." The Buddha enters nirvana (that is, passes into extinction, or dies) as an expedient means to lead people to enlightenment.

Nirvana indicates a state of tranquillity achieved by overcoming earthly desires. The early Buddhist teachings, moreover, put forth the goal of "complete nirvana," or "nirvana of no remainder," attained by not only overcoming earthly desires of the mind but by freeing oneself from the influence of the physical body through death. For this reason, a Buddha's death is referred to as "entering nirvana."

But the "Life Span" chapter indicates that the Buddha only appears to pass into extinction, or enter nirvana, as an expedient means. The truth is that, out of his compassion and wisdom, he eternally continues working to lead all people to happiness.

The profound stability of the Buddha's life derives from his ceaseless activity to save people, just as the stability of a top derives from the rapidity of its spin. The Buddha's state of life, pervaded with compassion and wisdom, is one of absolute serenity and tranquillity.

True nirvana lies not in physical and spiritual extinction but in the perfection of wisdom. Perfect wisdom is limitless and works in conjunction with compassion; it manifests as the Buddha's eternal activity to lead people to happiness.

The sutra passage mentions the Buddha's "transcendental powers." Basically, these are a function of the "compassion at one with wisdom" with which the Buddha's eternal life is endowed.

From the standpoint of Nichiren Buddhism, this perfect wisdom is an original attribute of our lives. We are eternally endowed with the Buddha's three bodies. Those who have forgotten this original self are, as the passage says, "befuddled."

Like a Concerned Parent Watching Over His Children

To the Buddha, "living beings in their befuddlement" are like children who have not yet reached the age of discernment. Mischievous children may resent and feel constrained by a parent who constantly watches over them. But if the parent momentarily disappears from the child's sight, the child cries out for and tries to find the parent.

Similarly, only when the Buddha passes into extinction can befuddled people truly appreciate their fortune in having encountered the Buddha. He regards all people as his own children. Like a parent, the Buddha understands the people well and exerts himself in various ways on their behalf, employing all manner of expedient means. Passing into extinction is the ultimate expedient means at the Buddha's disposal.

The Buddha in fact constantly watches over the people, close by their side. He is "always here, preaching the Law" but purposely does not allow himself to be seen. Thus Shakyamuni says he makes it so that people "do not see me even when close by."

Why does the Buddha go to such lengths? It is necessary in order to awaken people to their true selves and enable them to become self-reliant. Continuing this parent-child analogy, it is as though the Buddha is engaging us by playing a game of peek-a-boo or hide-and-seek. Such games are thought to be very important for the psychological development of children. They cultivate a sense of assurance and trust that even though someone is not immediately visible, they are still somewhere close and will definitely reappear.

The development of such awareness gives rise to the power of self-reliance. In a sense, the parent dwells within the child's heart. In the child's heart, there is someone in whom the child can firmly believe, even though that person may not currently be there. As a result, the child learns to take action with a sense of freedom and self-assurance.

The principle remains operative even after we become adults. Whether anyone else is aware of what we are doing, if there is but one person who truly trusts and understands us, we will have confidence and absolute peace of mind. This becomes a great source of encouragement and, above all, strength. Because of this, we can take action freely and to our heart's content.

Our relationship with the Buddha is not limited to this lifetime alone. The parent who constantly watches over the people is the eternal Buddha revealed in the "Life Span" chapter.

Yet befuddled people cannot even see the Buddha existing in their own hearts. For this reason, Nichiren Daishonin inscribed the life of the Buddha—his own identity—in the form of the Gohonzon. And this Gohonzon serves as a mirror for us to see the Gohonzon existing within ourselves.

In his letter "On the Treasure Tower," Nichiren writes:

> Abutsu-bo is therefore the treasure tower itself, and the treasure tower is Abutsu-bo himself. . . . You, yourself, are a Thus Come One who is originally enlightened and endowed with the three bodies. You should chant Nam-myoho-renge-kyo with this conviction. Then the place where you chant daimoku will become the dwelling place of the treasure tower. (WND-I, 299–300)

When we reverently pray to the Gohonzon, we manifest the life of the Gohonzon in ourselves. Illuminated by the bright mirror of the Gohonzon, the world of Buddhahood within spontaneously rises to the surface.

The Gohonzon, embodying Nichiren's very soul, is the essence of the Buddha's life. Even though the Buddha is always here in the world in the form of the Gohonzon, unless people have faith, the Gohonzon will appear to them only as paper or wood. But it is in fact the embodiment of the noble life of the Buddha.

Regarding "always here" in the passage "I am always here, preaching the Law," Nichiren says: "'Always here' refers to the place where the votaries of the Lotus Sutra abide. 'Here' is the saha world" (OTT, 134). The Buddha is present wherever a person of action overcomes difficulties based on faith and correctly advances in life.

He continues: "'Preaching the Law' is the sound of the words of all living beings, that is, the sound of preaching the Law through the wisdom that is freely received and used, a part of their original makeup. Now that we have entered the Latter Day of the Law, preaching the Law means Nam-myoho-renge-kyo" (OTT, 134).

The Buddha of limitless joy (the Buddha of compassion, at one with wisdom, who freely receives and uses the benefit of the Mystic Law) manifests in the lives of those who chant Nam-myoho-renge-kyo to the Gohonzon. Nichiren says that by basing ourselves on faith we can tap the Buddha's wisdom and manifest the Buddha's benefit in our lives.

When we have absolute confidence that we can overcome any and all sufferings through faith in the Gohonzon, our lives are bathed in the light of boundless hope, and limitless strength wells forth. This is the strongest and most secure way of life.

The passage "as an expedient means I appear to enter nirvana," according to President Toda, "sheds light on the question of why we die even though life is eternal." He taught that, viewed from the eternal state of one who perceives the oneness of birth and death, death is an expedient means.

President Toda often compared death to sleep. When we have been awake for a long time, we tire and go to sleep. And when we wake up after a sound sleep, our vitality is restored. After we have been alive for a long time, we grow weary and die. And then we set out on a new life with a fresh spirit.

Death is a period of "recharging" for our next existence. Those who dedicate themselves to the Mystic Law are immediately reborn, and in their new existences they rejoin their comrades struggling for kosen-rufu. They can lead fulfilling lives of mission according to their desires.

In Buddhism, therefore, there is neither fear of death nor a defiant attitude toward death accompanied by a sense of resignation. Firmly fixing our eyes on the truth that death is an expedient means, we can live through everything with dignity and composure. This is the way of life of a Buddhist. We can live with unremitting spirit and vigor in this lifetime and in every lifetime.

As President Toda emphasized, however, even though life is eternal, our rebirth does not entail any discontinuity from one existence to the next. From past existences to the present and from the present to the future, our lives are continuous. The law of cause and effect operates eternally over past, present and future. The good and evil causes engraved in our lives do not simply disappear.

President Toda taught that after we die, our lives merge with and melt into the universe:

> While our lives melt into the universe, they do not blend in with the lives of others. Each life retains its integrity and experiences joy or sadness depending on the person's actions while alive—as though crying or laughing in a dream. And then, like someone waking up from a dream on account of some disturbance, a person is born once again in concordance with the proper external causes.

Therefore, we must not give up in this life using the rationale that "there's always my next lifetime." Nor can irresponsible or erratic behavior be justified on the grounds that "you only live once."

One's actions in previous existences are all engraved and contained in this lifetime. The causes for our present suffering or joy, happiness or misery, all lie in our own past actions. But Nichiren Buddhism enables us to fundamentally reform our destiny. When we truly base ourselves on Buddhism's view of life's eternity, we realize the first thing to change is how we live in the present.

When we pray to the Gohonzon, change arises from the depths of our being. Strong, pure vitality wells forth in abundance. The iron chains of destiny are cut, and our original identity, the fresh and robust world of Buddhahood, appears.

Carrying out our human revolution means always living with exactly such new vitality.

▪31▪

Shu ken ga metsu-do.
Ko kuyo shari.
Gen kai e renbo.
Ni sho katsu-go shin.
Shujo ki shin-buku.
Shichi-jiki i nyunan.
Isshin yok ken butsu.
Fu ji shaku shinmyo.
Ji ga gyu shuso.
Ku shutsu ryojusen.

"When the multitude sees that I have passed into extinction,
far and wide they offer alms to my relics.
All harbor thoughts of yearning
and in their minds thirst to gaze at me.
When living beings have become truly faithful,
honest and upright, gentle in intent,
single-mindedly desiring to see the Buddha,
not hesitating even if it costs them their lives,
then I and the assembly of monks
appear together on Holy Eagle Peak."
(LSOC, 271)

I N WORKING on this lecture, I composed this poem:

Each morning and evening,
reciting the "Expedient Means"
and "Life Span" chapters,
we luxuriate in
the song of the universe.

In our morning and evening practice of gongyo and chanting dai-moku, the microcosm of our lives joins with the macrocosm of the universe in a melodious chorus. The sound of the Mystic Law, the sound of voices chanting Nam-myoho-renge-kyo, is the symphony of the universe.

Each morning and evening, we immerse ourselves in the symphony of the Mystic Law resounding throughout the universe. The Buddhas, bodhisattvas and Buddhist deities throughout eternity shower us with praise and protection. I hope each of you will have great conviction in this and lead a thoroughly joyous and cheerful existence. This is my ardent wish.

As I have mentioned, we who dedicate ourselves to kosen-rufu are always together with the Buddha. In an age that for many could be called a lonely hell, we are following an unparalleled path of peace, tranquillity and eternal joy. Moreover, there are now friends, Bodhisattvas of the Earth, in every part of the world. Comrades everywhere share our heartfelt aspirations. Truly, we lead the noblest and most wonderful lives.

We who dedicate ourselves to this unsurpassed path can encounter the noble Buddha at any time and in any place. From the sutra passage above, we gain a still deeper understanding of this point.

Yearning for the Buddha

From the Buddha's perspective, nirvana is an expedient means. In truth, the Buddha is always at our sides. People have a hard time grasping this truth. But when the Buddha dies, they develop a seeking spirit for—they yearn for and thirst to gaze upon—the Buddha. Having sought to quell people's worries by saying, "as an expedient means I appear to enter nirvana" (LSOC, 271), and thus revealing the meaning of his death, the Buddha now offers profoundly merciful words.

He says in effect: "After I die, people will make offerings to my relics and thirst to see me. Someone who arouses an earnest seeking mind for the Buddha can meet me without fail. I will appear here on Eagle Peak with many disciples." These words abundantly convey the Buddha's spirit of concern for all those in the world after his passing.

The relationship between the Buddha and his disciples is not limited to a single lifetime. The mentor-disciple relationship is maintained eternally throughout the past, present and future. I am always together with President Toda. This I understand from struggling as I have.

Although the Buddha is close at hand, we cannot sense the connection if we just sit around idly. This passage concretely elucidates the attitude we need to have toward the Buddha.

In the first place, it says, "far and wide they offer alms to my relics." This should not be taken as encouragement to make offerings to relics in a literal sense. Rather, it teaches the importance of having a direct connection in faith with the Buddha. The highest offering to the Buddha is not to worship something reminiscent of the Buddha. Rather, it is to inherit the Buddha's spirit. In other words, the highest offering lies in struggling to manifest, as one's own way of life, even a part of the spirit of the Buddha, who upheld the philosophy that everyone is a Buddha and tirelessly strove to save all from suffering.

Shakyamuni's spirit is embodied in the Lotus Sutra. Nichiren Daishonin's spirit is embodied in the Three Great Secret Laws and the great undertaking of kosen-rufu to lead all to happiness. For us today, "far and wide they offer alms to my relics" means chanting Nammyoho-renge-kyo to the Gohonzon and participating in activities for kosen-rufu.

Faith ultimately means wholeheartedly devoting oneself to the Gohonzon and arousing a spirit of yearning for and thirsting to gaze upon the Gohonzon. In a letter to the lay nun Myoichi, Nichiren Daishonin writes:

> What is called faith is nothing unusual. Faith means putting one's trust in the Lotus Sutra, Shakyamuni, Many Treasures, the Buddhas and bodhisattvas of the ten directions, and the heavenly gods and benevolent deities, and chanting Nam-myoho-renge-kyo as a woman cherishes her husband, as a man lays down his life for his wife, as parents refuse to abandon their children, or as a child refuses to leave its mother. (WND-1, 1036)

The love between husband and wife or parent and child is an expression of unadorned humanity, of the pure human heart. It may be that, in the present age, even such love has become weak and diluted. No matter how much honor or wealth someone may have, to lose touch with human affection is to become miserable. There is no greater anguish.

The lay nun Myoichi, the recipient of this letter, was a woman who treasured most highly this spirit Nichiren is talking about. While the circumstances she faced were severe, she possessed immense inner wealth. Moreover, for the lay nun Myoichi, these words from the Daishonin were more than simple metaphor.

Amid the whirlwind of attacks against Nichiren's followers that accompanied the Tatsunokuchi Persecution and the Sado Exile, the lay nun Myoichi and her husband steadfastly maintained their faith. They suffered various hardships due to their faith in the Lotus Sutra, including having their fief confiscated. Moreover, the lay nun Myoichi's husband died before word could reach them that Nichiren had been pardoned from exile. She and her children were also in poor health.

Still, she fought heroically, keeping alive the flame of faith and practicing for both herself and her late husband. While her life was difficult, she sent her own laborers to work for Nichiren at Sado and at Minobu. She fought hard, with the message of hope she received from Nichiren sustaining her spirits: "Those who believe in the Lotus Sutra are as if in winter, but winter always turns to spring" (WND-1, 536).

Nichiren also wrote her this encouragement:

> Your husband gave his life for the Lotus Sutra ... Therefore he must certainly have received blessings as great as theirs [the boy Snow Mountains and Bodhisattva Medicine King].
>
> He is probably watching his wife and children in the heavenly mirrors of the sun and moon every moment of the day and night. Since you and your children are ordinary persons, you cannot see or hear him. . . . But never doubt that he is protecting you. Moreover, he may be close at hand. (WND-1, 536)

What courage and strength these words must have given the lay nun Myoichi! The most miserable person deserves to become the happiest. This is Buddhism. This is the Daishonin's spirit.

Nichiren's writing that I quoted earlier, which begins with "What is called faith is nothing unusual," was sent to the lay nun Myoichi after she had continued her difficult struggle for as long as seven years without retreating a step. She struggled hard for both herself and her late husband, and she succeeded splendidly in raising her children. The Daishonin encouraged her to pray to the Gohonzon and chant Nam-myoho-renge-kyo with the same love and affection she felt toward her deceased husband and her children. This, he told her, is faith.

The ultimate meaning of faith is difficult to understand, and yet at the same time quite simple. Essentially, it is to maintain a seeking mind toward—and not to forget—the Gohonzon, no matter what our circumstances. When we seek the Buddha with an honest and pure spirit—like that of a child in search of her mother or a mother embracing her child—a palace of indestructible happiness arises in our hearts.

By contrast, someone whose inner life is shrouded in a thick smoke screen of doubt will be utterly incapable of connecting in faith with the great life of the Buddha. This is what the verse section of the "Life Span" chapter teaches. Faith means yearning for and thirsting to see the Buddha. It is to be "honest and upright, gentle in intent"; to be thoroughly honest and gentle in one's spirit toward the Buddha, toward the Gohonzon. We must not have the rigid attitude of those whose hearts are callous and closed.

The Object of Devotion of Faith

The passage further indicates the proper attitude we should have in faith where it says "single-mindedly desiring to see the Buddha, not hesitating even if it costs them their lives" (LSOC, 271). When we practice unstintingly with such honest faith, with such a seeking spirit, the Buddha appears together with his many disciples at Eagle Peak. In other words, we can then see the Buddha at any time.

President Toda once lectured on this passage as follows:

> When the Buddha solemnly manifests in our lives, we are
> undoubtedly free of all misery. In other words, when we

embrace the Gohonzon—even though we may not be aware of it—the Gohonzon appears within us. Our bodies become Eagle Peak. And the power of the Gohonzon, that is, the power of the Daishonin, fills our lives.

Those who practice with the attitude of "single-mindedly desiring to see the Buddha, not hesitating even if it costs them their lives" can definitely attain the state of life indicated by "I and the assembly of monks appear together on Holy Eagle Peak."

These two passages are joined by the word "then." What this reveals is that the moment we set our hearts firmly on our wish to see the Buddha, we are unfailingly embraced in the Buddha's immense compassion.

"Then" does not mean "eventually" or "in the future." It indicates the attainment of Buddhahood through the principle of embracing the Gohonzon is in itself observing one's own mind. When we stand up with strong faith in the Gohonzon, then—at that time, at that very instant—the life of the Buddha wells forth in our own lives. And the place where we are becomes Eagle Peak, the Buddha land, the place where the Buddha dwells.

Nichikan says:

When one chants Nam-myoho-renge-kyo with faith in this Gohonzon, [his or her] life immediately becomes the object of devotion of three thousand realms in a single moment of life; it becomes the life of Nichiren Daishonin.

The life of the Gohonzon, the life of Nichiren Daishonin, instantaneously manifests in our lives. There is no greater benefit than this.

All people, without exception, possess in their hearts the supreme hidden treasure of Buddhahood. The heart of the Lotus Sutra is found in such equality. And the heart of the Daishonin has made it possible for all people of the Latter Day of the Law to open this inner treasure chest. The key that opens it is the faith of "single-mindedly desiring to see the Buddha" and the practice of "not hesitating even if it costs them their lives." The basis for attaining enlightenment is a sincere seeking mind and an earnest practice.

"Not hesitating even if it costs them their lives" does not suggest any devaluation of life, however. To view life lightly goes against the spirit of the Lotus Sutra. The true meaning of this passage is that we should overcome, without hesitation, the ego that attaches to the lesser self and base our lives instead on the truly dignified and majestic greater self.

The true meaning of "not hesitating even if it costs them their lives" is to live in the real world while steadfastly basing oneself on the Mystic Law. It means to challenge oneself to realize one's fullest potential.

There is no limit to the extent to which we who uphold faith in the Mystic Law can expand and enrich our lives when we practice with this spirit. To this end, it is important in our practice of faith that we not hesitate or hold back. The Mystic Law enables us to lead the fullest and most brilliant of lives. The whole point of practicing this Buddhism is to ensure that we never find ourselves deadlocked in misery.

The Gohonzon is a "cluster of blessings"; it contains within it every kind of benefit. Our hearts, our faith, our practice hold the key to the benefits of the entire universe. The true "object of devotion for observing the mind" is the object of devotion of faith. Nothing is greater than faith. Therefore, a person of strong faith and seeking spirit shines. The life of such a person itself becomes a jewel. This is the benefit of Nichiren Buddhism.

As I have mentioned before, the verse section is a song praising the greater self. We ourselves—our own minds—open the object of devotion within our lives. Therefore, as long as we possess an unshakable mind of faith, we can build a dignified self and become like a great mountain that no storm can budge.

As the Daishonin says, "Regard both suffering and joy as facts of life, and continue chanting Nam-myoho-renge-kyo" (WND-I, 681). True faith, to truly uphold the Mystic Law, means to persevere in our practice in times of both suffering and joy.

The Assembly on Eagle Peak Has Not Yet Disbanded

This year (1996) marks the fiftieth year since President Toda began lecturing on the Lotus Sutra after the war. President Toda's lectures have always remained in my heart. I have composed each installment out of the desire to pass on to future generations my mentor's lectures, which were profound and lucid and resounded with his love of humanity.

Through this lecture series, people the world over have had a new opportunity to deeply study his guidance, which brims with wisdom and conviction. Inspiration and determination are spreading. I feel as though I can see him smiling broadly on Eagle Peak.

Speaking of Eagle Peak, the passage we're studying reads in part:

When living beings have become truly faithful,
honest and upright, gentle in intent,
single-mindedly desiring to see the Buddha,
not hesitating even if it costs them their lives,
then I and the assembly of monks
appear together on Holy Eagle Peak.
(LSOC, 271)

This passage reveals the key to attaining Buddhahood for people in the Latter Day of the Law. President Toda's enlightenment in prison, which became the origin of the Soka Gakkai's development in the postwar period, means he read this passage with his whole life.

From the standpoint of Nichiren Buddhism, we will discuss the meaning of these lines on a still-deeper level.

As I have already mentioned, the verse section of the "Life Span" chapter is a song calling out to the people in the world after Shakyamuni's passing, especially to those of the Latter Day. And within the verse section, the above passage in particular reveals the key for people of the Latter Day to attain Buddhahood.

That key is contained in the phrase "single-mindedly." Nichiren Buddhism elucidates and makes available the secret of "single-mindedly" to all people of the Latter Day in the form of Nam-myoho-renge-kyo.

Thus, in "Letter to Gijo-bo," Nichiren writes:

> The verse section of the chapter states, "single-mindedly desiring to see the Buddha, not hesitating even if it costs them their lives." As a result of this passage, I have revealed the Buddhahood in my own life. The reason is that it is this sutra passage that has enabled me to embody the Three Great Secret Laws, or the reality of three thousand realms in a single moment of life, that is found in the "Life Span" chapter. (WND-I, 389)

He then clarifies the implicit meaning of single-mindedly, saying: "'Single-mindedly desiring to see the Buddha' may read as follows: single-mindedly observing the Buddha, concentrating one's mind on seeing the Buddha, and when looking at one's own mind, perceiving that it is the Buddha" (WND-I, 389–90).

Nichiren interprets single-mindedly desiring to see the Buddha as meaning "to see one's own mind is to see the Buddha." He thus indicates that the mind of an ordinary person who seeks the Buddha becomes and manifests the mind of the Buddha. Nichiren says that to perceive Buddhahood within one's own mind is to attain the effect of the Buddha eternally endowed with the three bodies.

Herein lies life's most profound secret. In this mind of faith, the ordinary person is a Buddha embodying the mystic principles of the mutual possession of the Ten Worlds and the reality of three thousand realms in a single moment of life.

For all of us in the Latter Day, the Daishonin manifested the "mind of the Buddha" and the "effect of the Buddha eternally endowed with the three bodies," which are inherent in his life, as the Gohonzon. In the Latter Day, the Buddha whom we should seek single-mindedly is none other than the Gohonzon.

Accordingly, the lines that follow, "then I and the assembly of monks appear together on Holy Eagle Peak," allude to the Gohonzon. This is clarified in Nichiren's words, "The Gohonzon is the realization and manifestation of this passage" (OTT, 135).

The ceremony at Eagle Peak in the Lotus Sutra is a ceremony of life that reveals the world of Buddhahood existing in Shakyamuni's own heart. It reveals the Buddha's life, which is as vast as the universe.

In this passage, "I" indicates Shakyamuni or the world of Buddhahood; "the assembly of monks" refers to the bodhisattvas and people of the two vehicles; and "together" means all beings of the Ten Worlds. In short, the ceremony at Eagle Peak reveals the Buddha's life embodying the mutual possession of the Ten Worlds and three thousand realms in a single moment of life.

Making use of the imagery of the ceremony at Eagle Peak (i.e., the Ceremony in the Air), Nichiren manifested the world of Buddhahood existing in his life as the Gohonzon.

Therefore, he says, "This passage refers to 'the assembly on Holy Eagle Peak which continues in solemn state and has not yet disbanded'" (OTT, 135). In other words, the ceremony at Eagle Peak is still being solemnly conducted and has not ended.

Nichiren also says:

Wherever we dwell and practice the single vehicle, that place will be the Capital of Eternally Tranquil Light. And, without having to take a step, those who are our disciples and lay supporters can view Eagle Peak in India and day and night will go to and from the Land of Eternally Tranquil Light that has existed for all time. (WND-1, 313)

When we chant Nam-myoho-renge-kyo to the Gohonzon, we are taking our places at the solemn ceremony of the assembly at Eagle Peak. When we earnestly chant Nam-myoho-renge-kyo, the Eagle Peak in our hearts comes to brilliantly illuminate our lives. Our very existence becomes the Ceremony in the Air. Our daily activities become in every respect the conduct of persons gathered at Eagle Peak. How wondrous!

Also, broadly speaking, it could be said that the SGI itself represents "the assembly on Holy Eagle Peak which continues in solemn state and has not yet disbanded," because its members, as Nichiren's followers, are advancing kosen-rufu in the unity of many in body, one in mind.

While incarcerated during the war, President Toda had an experience in which he perceived himself at the Lotus Sutra's Ceremony in the Air as a Bodhisattva of the Earth. He experienced with his own life "the assembly on Holy Eagle Peak which continues in solemn state and has not yet disbanded." At that time, President Toda realized his mission as a Bodhisattva of the Earth, a realization that became the origin of the Soka Gakkai's postwar development.

After President Toda's death, Nichijun, hearing us vow to advance one in mind toward kosen-rufu, said: "It seems to me that this body [the Soka Gakkai] truly represents 'the assembly on Holy Eagle Peak which continues in solemn state and has not yet disbanded.' To put it another way, this body is the true pure land of Eagle Peak. It is the Buddha's great gathering and as such commands my deepest respect."

The SGI is truly a sublime gathering of the Buddha's children. It is the assembly on Holy Eagle Peak that continues in solemn state and has not yet disbanded. The SGI is a gathering of Bodhisattvas of the Earth who, just as in the ceremony on Eagle Peak, have appeared to lead all people of the Latter Day to enlightenment and so fulfill their eternal vow. We are eternal comrades advancing together over the three existences toward kosen-rufu.

▪32▪

Ga ji go shujo.
Jo zai shi fu-metsu.
I ho-ben-rik ko.
Gen u metsu fu-metsu.
Yo-koku u shujo.
Kugyo shingyo sha.
Ga bu o hi chu.
I setsu mujo ho.
Nyoto fu mon shi.
Tan ni ga metsu-do.
Ga ken sho shujo.
Motsu-zai o kukai.
Ko fu i gen shin.
Ryo go sho katsu-go.
In go shin renbo.
Nai shutsu i seppo.

"At that time I tell the living beings
that I am always here, never entering extinction,
but that because of the power of expedient means
at times I appear to be extinct, at other times not,
and that if there are living beings in other lands
who are reverent and sincere in their wish to believe,

then among them too
I will preach the unsurpassed Law.
But you have not heard of this,
so you suppose that I enter extinction.
When I look at living beings
I see them drowned in a sea of suffering;
therefore I do not show myself,
causing them to thirst for me.
Then when their minds are filled with yearning,
at last I appear and preach the Law for them." (LSOC, 271)

THE BUDDHA APPEARS wherever people with seeking minds may be and illuminates their lives with sunlike brilliance. One of Shakyamuni's disciples composed a poem praising the greatness of his mentor: "Behold the brilliance of the Great One! Does he not shine like the sun in the sky?"

The sun is always solemnly shining, even though at times obscured by clouds and not visible from earth. The Buddha, likewise, is always present in the world. "I am always here, never entering extinction"—this describes the true aspect of the Buddha's life.

But if the Buddha were to remain constantly at people's sides, they would become utterly dependent on him. And so, to cause his disciples to become self-reliant, Shakyamuni, employing the "power of expedient means," at times appears "to be extinct, at other times not." That is, he gives the appearance of sometimes dying, sometimes living.

Just because the sun is obscured by dark clouds in one place does not mean it is hidden from sight in another. "Other lands" in this passage indicates that the sunlight of the Buddha's compassion shines also on other worlds.

"If there are living beings in other lands who are reverent and sincere in their wish to believe, then among them too I will preach the unsurpassed Law." This indicates that the Buddha appears and expounds the unsurpassed Law where there are people who sincerely believe in him, wherever they may be.

In terms of Nichiren Buddhism, the Buddha who is always here in the world and never enters extinction is the Gohonzon, or the Nam-myoho-renge-kyo Thus Come One. The unsurpassed Law that this eternal Buddha expounds is none other than Nam-myoho-renge-kyo. When we chant with unhesitant faith, our voices, just as they are, become the voice of the Buddha who is always here expounding the unsurpassed Law. Through relating actual proof of benefit, for example, this voice of the Buddha teaches us the unsurpassed power of the Mystic Law.

"I see them drowned in a sea of suffering" means that the great light of the Buddha's compassion shines upon all those whose lives are submerged in suffering. The Buddhist Law illuminates society—which is a sea of suffering—with the light of the sun of eternal joy.

Lecturing on "Life Span," President Toda said:

At least among those active as adult members of society, there is probably no one who today could unequivocally and sincerely say that life in the real world is "joyful." True joy in life is not merely a matter of having money or good health; it is a state where joy wells forth from the very depths of one's being.

President Toda's prayer was for all members to attain the state of absolute happiness in which living is itself a great joy.

The Buddha's prayer is for all people to develop the same state of life he possesses. The Lotus Sutra is the scripture in which he reveals the path to this end. "I want each of you to become a sunlike existence just like me"—this is Shakyamuni's spirit expressed in the "Life Span" chapter.

Nichiren Buddhism is the teaching that enables each person to become a "sun." It reveals the great path to true self-reliance.

The Russian poet Aleksandr Pushkin sings:

> *Before the bright dawn, even so*
> *Shall flicker and die every sophistry jaded*
> *At reason's unperishing spark.*
> *Salute to the sunrise, and vanish the dark!*[6]

Life is not all sunshine. There are cloudy days and days that are cold and wet. There are times when we are chilled to the bone by blowing snow. But at all times, and no matter what happens, let us dauntlessly advance with the sun in our hearts blazing ever brilliantly. Even in the coldest months of winter, the sunlight of spring is definitely drawing near. And with the arrival of spring, even the thickest walls of ice melt away, turning into water that moistens the earth, producing the floral pageantry of spring.

▪33▪

Jin-zu-riki nyo ze.
O asogi ko.
Jo zai ryojusen.
Gyu yo sho jusho.
Shujo ken ko jin.
Dai ka sho sho ji.
Ga shi do annon.
Tennin jo juman.
Onrin sho do-kaku.
Shuju ho shogon.
Hoju ta keka.
Shujo sho yu-raku.
Shoten gyaku tenku.
Jo saŝshu gi-gaku.
U mandara ke.
San butsu gyu daishu.

"Such are my transcendental powers.
For asamkhya kalpas
constantly I have dwelled on Holy Eagle Peak
and in various other places.
When living beings witness the end of a kalpa
and all is consumed in a great fire,
this, my land, remains safe and tranquil,

constantly filled with heavenly and human beings.
The halls and pavilions in its gardens and groves
are adorned with various kinds of gems.
Jeweled trees abound in flowers and fruit
where living beings enjoy themselves at ease.
The gods strike heavenly drums,
constantly making many kinds of music.
Mandarava blossoms rain down,
scattering over the Buddha and the great assembly."
(LSOC, 271–72)

WHAT IS life's purpose? It is happiness. And what is the aim of religion or belief? Again, it must be human happiness.

What, then, is happiness? What is a happy life?

If happiness lay in fleeting pleasures, then the world would abound with happiness. If true happiness could be found in a life of amusement, then devoting ourselves to such an existence would be most appropriate. But viewed from the standpoint of life's eternity over the past, present and future, such happiness is an illusion and in the end will prove hollow.

Buddhism teaches how we can realize eternally indestructible happiness or, as President Toda put it, a "state of life of absolute happiness." The passage above clarifies what this essentially entails.

To begin with, "For asamkhya kalpas constantly I have dwelled on Holy Eagle Peak and in various other places" literally means that the Buddha has dwelled at Eagle Peak for an extremely long time, and that he has also appeared in various worlds in the ten directions.

From the standpoint of Nichiren Buddhism, this indicates that the Gohonzon solemnly exists in our lives at all times, wherever we may be. The Gohonzon is always with us at our sides, not parting from us for even an instant. It is always with us. Let us engrave this in our hearts.

From the next line, "When living beings witness the end of a kalpa . . .," we get a description of two completely different worlds.

"When living beings witness the end of a kalpa and all is consumed in a great fire" describes a world of suffering that reflects the state of people's lives. It is truly a hellish condition of suffering and fear.

But from the line, "this, my land, remains safe and tranquil," the scene changes completely. Here, there is peace, tranquillity and vibrancy. There is joy and brilliance, lively music and rich culture. This is the true world as perceived by the Buddha with his vast state of life.

These two worlds are in fact one and the same. Ordinary people and the Buddha perceive and experience the same world in totally different ways.

Nichiren says that the "great fire" people perceive is the "great fire of earthly desires" (OTT, 136). It is not the world itself but their lives being consumed in flames. At this they tremble in fear. And so the Buddha counsels them, saying in effect: "What do you have to fear or lament? The truth is not at all what you perceive!" And he tells them, "This land where I dwell is eternally peaceful and tranquil."

With these few words, the Buddha shatters people's illusions and opens up their shallow, limited states of life. These words of great compassion express the Buddha's desire to elevate all people, all humankind, to the great state of life of Buddhahood.

The pre-Lotus Sutra teachings taught that the Buddha and ordinary people lived in different worlds. They explained that people had to cross over from this world, the saha world, to the other world where the Buddha was said to dwell—and that this was only possible by practicing for an extremely long time.

But the "Life Span" chapter explains that the Buddha eternally expounds the Law in this saha world. It teaches that this world is the Buddha land, and that the Buddha and ordinary people dwell in the same saha world.

Nichiren writes:

> Hungry spirits perceive the Ganges River as fire, human beings perceive it as water, and heavenly beings perceive it as amrita. Though the water is the same, it appears differently according to one's karmic reward from the past. (WND-1, 486)

What we see differs depending on our state of life. Moreover, when our state of life changes, the world in which we live also changes. This is the ultimate principle of actual three thousand realms in a single moment of life found in the Lotus Sutra.

Nichiren says of his life of repeated persecution:

> Day after day, month after month, year after year I have been subjected to repeated persecutions. Minor persecutions and annoyances are too numerous even to be counted, but the major persecutions number four. (WND-1, 240)

During his exile to Sado—by any standard a persecution of the greatest severity—Nichiren Daishonin calmly proclaimed: "I feel immeasurable delight even though I am now an exile" (WND-1, 386). From the vantage of a state of life as vast as the universe, he took in everything with imperturbable composure.

President Makiguchi endured life in prison with the thought, "When I reflect on the Daishonin's sufferings on Sado, my difficulties are as nothing." He also wrote in a letter, "Even hell has its enjoyments, depending on one's outlook."

A vast state of life is the product of profound humanity. I recall how President Toda looked on the day his publishing company, having fallen on hard times, finally had to curtail its operations. I described the scene in my narrative history, *The Human Revolution*.

I was then twenty-one. As editor of the monthly magazine *Boys' Japan*, I had been filled with enthusiasm. Then suddenly the magazine was discontinued. It came as truly a great shock—like being aboard a jet that halted suddenly in midair.

But when I happened to glance at President Toda, I saw that he was enjoying a game of *shogi* (Japanese chess) with a friend. He looked completely calm and untroubled. For a moment, I couldn't understand how he could carry on so at such a dire time. But a moment later, I understood: "He's fine. Nothing in him has changed. His appearance is a declaration that he will carry on the struggle." The inspiration I felt is still fresh in my mind.

No matter what violent storms of destiny might assail us, our fighting spirit should not falter in the least. Our mind of faith must not be destroyed at any cost. "This, my land, remains safe and tranquil" describes such a state of life.

I am Josei Toda's disciple. From the time I rallied under him at age nineteen until today, I have created a history, time and again weathering storms and navigating rough seas. I have as a result developed the fortitude to withstand any and all difficulties without wavering in the least.

President Toda taught that "this, my land, remains safe and tranquil" refers to our homes, where the Gohonzon is enshrined—that our homes will definitely become safe and tranquil as a result of our practice.

No matter what, we absolutely must not be defeated. Let us proudly advance with a lofty state of life, with the great spirit that "solid is the castle of my heart!"

The Wonderful Workings of One's Mind

The passage that begins "constantly filled with heavenly and human beings" and ends "scattering over the Buddha and the great assembly" is like a poem to gladden our hearts when we recite the "Life Span" chapter every morning and evening. It is a pageant of truly dazzling images—of shapes, colors and sounds vying to outshine one another. So joyous, bright and lively is the world of the Buddha of the Lotus Sutra!

When he lectured on this passage, President Toda had a look of true elation. He seemed to embrace everyone with his merciful, warm voice. It was the 1950s, and everyone was poor and had various worries. "Consumed in a great fire" indeed described the state of their lives. Therefore, even though morning and evening they read the lines "The halls and pavilions in its gardens and groves are adorned with various kinds of gems . . .," it probably seemed to them no more than a fairy tale.

But President Toda explained:

We must not suppose that this passage has nothing to do with us. Even though we may be poor, we can all still lead splendid daily lives—lives in which "the halls and pavilions in its gardens and groves are adorned with various kinds of gems."

To illustrate, if you plant some saplings in an orange crate and enjoy watering and tending to them every day, then isn't that having a splendid garden or grove? And as for halls and pavilions, while your home may only be a tiny four-and-a-half tatami mat room, it is still your palace. With this confidence, you solemnly adorn it with gems. When a child brings home an outstanding report card, if the father and mother post it on the wall and take pleasure in it, then they are adorning their palace with a gem from their child. The treasures with which we adorn our palaces are the treasures of the heart.

Hearing him discuss the passage with such rich humor opened and brightened the listeners' hearts. They determined: "While we may be poor, what do our happy homes really lack?" "Let's splendidly adorn our homes with 'treasures of the heart.'" "I will turn my home into a 'jeweled palace of happiness.'"

Even a single flower can completely transform a room that was previously desolate. The important thing is that we possess the spirit and determination to change and improve our environment, even just a little.

Moreover, it is absolutely impossible that someone with a spirit of earnest faith could fail to become happy and prosperous or that his or her environment could fail to be revitalized. This is the universal principle of Buddhism.

Your heart changes everything. This is the mystic nature of life. It is an unmistakable truth. The Swiss philosopher Carl Hilty included in his book of sayings, *Bausteine*: "Rather than being upset that the rose has thorns, we should delight that a thorny shrub puts forth flowers."[7] A single change in perspective can change everything, giving rise to brightness, beauty and vast possibilities.

Nichiren speaks of the "wonderful workings of one mind" (OTT, 30). There is marvelous power and activity in the mind of someone who believes in the Gohonzon. Once we activate the fundamental energy of our minds, the gears of the three thousand phenomena immediately engage. Everything changes. We can use every situation to create hope and good.

"Adorned with various kinds of gems" could also refer to cleaning and caring for our local Buddhist centers. Local members, motivated by tremendous sincerity, are always cleaning, planting lovely flowers and trees and beautifully adorning these centers. Their sincerity is itself a supreme gem.

Moreover, pure-minded fellow Bodhisattvas of the Earth joyfully gather at these palaces of the Law, earnestly seeking a correct way of life and singing a song of hope and courage. These are indeed the joyful gardens the sutra describes as a gathering of "heavenly and human beings."

The SGI itself perfectly matches the description in this sutra passage. It is a gathering of fine people who are always bright, high-spirited and lively. "Constantly filled with heavenly and human beings" describes well this organization.

The purpose of the SGI's advance, bright and jubilant, is to turn our homes and communities, society, the world and this precious planet Earth into a paradise "adorned with various kinds of gems."

When we are embraced in the Buddha's immense state of life, then we ourselves, those around us and the land itself all shine with the light of happiness and hope. This is the power of Nam-myoho-renge-kyo of three thousand realms in a single moment of life—it is the dynamic principle of change.

Attuning ourselves with this great principle, we are struggling in the very midst of society to change the world into a paradise of happiness. This is our movement of kosen-rufu.

A Life Dedicated to the Mystic Law, a Life of True Happiness

The Lotus Sutra speaks directly to the human heart. It calls upon people to ask themselves: For what purpose was I born in this world?

Are people born to suffer, to worry? No. Are they born to lament their destiny? No, definitely not.

In connection with the passage "where living beings enjoy themselves at ease," President Toda always said: "We are born in the world to enjoy life. We are not born to suffer."

We have come here to enjoy ourselves, to live at ease. The sutra says this world is a place "where living beings enjoy themselves at ease." These wonderful words overturn shallow views about the nature of life and happiness.

Of course, "enjoy themselves at ease" does not mean indulging in superficial or hedonistic pleasures. In the face of reality's turbulent waves, such pleasures prove all too empty. The saha world, moreover, is a "world of endurance." How truly difficult it is to live, to endure life, in a world so replete with suffering and fear! If our life state is low, ultimately we will be defeated.

As seen with the Buddha eye, when we ordinary people open up the state of Buddhahood in our lives, this saha world itself becomes a paradise where living beings enjoy themselves at ease. It could be said that we are enacting a human drama of joyfully living out our lives on the stage of the saha world.

Nichiren Daishonin says, "There is no true happiness for human beings other than chanting Nam-myoho-renge-kyo" (WND-1, 681). When deep in our hearts we base ourselves on the Mystic Law, we can lead lives of supreme happiness in which we thoroughly savor both the sufferings and joys of this world.

Again, to analyze "enjoy themselves at ease," it could be said that "at ease" means "freely," and "enjoy themselves" means to "enjoy life thoroughly and wholeheartedly." In any event, our life state is the key.

In nature, there is drama. There is great joy in spring precisely because the severe winter has been withstood. The year is beautiful because of the changing seasons.

The same is true of human life. In the course of living, we encounter mountains and valleys. Because there are steep mountains, we can enjoy mountain climbing. And because there are waves, we can enjoy surfing. Similarly, as long as we possess strong life force and abundant wisdom, we can enjoy ourselves as we overcome all of life's difficulties. And we come to possess unshakable selves, secure lives endowed with the four virtues—eternity, happiness, true self and purity. President Toda called this free, indestructible, diamond-like condition a "life state of absolute happiness."

Furthermore, the Daishonin says that "enjoy themselves at ease" refers to the "boundless joy of the Law" and goes on, "Could 'enjoy themselves at ease' mean anything but that both our bodies and minds, lives and environments, are entities of three thousand realms in a single moment of life and Buddhas of limitless joy?" (WND-1, 681).

True happiness enriches our bodies and minds, our selves and our environment, and all those around us with the benefits of faith. We pray and take action not merely for our own happiness but for the happiness of others. This is the spirit of the Lotus Sutra.

We are advancing along the path of supreme happiness and leading lives of true enjoyment and ease.

"Constantly Making Many Kinds of Music"

In the line "The gods strike heavenly drums," the original meaning of "heavenly drums" is thunder. It seems that in ancient India thunder was regarded as the joyful music of heaven announcing a merciful rainfall. On one level, it could be said that this line indicates a heart of joy reverberating with supreme happiness.

President Toda explained "The gods strike heavenly drums, constantly making many kinds of music" as follows:

> Where it says that they are constantly making music, this is not like having a radio going. Let's say a father comes home and says something like, "I had a really pleasant day today"; the wife, commenting on her day, says something like, "Darling, today, I happened to hear our neighbor's cat meowing"; the son says, "I saw my teacher out walking"; and so on. A family living amid joyful conversation and

laughter—that is "constantly making many kinds of music."
But if the father is always yelling with a voice like a broken
drum, the mother is constantly screaming and the children
break down in tears, it doesn't make for very good music.

In our lives, from moment to moment and day to day, we are constantly making many kinds of music. Everything is music in the key of
our life state. Since we are alive, let's make our lives resound with the
marvelous music of hope and happiness. Let us sing the triumphant
song of a splendid life.

The SGI constantly rings with the joyous, hope-filled and confident voices of people striving to live life to the fullest. It is truly
a place where "the gods strike heavenly drums, constantly making
many kinds of music." Each voice is a "sutra" embracing people in
tones of happiness, a living expression of the principle that "the voice
carries out the work of the Buddha" (OTT, 4).

Nichiren says, "Nam-myoho-renge-kyo is like the roar of a lion"
(WND-1, 412). The great sound of our voices chanting Nam-myoho-
renge-kyo each day dispels the sad music of sorrow and lamentation;
it is steadily and surely creating an age resounding widely with the
triumphant song of the people.

The text then reads, "Mandarava blossoms rain down." Mandarava
are heavenly flowers said to delight the heart. They float down from
heaven to the world of the Mystic Law. We who dwell in the realm
of the Mystic Law—that is, we who steadily persevere in faith—are
certain to be embraced by flowers of happiness and good fortune and
celebrated by the Buddhist deities.

"Mandarava blossoms rain down" also indicates causing joy in
people's hearts. To illustrate: When a child works hard at something
and the parents praise him or her, saying, "You did a really fine job,"
the child can then take further action with joy, in high spirits, and
show still greater ability.

"Scattering over the Buddha and the great assembly" means that these flowers of good fortune and benefit fall equally upon the Buddha and all people. There is no discrimination.

As this suggests, the Buddha and the people dwell in the same saha world. Our stage for realizing eternal happiness is here and now.

▪34▪

Ga jodo fu ki.
Ni shu ken sho jin.
Ufu sho kuno.
Nyo ze shitsu juman.
Ze sho zai shujo.
I aku-go innen.
Ka asogi ko.
Fu mon sanbo myo.

"My pure land is not destroyed,
yet the multitude sees it as consumed in fire,
with anxiety, fear, and other sufferings
filling it everywhere.
These living beings with their various offenses,
through causes arising from their evil actions,
spend asamkhya kalpas
without hearing the name of the three treasures."
(LSOC, 272)

"MY PURE LAND is not destroyed." What power these words convey! This saha world is the true land of the eternal Buddha. It is the true stage on which the undying Buddha resolutely struggles to lead all people to happiness. Therefore, it absolutely cannot be destroyed. So the Buddha declares.

When we firmly base ourselves on these words of the Buddha, we are fearless. Our confidence that we dwell in an indestructible pure land manifests as indestructible courage and inexhaustible hope. And the power to transform an impermanent and impure world into an eternal pure land wells forth in our lives.

Nichiren says: "There are not two lands, pure or impure in themselves. The difference lies solely in the good or evil of our minds" (WND-I, 4).

He also writes:

> You must quickly reform the tenets that you hold in your heart and embrace the one true vehicle, the single good doctrine [of the Lotus Sutra]. If you do so, then the threefold world will become the Buddha land, and how could a Buddha land ever decline? The regions in the ten directions will all become treasure realms, and how could a treasure realm ever suffer harm? (WND-I, 25)

The world changes completely depending on one's mindset or single-minded determination. On the most fundamental level, peace can only be realized through a revolution in people's lives.

"Yet the multitude sees it as consumed in fire" refers to the saha world as it appears to those who wander from illusion to illusion, from darkness to darkness. At the end of such wandering, they see only an abyss of despair. Therefore it appears to them that the world is consumed in the flames of an all-destroying fire that spells the world's end. But it is not actually an all-destroying fire; the flames they see are merely the fires of their own earthly desires.

Again, as indicated by the lines "with anxiety, fear, and other sufferings filling it everywhere," to those who labor under such delusion, this world is rife with anxiety, fear and all manner of suffering.

The word "sees" is central to the meaning of this section. It appears to people that the world is filled with suffering, but this is not the reality. As observed by the Buddha, this world is a solemn Buddha land, a pure land. Therefore the Daishonin says, "Whatever trouble occurs, regard it as no more than a dream, and think only of the Lotus Sutra" (WND-I, 502).

Viewing the troubles and hardships of life as "transitory as a dream" requires an immense spirit. This is the power of single-minded determination, the power of faith. Belief entails a great revolution in our frame of mind. And this revolution constitutes the driving force for transforming our lives and our surroundings.

Those unaware of this power are miserable. They are referred to in the subsequent passage: "These living beings with their various offenses, through causes arising from their evil actions, spend asamkhya kalpas without hearing the name of the three treasures."

"Offenses" basically means disbelief in the Mystic Law. "Causes arising from their evil actions" means endless wandering through earthly desires, karma and suffering.

Such people, while physically dwelling in the Buddha land, enshroud themselves in a fog and so fail to see the Buddha who is before their very eyes. Owing to disbelief, they firmly close the doors to their hearts and, as a result, cannot even hear about the three treasures, even after a duration of asamkhya kalpas.

The three treasures are: the Buddha, the Law (the Buddha's teachings) and the Buddhist Order (community of believers). The three treasures hold the key to people's salvation. Therefore, they are most highly revered in Buddhism as treasures that lead people to happiness.

We solemnly recognize the correct three treasures of the Latter Day of the Law. The treasure of the Buddha is Nichiren Daishonin, the Buddha of the Latter Day. The treasure of the Law is Nam-myoho-renge-kyo of the Three Great Secret Laws. And the treasure of the Buddhist Order refers to the harmonious gathering of people who correctly uphold and spread Nichiren Buddhism, exerting themselves to lead others to happiness and realize peace. Today, this harmonious gathering of people is of course the SGI.

The Unity of the Three Mystic Principles

Here I will mention something about the doctrine of the unity of the three mystic principles found in the "Life Span" chapter. The passage that begins "When living beings witness the end of a kalpa," which we studied earlier, explains that the saha world is in truth an indestructible pure land. This is the revelation of the mystic principle of the true land. It was indicated in the earlier prose section in such passages as "I have been constantly in this saha world, preaching the Law, teaching, and converting" (LSOC, 266).

Again, passages like "it has been immeasurable, boundless hundreds, thousands, ten thousands, millions of nayutas of kalpas since I in fact attained Buddhahood" (LSOC, 265–66) and "since I attained Buddhahood, an extremely long period of time has passed" (LSOC, 267) explain that the Buddha is always in this world and that his life is inextinguishable. This is the mystic principle of true effect.

Finally, "originally I practiced the bodhisattva way, and the life span that I acquired then has yet to come to an end but will last twice the number of years that have already passed" (LSOC, 268) explains the permanence of the life of the nine worlds. This is the mystic principle of the true cause.

These three mystic principles are all expounded in "Life Span," and this is termed the unity of the three mystic principles.

The unity of the three mystic principles in the essential teaching indicates that the Buddha, the beings of the nine worlds and the land are all eternal and indestructible. This concept completes the Lotus Sutra's doctrine of three thousand realms in a single moment of life. This doctrine, transcending distinctions among the Ten Worlds and between life and its environment, clarifies that the three thousand realms of all phenomena are eternal and everlasting. It reveals the great and eternal entity of life that encompasses within it the three thousand realms of all phenomena.

Nichiren's teaching of actual three thousand realms in a single moment of life opens the path whereby all people of the Latter Day can manifest this great and eternal life, which he identified as Nam-myoho-renge-kyo. We who earnestly embrace Nichiren Buddhism are therefore noble emissaries of the Buddha who put into practice in society this unity of the three mystic principles.

▪35▪

Sho u shu ku-doku.
Nyuwa shichi-jiki sha.
Sokkai ken gashin.
Zai shi ni seppo.
Waku-ji i shi shu.
Setsu butsu-ju muryo.
Ku nai ken bussha.
I setsu butsu nan chi.

"But those who practice meritorious ways,
who are gentle, peaceful, honest, and upright,
all of them will see me
here in person, preaching the Law.
At times for this multitude
I describe the Buddha's life span as immeasurable,
and to those who see the Buddha only after a long time
I explain how difficult it is to meet a Buddha."
(LSOC, 272)

THE PASSAGE we studied earlier describes how human beings befuddled with illusion see the world around them as filled with suffering and engulfed in an all-consuming fire.

The above passage teaches that, by steadfastly maintaining honest and upright faith, we can receive the great benefit of the Mystic Law.

It indicates that those who have accumulated benefit and who are gentle, peaceful and honest can see the Buddha expounding the Law for people's happiness.

"Gentle" and "peaceful" mean possessing an open mind free of all obstinacy or narrow-mindedness. This is not by any means to say weak-willed. It is the spirit to see the truth exactly as it is, without being swayed by prejudice, bias, appearances and the like. "Honest and upright," as these words suggest, mean an attitude of directly approaching and seeking out that which is good and great.

The eternal Buddha is visible to those who are gentle, peaceful, honest and upright. The Buddha's life is eternal and indestructible. Those whose minds are gentle, peaceful and upright can continuously live with a sense of absolute peace of mind in being together with the Buddha. And those who are always with the Buddha will be liberated from loneliness and impatience, anxiety and despair. They can abide in a state of eternal happiness.

For us, "gentle, peaceful, honest, and upright" refers to our attitude of faith in the Gohonzon. From a literal standpoint, to "practice meritorious ways" means to accumulate benefit by carrying out various Buddhist practices. But our practice is none other than the practice of chanting Nam-myoho-renge-kyo to the Gohonzon for ourselves and others.

Nichiren says that "the five characters of Myoho-renge-kyo, the heart of the essential teaching of the Lotus Sutra, contain the benefit amassed through the countless practices and meritorious deeds of all Buddhas throughout the three existences" (WND-1, 481). Chanting Nam-myoho-renge-kyo confers the ultimate benefit and is the wellspring of all benefit.

Accordingly, this sutra passage teaches that we should always chant the Mystic Law with a pure and earnest seeking mind toward the Gohonzon. When we possess such sincere faith, a life state identical to that of the eternal Buddha manifests within us. An open and upright mind connects us directly with the life of the Buddha.

In the above passage, this is explained by the lines "all of them will see me here in person, preaching the Law." The Buddha is always here preaching the Law. In other words, at all times we can live embraced by the Buddha's compassion and in perfect accord with the Buddha's wisdom.

When we base ourselves on the great conviction that we are always together with the Gohonzon, that we are always together with the Daishonin, we are fearless. When something happens, we calmly challenge the situation, fully exercising our wisdom and all the while chanting Nam-myoho-renge-kyo. By doing so, we cannot fail to be protected; we are certain to realize a life of victory.

Also, "all of them will see me here in person" indicates the principles of the mutual possession of the Ten Worlds and three thousand realms in a single moment of life. The beings of the nine worlds perceive and are embraced by the world of Buddhahood. That is, the nine worlds are endowed with the world of Buddhahood, and the world of Buddhahood is endowed with the nine worlds.

In *The Record of the Orally Transmitted Teachings*, Nichiren says:

> The revelations in this "Life Span" chapter make clear that "all of them will see me," that is, they make clear the principle of three thousand realms in a single moment of life. Now Nichiren and his followers, who chant Nam-myoho-renge-kyo, are the very persons referred to here. (p. 137)

Certainly SGI members are carrying out "gentle, peaceful, honest, and upright" faith just as the Daishonin teaches. The SGI is a gathering of "those who practice meritorious ways, who are gentle, peaceful, honest, and upright." It is a body dedicated to accomplishing the

Buddha's will and decree, whose members honestly put the Buddha's spirit into practice.

The SGI therefore abounds with the power of the Mystic Law and the strength of justice. Nichiren says, "When the lion king . . . roars; the hundred cubs will then feel emboldened" (WND-1, 949). Nam-myoho-renge-kyo is the lion's roar. We are a gathering of lions.

Our benefits from exerting ourselves for kosen-rufu are immense. Our efforts are definitely known to the Gohonzon. As long as we possess the roar of the lion, the SGI is certain to prosper and develop eternally.

The next part reads, "At times for this multitude I describe the Buddha's life span as immeasurable, and to those who see the Buddha only after a long time I explain how difficult it is to meet the Buddha." This reveals the Buddha's immense wisdom to save people on the most fundamental level. From the standpoint of Nichiren Buddhism, it indicates the great power of the Gohonzon.

President Toda said, "When we read this passage with a clear understanding, we develop great confidence in our own lives."

To those who are gentle, peaceful, honest and upright, Shakyamuni reveals that the Buddha's life is infinite; to those who see the Buddha only after much time has elapsed, he teaches that the Buddha is difficult to meet. The Buddha always exists, but he is rarely encountered. While seemingly contradictory, this is the main theme of the verse section of "Life Span," as I've previously noted.

If Shakyamuni were to say only that the Buddha always exists, then people would come to depend entirely on the Buddha. Such an outcome is inconsistent with Buddhism, whose purpose is to enable all people to become Buddhas.

The Buddha wants people to become self-reliant. He wants them to develop the state of Buddhahood in their own lives. This is the Buddha's wish. And so, as the ultimate expedient means, the Buddha appears to enter extinction. He thereby causes people to sense that the Buddha is difficult to encounter and arouses in them a seeking mind.

We can achieve absolute happiness only when we perceive the eternal nature of our lives. And this sutra passage reveals the Buddha's skillful and wise way of preaching toward that end. It remains theory if we say that only the Buddha's life is eternal. From the standpoint of Nichiren Buddhism, all of our lives are eternal. The important thing is that we—right now, in our present lives—become profoundly aware of this.

To lead all people of the Latter Day of the Law to enlightenment, Nichiren manifested his own eternal life in the form of the Gohonzon. From the standpoint of his teaching, this is the meaning of "I describe the Buddha's life span as immeasurable."

With gentle, peaceful, honest and upright faith, we embrace the Gohonzon as the manifestation of the Daishonin's supreme life. When we possess such faith, such a seeking spirit, we can see the Gohonzon, the life of the Daishonin, in our own lives. And we can profoundly sense the eternal and indestructible benefit we possess. Unless we arouse a heart of faith, we cannot truly see the Gohonzon. This is the implicit meaning of the statement "I explain how difficult it is to meet the Buddha."

President Toda explained:

> We are taught that our lives are eternal. But when we truly understand the meaning of eternal, we realize that our present existence in this world is what is important. We must not waste our lives. That's why we chant Nam-myoho-renge-kyo and carry out the practice of propagation.

Because our lives are eternal, the present moment is precious. Neglecting this existence means neglecting our lives eternally. It is always our actions from this moment on that matter most.

Our lives are eternal and endowed with indelible nobility, as is the life of the Buddha. The Ten Worlds all exist in our lives and minds at each moment. We have infinite potential. This is the fundamental spirit of Buddhism, which places high value on the present, and is the basis for the idea of life's sanctity.

▪36▪

Ga chi-riki nyo ze.
Eko sho muryo.
Jumyo mushu ko.
Ku shugo sho toku.
Nyoto u chi sha.
Moĩ to shi sho gi.
To dan ryo yo jin.
Butsu-go jip̃ puko.

"Such is the power of my wisdom
that its sagacious beams shine without measure.
This life span of countless kalpas
I gained as the result of lengthy practice.
You who are possessed of wisdom,
entertain no doubts on this point!
Cast them off, end them forever,
for the Buddha's words are true, not false."
(LSOC, 272)

THIS PASSAGE DESCRIBES the Buddha's boundless wisdom that, like the spring sunshine, rejuvenates and nourishes all life. Spring causes a full-fledged explosion of life—of beautiful flowers and fresh young leaves, which, bathed in bright sunlight, display such unreserved vibrancy that they seem to be vying to outdo one another.

In the same way, the buds of Buddhahood in the lives of all people are illuminated and nourished by the great light of the Buddha's wisdom.

As in the previous section, "Such is the power of my wisdom" describes how the Buddha uses his wisdom to skillfully lead people to attain Buddhahood by sometimes preaching the truth and sometimes employing expedient means.

The Buddha's wisdom is limitless and therefore "its sagacious beams shine without measure." The light of the Buddha's wisdom dispels the darkness in the lives of countless people, the darkness in the world. The great light of the benefit of the Gohonzon shines throughout the universe and upon all people eternally, transcending life and death.

"This life span of countless kalpas" refers to the Buddha's eternal life. The Buddha's life of infinite wisdom and compassion is eternal. The Buddha's great wish is for all people to possess the light of this wisdom and recognize the infinite span of their lives. Daily we encourage people to become happy—and to do so through their own efforts.

Every person is different. Life is complicated. We worry about how to encourage everyone in light of his or her unique circumstances. Making strenuous efforts each day, we continue giving people courage and hope. Nothing is more praiseworthy. We lead truly noble and wonderful lives. Each day, we manifest boundless wisdom and illuminate the lives of friends with the light of hope.

In this sense, the passage "its sagacious beams shine without measure. This life span of countless kalpas" refer to us, "professors of humanity," who illuminate a confused society with our sunlike life states. These lines also express the noble function of the lives of all SGI members, who having received great life force from the Gohonzon, are continuously working to bring people happiness.

"The Buddha's Words Are True, Not False"

The Buddha's limitless life was "gained as the result of lengthy practice." This corresponds to the passage in the earlier prose section "originally I practiced the bodhisattva way, and the life span that I acquired then . . ." (LSOC, 268).

But, as President Toda said, "In terms of the implicit meaning, it is not something that was attained as a result of practicing for a long time but something originally possessed and eternal, something innate in life." In other words, each of us originally possesses a life identical to the eternal Buddha's.

Shakyamuni further proclaims: "You who are possessed of wisdom, entertain no doubts on this point! Cast them off, end them forever, for the Buddha's words are true, not false" (LSOC, 272). He is saying we should be confident that the Buddha's eternal and undying life exists within us.

You must "entertain no doubts on this point!" These are strong words, the words of someone speaking wholly in earnest; they are vigorous. At the same time, they overflow with compassion. The Buddha is a person without falsehood, a person of truth. And his true disciples are honest and upright.

The Buddha is upright. He is earnest. Disciples who follow the Buddha directly, uprightly and without any distortion or hesitation can manifest the Buddha's boundless wisdom and life force as their own. There is absolutely no doubt about this—so the Buddha assures us in this passage. How truly fortunate we are!

▪37▪

Nyo i zen hoben.
I ji o shi ko.
Jitsu zai ni gon shi.
Mu no sek͡ komo.
Ga yaku i se bu.
Ku sho kugen sha.

"He is like a skilled physician
who uses an expedient means to cure his deranged sons.
Though in fact alive, he gives out word he is dead,
yet no one can say he speaks falsely.
I am the father of this world,
saving those who suffer and are afflicted."
(LSOC, 272–73)

THE VERSE SECTION communicates the essence of the Buddha's eternal life with the resonance of a beautiful poem. Philosophically speaking, "Life Span" is replete with important principles, as distilled in the studies of T'ien-t'ai and others. Rather than expounding these principles directly, however, Shakyamuni sought to communicate them to people's hearts more profoundly and abundantly by committing them to resonant verse. He issues a cry from the heart, to reach the hearts of others. Herein lies Shakyamuni's greatness.

Coming into contact with the pulse of the verse section of the "Life Span" chapter, which embodies the essence of the Buddha's life state, those living after Shakyamuni have without doubt felt they could hear his voice and the sound of his heart across the great remove of time and space. This is a very important part of why the Lotus Sutra has been widely loved and recited by people over the ages.

Leaders should study poetry and possess a poetic spirit. Those lacking a poetic spirit will eventually lose touch with the hearts of the people. As a result, they will be unable to transform people's hearts or truly lead them to happiness. That is why I have repeatedly stressed this point.

We now approach the close of the verse section. In this passage, Shakyamuni passionately restates the conclusion of the parable of the Excellent Physician and His Sick Children. To save his children who have drunk poison and lost their right minds, the father, the skilled physician, employs an expedient means: He has someone announce to the children that he has died and so causes them to drink the medicine. But, as Shakyamuni says, "No one can say he speaks falsely."

He continues, "I am the father of this world, saving those who suffer and are afflicted." In this way, Shakyamuni loudly proclaims that he is the "father" who leads all people to enlightenment. This is a grand declaration. The Buddha's mission is to save all people, on the most fundamental level, from the sufferings under which they labor.

What does "I am the father of this world" mean from the standpoint of Nichiren Buddhism? Nichiren indicates that the verse section contains the virtues of sovereign, teacher and parent possessed by the Buddha of the essential teaching. "This, my land, remains safe and tranquil" attests to the virtue of the sovereign; "constantly I have preached the Law, teaching, converting" attests to that of the teacher; and "I am the father of this world" attests to that of the parent (see OTT, 137).

In addition, the Daishonin declares, "Now Nichiren and his followers, who chant Nam-myoho-renge-kyo, are the fathers of all living beings, for we save them from the torments of the hell of incessant suffering" (OTT, 138). In other words, he and his disciples who chant and propagate the Mystic Law are the "parents" who lead all people to happiness. He is telling us, in effect, to advance kosen-rufu with this awareness, carrying on his spirit. These are wonderful words—words of the greatest encouragement.

The Record of the Orally Transmitted Teachings clarifies that the Lotus Sutra is the great teaching for the salvation of all people of the Latter Day of the Law. With this work, Buddhism for the first time becomes truly a philosophy for the happiness of the people, for all humankind.

It is easy to speak of acting in the interest of the world, of humankind or of peace. But who will earnestly undertake such action, even at the cost of their lives? Society is ruled by egoism and desire. All too many people have the attitude, "Ultimately, I'm the only one who counts." Who in such a society is steadfastly working for the happiness of all people, while enduring calumny and persecution at the hands of those beset with delusion?

It is Shakyamuni. It is Nichiren Daishonin. And today it is the SGI members who directly carry on the Buddha's spirit in the modern age. The SGI is the pillar of society and the sun itself. Many fine people in the world, while perhaps not embracing faith in the Mystic Law, are earnestly struggling for the good of humankind. Joining hands with such people of conscience, let us fulfill our great mission to save those "who suffer and are afflicted."

Incidentally, let us recall how the parable of the Excellent Physician and His Sick Children concludes. The children, in their sadness from believing their father has died, open their eyes and take the medicine he has left for them. As a result they are cured of the effects of the poison. Upon hearing this, the father returns and is happily reunited with his children. What does this closing scene signify?

It means that when people (the children) honestly believe in and uphold (drink) Shakyamuni's teaching (the good medicine), the Buddha (the skilled physician) appears in (returns to) their hearts.

From our standpoint, the parable describes the great benefit of practicing Buddhism; that if we carry through with strong faith in the Gohonzon, the Buddha's life will certainly manifest within us. It is not a matter of something foreign suddenly appearing in our lives. Rather, the life of the Buddha that we originally possess wells forth. It is revived, rediscovered. We experience a renaissance of life.

In lecturing on the lines "I am the father of this world, saving those who suffer and are afflicted," President Toda said:

> We can take these to be the words of the Gohonzon—"I" is the Daishonin, the Gohonzon—promising to save people from all sufferings and afflictions. We need to be deeply cognizant of this promise when we read the verse section. The Gohonzon absolutely beyond any doubt leads to happiness those experiencing various worries and sufferings.

These words represent the solemn promise of the original Buddha. Therefore, whatever happens, it is enough that we merely continue advancing straight ahead with gentle, peaceful, honest and upright faith. Then we are certain to overflow with boundless life force, and we will develop the greater self—a life state of complete and total fulfillment. With this confidence, together let us continue to joyfully advance.

38

I bonbu tendo.
Jitsu zai ni gon metsu.
I joken ga ko.
Ni sho kyoshi shin.
Ho-itsu jaku go-yoku.
Da o aku-do chu.
Go jo chi shujo.
Gyo do fu gyo do.
Zui o sho ka do.
I ses̄ shuju ho.

"Because of the befuddlement of ordinary people,
though I live, I give out word I have entered extinction.
For if they see me constantly,
arrogance and selfishness arise in their minds.
Abandoning restraint, they give themselves up to the five desires
and fall into the evil paths of existence.
Always I am aware of which living beings
practice the way, and which do not,
and in response to their need for salvation
I preach various doctrines for them."
(LSOC, 273)

THE POINT HERE regarding "befuddlement of ordinary people" is the same as that in previous sections. Namely, if people think that the Buddha is always present, they may come to be arrogant or grow dependent on him and ultimately fall into the evil paths of existence owing to attachment to the five desires. In that scenario, they cannot possibly attain Buddhahood.

Therefore, as an expedient means, the Buddha explains that he will enter extinction. Out of immense compassion, the Buddha always preaches the Law in such a way as to enable people to grow and develop self-reliance.

Although they yearn to see the Buddha and attain salvation through the Law, people may become dependent on the Buddha and gradually be consumed and destroyed by their own inner weaknesses. As a result, they neglect their Buddhist practice and finally fall into the evil paths of existence. While fortunate enough to have met the Law existing eternally, they vacillate between believing and doubting, blinded by immediate interests and desires.

President Toda said:

> Those who doubt the Gohonzon because they view it from society's perspective and not from that of Buddhism have an upside-down view of the affairs of the world. Their view of life is similarly distorted; although life is eternal, they see only that there is death.

One can imagine how the Buddha, seeing deep into the highly unstable nature of the human heart, must have struggled to somehow raise people up to his enlightened life state.

Nichiren writes to the Ikegami brothers and their wives: "Among those who believed at first, many later discarded their faith, fearing that society would reject them. Among these are some who oppose me more furiously than those who slandered from the beginning" (WND-I, 502).

This is a pattern typical of the "befuddled."

To Shijo Kingo, Nichiren writes, "Though worldly troubles may arise, never let them disturb you" (WND-I, 681). The important thing is to advance cheerfully along the direct path to attaining Buddhahood, without being disturbed each time there is frivolous slander or name-calling—to construct a solid and unshakable self.

President Toda said, "Return to the common mortal of beginningless time." He proudly referred to himself as a "great common mortal." Let us always be "common mortals of the Mystic Law," magnanimous champions of humanity.

Next the passage says, "Always I am aware of which living beings practice the way, and which do not, and in response to their need for salvation I preach various doctrines for them." The Buddha always knows whether people are striving to excel in Buddhist practice and expounds the Law while freely employing appropriate means of leading them to enlightenment.

Regarding "which living beings practice the way, and which do not," Nichiren says, "Now Nichiren and his followers, who chant Nam-myoho-renge-kyo, are those who 'practice the way,' while those who do not chant it are those who 'do not [practice the way]'" (OTT, 139). In the same place, he explains that "the way" indicates the Lotus Sutra.

President Toda interpreted this sutra passage as explaining the immense power of the Gohonzon:

> Practicing the way means believing in and propagating faith in the Gohonzon. Not practicing the way means not doing so. The Gohonzon knows what people are doing and considers how best to save them, producing punishment or

reward according to their stance. The Gohonzon does not frown upon people simply because they do not have faith but contrives to lead them to happiness on that basis. This passage says that the Buddha definitely knows whether one is practicing the way.

Who is fighting hard? Who is slacking off? The Gohonzon knows everything about us, down to the very core of our being. We need simply to continue advancing, fully confident that the Gohonzon is watching over us.

This is "the way." We are advancing along the way called the Mystic Law. And the way of kosen-rufu, which lies in spreading faith in the Mystic Law throughout the world, is the unsurpassed way. It is the great way of happiness.

The resonant strains of "Song of the Open Road" by the poet of the people, Walt Whitman, again come to mind. Whitman is our comrade in spirit:

> *Afoot and light-hearted I take to the open road, . . .*
> *Henceforth I ask not good-fortune, I myself am good fortune, . . .*
> *Done with indoor complaints, libraries, querulous criticisms,*
> *Strong and content I travel the open road.*[8]

Whitman blasts complaints and "querulous criticisms." A poet knows well the nature of the world of human beings. He urges us to laugh off such low-level distractions.

Happiness does not lie somewhere else. "I myself am good fortune," he says. With this spirit, let us advance straight ahead along the great path of contributing to the well-being of humankind, jubilantly whistling songs of joy and friendship.

▪39▪

Mai ji sa ze nen.
I ga ryo shujo.
Toku nyu mu-jo do.
Soku joju busshin.

"At all times I think to myself:
How can I cause living beings
to gain entry into the unsurpassed way
and quickly acquire the body of a Buddha?"
(LSOC, 273)

THIS PASSAGE CLARIFIES the Buddha's eternal determination, his great wish from beginningless time. The Buddha yearns for only one thing: to help people gain unsurpassed happiness. This, Shakyamuni says, is his constant thought.

With crystal-clear thought and intent, the Buddha envisions the path that people need to follow to attain this happiness. And he points people in this direction, saying, "Go forward along this path."

Reading this passage, we sense that the wondrous, direct path to a state of boundlessly expanding happiness has at last come into view, illuminated by the sunlight of the Buddha's compassion.

These resounding, merciful words conclude the verse section, as well as the entire "Life Span" chapter. It is a soulful passage, an appropriate conclusion to the epic poem for the salvation of humankind that crystallizes the heart of the Lotus Sutra and the spirit of Shakyamuni.

Nichiren speaks of how we should never allow ourselves to forget the "compassionate vow of the Buddha, who declared, 'At all times I think to myself: [How can I cause living beings to gain entry into the unsurpassed way and quickly acquire the body of a Buddha?]'" (WND-1, 62). This vow constitutes the essential entity of the eternal Buddha. The eternity of the Buddha's life is inseparable from this great vow.

The Buddha appears in this world because of this great vow. In the "Expedient Means" chapter, this is referred to as the "one great reason for which the Buddhas appear in the world" (LSOC, 64). And the Buddha enters extinction as an expedient means because of this great vow. This is indicated by the line in the "Life Span" chapter that reads, "as an expedient means I appear to enter nirvana" (LSOC, 271).

Both the Buddha's appearance and extinction accord with this great vow. Both the Buddha's birth and death are incorporated in this "constant thought." Nichiren Daishonin says, "The two phases of life and death are the wonderful workings of one mind" (OTT, 30). The concluding lines of the verse section clarify the substance of this "one mind."

Regarding the Buddha's thought, as in "At all times I think to myself," Nichiren refers to "one instant of thought or a single moment of life comprising three thousand realms that is originally inherent in Buddhas and all living beings" (WND-2, 909).

"I want to become happy and for everyone else to become happy too." This is the original mind, the pure wish, functioning in the depths of life since beginningless time. Those who totally embrace this spirit are Buddhas. Because it is the Buddha's all-encompassing wish, it is the great vow.

Nichiren Daishonin, the Buddha of the Latter Day of the Law, lived his life according to this vow. The people's happiness was always the Daishonin's sole concern. In his epochal treatise "On Establishing the Correct Teaching for the Peace of the Land," Nichiren begins by depicting the miserable conditions of the people, who were suffering from one calamity after another.

Nichiren always fixed his gaze on the people. In this writing he called out to Hojo Tokiyori, the most powerful person in the country, and invited him to join in considering what could be done to alleviate the people's sufferings.

Whether warmly encouraging a hapless believer or strictly admonishing the country's rulers, Nichiren's spirit was always focused on the happiness of the people. He writes, "From the time that I was born until today, I have never known a moment's ease; I have thought only of propagating the daimoku of the Lotus Sutra" (WND-1, 965). His life was a succession of hardships he willingly took on for the people's happiness, a life that epitomized the spirit of the passage "At all times I think to myself . . ."

Living for the great vow of accomplishing kosen-rufu means basing one's life on the Buddha's eternal determination. "At all times" does not mean only in this lifetime. The Daishonin says, "'At all times' means eternally over the three existences" (GZ, 840).

President Toda said:

"At all times" means over past, present and future. "At all times I think to myself" indicates Nichiren Daishonin's constant prayer—since beginningless time—for the salvation of all of us. This is a very important passage.

The pulse of the Buddha's constant thought is found only in the life-to-life bonds of mentor and disciple. That's why the Daishonin called upon his disciples to cherish the same great desire he did. "My disciples," he in effect urges them, "dedicate your lives to accomplishing the Buddha's great vow. Maintain the spirit of the oneness of mentor and disciple."

He encourages us to dedicate our lives to the Lotus Sutra, saying,

"Think of this offering as a drop of dew rejoicing the ocean, or a speck of dust returning to the earth" (WND-1, 1003). When we base ourselves on this great wish, our own lives, which might seem as light and insubstantial as a drop of dew or speck of dust, become in actuality one with the eternal life of the Buddha, as immense and formidable as the ocean or earth.

The path of the oneness of mentor and disciple, which in practice means basing ourselves on the same wish as the Buddha, is the very essence of Buddhism.

May 3, 1951, the day Josei Toda became Soka Gakkai president, was an unforgettable day for me—it was then that the eternal bond of mentor and disciple was formed. On that day, a new structure for the Soka Gakkai organization was announced. The headline in the *Seikyo Shimbun* reported, "A New Organization to Lead All People to Happiness." To work for the happiness of all people—this was President Toda's spirit.

At the time, there was a membership of several thousand. Society was still very confused in the aftermath of the war, and the Soka Gakkai was by and large a gathering of people who were hard-pressed financially. But Mr. Toda's impassioned appeal upon becoming president, like the roar of a lion, lit a flame in each person's heart, the yearning to lead all people to happiness.

And so, while practicing with the spirit that "faith expresses itself in society" and "faith equals daily life," we embarked on a journey to become a religion for all humankind. In the brief span of several decades, we have constructed an unprecedented foundation for global kosen-rufu. We have sown the seeds of happiness in the hearts of people the world over. Who could have foreseen this? In the popular history of the era, this certainly qualifies as the "miracle of the twentieth century."

All the members were serious, giving it their all. They fought with the resolve that they would definitely accomplish kosen-rufu, thus fulfilling the Daishonin's will.

Nichiren says, "'Myself' [in 'I think to myself'] refers specifically to Shakyamuni Buddha, and in a more general way to the [beings of the] Ten Worlds" (OTT, 139). In this latter sense, "I think to myself" refers to us. The thoughts of those who at all times think to themselves about kosen-rufu are at one with Nichiren's immensely compassionate thoughts.

Advancing along the "unsurpassed way" of the Buddha means sharing the Buddha's "constant thought" to enable all people to attain enlightenment. The "unsurpassed way" is in contrast to a "limited way." It signifies a way of life based on supreme philosophy and imbued with supreme happiness.

Nichiren says:

"Unsurpassed way" refers to the Buddha eternally endowed with the three bodies who is revealed in the "Life Span" chapter. Outside of this, there is no other "body of a Buddha" to be acquired.

Now Nichiren and his followers, who chant Nam-myoho-renge-kyo, will without doubt "[quickly] acquire the body of a Buddha." (OTT, 140)

Nichiren thus declares that those who chant Nam-myoho-renge-kyo are certain to "quickly acquire the body of a Buddha." That is, they will become Buddhas possessing the three bodies and acquire the body of a Buddha. "Quickly" means that we will do so just as we are—as ordinary people. This is because the three bodies of the Buddha are inherent in our lives.

The Buddha, in other words, is telling people: "Become happy!" He promises the happiness of all humankind. The gate to true happiness has been opened for all. And it is through faith that one can enter this gate.

Nothing delighted President Toda more than hearing members' experiences of benefit. Whenever he heard someone's happy experience, he would call out to those nearby: "I hope you will further solidify your faith so that we can hear many more such delightful testimonials. That is my sole wish. I desire nothing but for all of you to become truly happy.

"As president, I stand up together with you out of the desire to help all people become happy. That is my sole wish."

My spirit is the same.

This is why it is the important duty of the Buddha's children to stand up to those with evil intentions who seek to obstruct the path to people's happiness. Many years have now passed since March 16, 1958, the historic youth division ceremony at which President Toda passed on the responsibility for achieving kosen-rufu to his young successors. President Toda's final guidance was: "Fight resolutely against evil. . . . You must never let up in your struggle against evil."

Needless to say, those who fight for the people's happiness with the same spirit as the Buddha, who fight to crush the forces seeking to obstruct the people's happiness, are certainly emissaries of the Buddha and the Buddha's children.

Carrying out the practice of "At all times I think to myself: How can I cause living beings to gain entry into the unsurpassed way and quickly acquire the body of a Buddha?" is the vow of the Buddha and the determination of the Buddha's disciples. If we always make the people's happiness our goal, the SGI will continue to flourish eternally.

On the Silent Prayers

At the close of these lectures, I would like to touch upon the silent prayers that we offer during morning and evening gongyo.

Silent prayers are offered in the heart. Accordingly, even though we may read their words, it is what we actually think—the thoughts occurring to us—that become our prayers.

President Toda said:

Since we are human, it is only natural that various thoughts occur to us while we are chanting Nam-myoho-renge-kyo. But if we chant earnestly, then gradually we can focus entirely on the Gohonzon. If we chant with an earnest frame of mind, various worries about our daily lives will be resolved. At that time, for example, the complaints of a spouse can sound as soothing as a lullaby.

But let's be careful when offering silent prayers. The thoughts in our heart are clearly expressed to the Gohonzon. If during the silent prayers we think, "That guy's a real jerk," then even though we may be reading the silent prayers' words, it is the thought in our heart, "He's a real jerk," that becomes our prayer to the Gohonzon.

Offering the silent prayers properly is a decisive struggle. The prayers that someone offers reflect his or her life state. Prayers have to be concrete, and they must be earnest and made with determination.

Whether chanting Nam-myoho-renge-kyo or offering silent prayers, the most important thing is to pray with a resolute mind. Prayers should not be abstract. The Buddhas and Buddhist deities respond to earnest, strong prayers arising from the very depths of one's life.

I've now completed my lectures on the "Expedient Means" and "Life Span" chapters, which clarify the very essence of the Lotus Sutra, the scripture of humankind.

In my heart, I see President Toda discussing the essence of Buddhism while calmly taking in the storms of society. Mentor and disciple are always together. "Today, once again, I can fight! Today, once again, I can advance kosen-rufu!"—I start out each day with this sense of elation. In my heart, I greet President Toda and begin an all-out struggle. For me, every day is like an exuberant morning.

Based on my daily gongyo and daimoku, together with friends and comrades throughout the world, still I continue to fight vigorously with the spirit of the rising sun.

As we have learned thus far, we who recite the Mystic Law dwell in the eternal dimension of the three existences, the dimension of all humankind and the entire world. And with a grand spirit, we advance sure-footedly through the realities of our lives. This is our path.

Appendix: Excerpts From the Lotus Sutra

THE FOLLOWING is the English translation of the passages from the "Expedient Means" and "Life Span" chapters covered in this book. The numbers next to each passage correspond to the preceding numbered lectures. Page numbers where the lecture for each passage can also be found here.

Excerpts From the "Expedient Means" Chapter (LSOC, 56–57)

(1) At that time the World-Honored One calmly arose from his samadhi and addressed Shariputra, saying: "The wisdom of the Buddhas is infinitely profound and immeasurable. The door to this wisdom is difficult to understand and difficult to enter. Not one of the voice-hearers or pratyekabuddhas is able to comprehend it." (p. 23)

(2) "What is the reason for this? The Buddhas have personally attended a hundred, a thousand, ten thousand, a million, a countless number of Buddhas and have fully carried out an immeasurable number of Buddhas' ways and doctrines. They have exerted themselves bravely and vigorously, and their names are universally known. They have realized the Law that is profound and never known before, and preach it in accordance with what is appropriate, yet their intentions are difficult to understand." (p. 37)

(3) "Shariputra, ever since I attained Buddhahood I have through various causes and various similes widely expounded my teachings and have used countless expedient means to guide living beings and cause them to renounce their attachments." (p. 57)

(4) "Why is this? Because the Thus Come Ones are fully possessed of both expedient means and the paramita of wisdom." (p. 71)

(5) "Shariputra, the wisdom of the Thus Come Ones is expansive and profound. They have immeasurable [compassion], unlimited [eloquence], power, fearlessness, concentration, emancipation, and samadhis, and have deeply entered the boundless and awakened to the Law never before attained." (p. 79)

(6) "Shariputra, the Thus Come Ones know how to make various distinctions and to expound the teachings skillfully. Their words are soft and gentle and can delight the hearts of the assembly.
    "Shariputra, to sum it up: the Buddhas have fully realized the Law that is limitless, boundless, never attained before." (p. 89)

(7) "But stop, Shariputra, I will say no more. Why? Because what the Buddhas have achieved is the rarest and most difficult-to-understand Law." (p. 99)

(8) "The true aspect of all phenomena can only be understood and shared between Buddhas. This reality consists of the appearance, nature, entity, power, influence, internal cause, relation, latent effect, manifest effect, and their consistency from beginning to end." (p. 103)

The "Life Span" Chapter Prose Section
(LSOC, 265–70)

(9) At that time the Buddha spoke to the bodhisattvas and all the great assembly: "Good men, you must believe and understand the truthful words of the Thus Come One." And again he said to the great assembly: "You must believe and understand the truthful words of the Thus Come One." And once more he said to the great assembly: "You must believe and understand the truthful words of the Thus Come One."

At that time the bodhisattvas and the great assembly, with Maitreya as their leader, pressed their palms together and addressed the Buddha, saying: "World-Honored One, we beg you to explain. We will believe and accept the Buddha's words." They spoke in this manner three times, and then said once more: "We beg you to explain it. We will believe and accept the Buddha's words."

At that time the World-Honored One, seeing that the bodhisattvas repeated their request three times and more, spoke to them, saying: "You must listen carefully and hear of the Thus Come One's secret and his transcendental powers." (p. 147)

(10) "In all the worlds the heavenly and human beings and asuras all believe that the present Shakyamuni Buddha, after leaving the palace of the Shakyas, seated himself in the place of enlightenment not far from the city of Gaya and there attained supreme perfect enlightenment. But good men, it has been immeasurable, boundless hundreds, thousands, ten thousands, millions of nayutas of kalpas since I in fact attained Buddhahood." (p. 159)

(11) "Suppose a person were to take five hundred, a thousand, ten thousand, a million nayuta asamkhya major world systems and

grind them to dust. Then, moving eastward, each time he passes five hundred, a thousand, ten thousand, a million nayuta asamkhya worlds he drops a particle of dust. He continues eastward in this way until he has finished dropping all the particles. Good men, what is your opinion? Can the total number of all these worlds be imagined or calculated?"

The bodhisattva Maitreya and the others said to the Buddha: "World-Honored One, these worlds are immeasurable, boundless—one cannot calculate their number, nor does the mind have the power to encompass them. Even all the voice-hearers and pratyekabuddhas with their wisdom free of outflows could not imagine or understand how many there are. Although we abide in the stage of non-regression, we cannot comprehend such a matter. World-Honored One, these worlds are immeasurable and boundless." (p. 173)

(12) At that time the Buddha said to the multitude of great bodhisattvas: "Good men, now I will state this to you clearly. Suppose all these worlds, whether they received a particle of dust or not, are once more reduced to dust. Let one particle represent one kalpa. The time that has passed since I attained Buddhahood surpasses this by a hundred, a thousand, ten thousand, a million nayuta asamkhya kalpas." (p. 177)

(13) "Ever since then I have been constantly in this saha world, preaching the Law, teaching, and converting. And elsewhere I have led and benefited living beings in hundreds, thousands, ten thousands, millions of nayutas and asamkhyas of lands." (p. 181)

(14) "Good men, during that time I have spoken about the Buddha Burning Torch and others, and described how they entered

nirvana. All this I employed as an expedient means to make distinctions.

"Good men, if there are living beings who come to me, I employ my Buddha eye to observe whether their faith and other faculties are keen or dull, and then depending upon how receptive they are to salvation, I appear in different places and preach to them under different names, and describe my life span as long or short. Sometimes when I make my appearance I say that I am about to enter nirvana, and also employ different expedient means to preach the subtle and wonderful Law, thus causing living beings to awaken joyful minds." (p. 189)

(15) "Good men, the Thus Come One observes how among living beings there are those who delight in lesser teachings, meager in virtue and heavy with defilement. For such persons I describe how in my youth I left my household and attained supreme perfect enlightenment. But in truth the time since I attained Buddhahood is extremely long, as I have told you. It is simply that I use this expedient means to teach and convert living beings and cause them to enter the Buddha way. That is why I speak in this manner." (p. 197)

(16) "Good men, the scriptures expounded by the Thus Come One are all for the purpose of saving and emancipating living beings. Sometimes I speak of myself, sometimes of others; sometimes I present myself, sometimes others; sometimes I show my own actions, sometimes those of others. All that I preach is true and not false." (p. 203)

(17) "Why do I do this? The Thus Come One perceives the true aspect of the threefold world exactly as it is. There is no ebb or

flow of birth and death, and there is no existing in this world and later entering extinction. It is neither substantial nor empty, neither consistent nor diverse. Nor is it what those who dwell in the threefold world perceive it to be. All such things the Thus Come One sees clearly and without error." (**p. 207**)

(18) "Because living beings have different natures, different desires, different actions, and different ways of thinking and making distinctions, and because I want to enable them to put down good roots, I employ a variety of causes and conditions, similes, parables, and phrases and preach different doctrines. This, a Buddha's work, I have never for a moment neglected." (**p. 221**)

(19) "Thus, since I attained Buddhahood, an extremely long period of time has passed. My life span is an immeasurable number of asamkhya kalpas, and during that time I have constantly abided here without ever entering extinction. Good men, originally I practiced the bodhisattva way, and the life span that I acquired then has yet to come to an end but will last twice the number of years that have already passed." (**p. 229**)

(20) "Now, however, although in fact I do not actually enter extinction, I announce that I am going to adopt the course of extinction. This is an expedient means that the Thus Come One uses to teach and convert living beings.

"Why do I do this? Because if the Buddha remains in the world for a long time, those persons with shallow virtue will fail to plant good roots but, living in poverty and lowliness, will become attached to the five desires and be caught in the net of deluded thoughts and imaginings. If they see that the Thus Come One is constantly in the world and never enters extinction, they will grow arrogant and selfish, or become discouraged and neglectful. They will fail to realize how difficult it is to encounter the Buddha and will not approach him with a respectful and reverent mind." (p. 245)

(21) "Therefore as an expedient means the Thus Come One says: 'Monks, you should know that it is a rare thing to live at a time when one of the Buddhas appears in the world.' Why does he do this? Because persons of shallow virtue may pass immeasurable hundreds, thousands, ten thousands, millions of kalpas with some of them chancing to see a Buddha and others never seeing one at all. For this reason I say to them: 'Monks, the Thus Come One is hard to get to see.' When living beings hear these words, they are certain to realize how difficult it is to encounter a Buddha. In their minds they will harbor a longing and will thirst to gaze upon the Buddha, and then they will work to plant good roots. Therefore the Thus Come One, though in truth he does not enter extinction, speaks of passing into extinction.

"Good men, the Buddhas, the Thus Come Ones, all act in such a manner. They act in order to save living beings, so what they say is true and not false." (p. 253)

(22) "Suppose, for example, that there is a skilled physician who is wise and understanding and knows how to compound medicines to effectively cure all kinds of diseases. He has many sons, perhaps ten, twenty, or even a hundred. He goes off to some other land far away to see about a certain affair." (p. 257)

(23) "After he has gone, the children drink some kind of poison that makes them distraught with pain and they fall writhing to the ground.

"At that time the father returns to his home and finds that his children have drunk poison. Some are completely out of their minds, while others are not. Seeing their father from far off, all are overjoyed and kneel down and entreat him, saying: 'How fine that you have returned safely. We were foolish and by mistake drank some poison. We beg you to cure us and let us live out our lives!'" (p. 261)

(24) "The father, seeing his children suffering like this, follows various prescriptions. Gathering fine medicinal herbs that meet all the requirements of color, fragrance, and flavor, he grinds, sifts, and mixes them together. Giving a dose of these to his children, he tells them: 'This is a highly effective medicine, meeting all the requirements of color, fragrance, and flavor. Take it and you will quickly be relieved of your sufferings and will be free of all illness.'" (p. 267)

(25) "Those children who have not lost their senses can see that this is good medicine, outstanding in both color and fragrance, so they take it immediately and are completely cured of their sickness. Those who are out of their minds are equally delighted to see their father return and beg him to cure their sickness, but when they are given the medicine, they refuse to take it. Why? Because the poison has penetrated deeply and their minds no longer function as before. So although the medicine is of excellent color and fragrance, they do not perceive it as good." (p. 275)

(26) "The father thinks to himself: My poor children! Because of the poison in them, their minds are completely befuddled. Although they are happy to see me and ask me to cure them, they refuse to take this excellent medicine. I must now resort to some expedient means to induce them to take the medicine. So he says to them: 'You should know that I am now old and worn out, and

the time of my death has come. I will leave this good medicine here. You should take it and not worry that it will not cure you.'"
(p. 281)

(27) "Having given these instructions, he then goes off to another land, where he sends a messenger home to announce, 'Your father is dead.'

"At that time the children, hearing that their father has deserted them and died, are filled with great grief and consternation and think to themselves: If our father were alive he would have pity on us and see that we are protected. But now he has abandoned us and died in some other country far away. We are shelterless orphans with no one to rely on!

"Constantly harboring such feelings of grief, they at last come to their senses and realize that the medicine is in fact excellent in color and fragrance and flavor, and so they take it and are healed of all the effects of the poison. The father, hearing that his children are all cured, immediately returns home and appears to them all once more." (p. 285)

(28) "Good men, what is your opinion? Can anyone say that this skilled physician is guilty of lying?"

"No, World-Honored One."

The Buddha said: "It is the same with me. It has been immeasurable, boundless hundreds, thousands, ten thousands, millions of nayuta asamkhya kalpas since I attained Buddhahood. But for the sake of living beings I employ the power of expedient means and say that I am about to pass into extinction. In view of the circumstances, however, no one can say that I have been guilty of lies or falsehoods."

At that time the World-Honored One, wishing to state his meaning once more, spoke in verse form, saying: . . . (p. 291)

The "Life Span" Chapter Verse Section
(LSOC, 270–73)

(29) "Since I attained Buddhahood
  the number of kalpas that have passed
  is an immeasurable hundreds, thousands, ten thousands,
  millions, trillions, asamkhyas.
  Constantly I have preached the Law, teaching, converting
  countless millions of living beings,
  causing them to enter the Buddha way,
  all this for immeasurable kalpas." (p. 309)

(30) "In order to save living beings,
  as an expedient means I appear to enter nirvana
  but in truth I do not pass into extinction.
  I am always here, preaching the Law.
  I am always here,
  but through my transcendental powers
  I make it so that living beings in their befuddlement
  do not see me even when close by." (p. 317)

(31) "When the multitude sees that I have passed into extinction,
  far and wide they offer alms to my relics.
  All harbor thoughts of yearning
  and in their minds thirst to gaze at me.
  When living beings have become truly faithful,
  honest and upright, gentle in intent,
  single-mindedly desiring to see the Buddha,
  not hesitating even if it costs them their lives,
  then I and the assembly of monks
  appear together on Holy Eagle Peak." (p. 325)

(32) "At that time I tell the living beings
       that I am always here, never entering extinction,
       but that because of the power of expedient means
       at times I appear to be extinct, at other times not,
       and that if there are living beings in other lands
       who are reverent and sincere in their wish to believe,
       then among them too
       I will preach the unsurpassed Law.
       But you have not heard of this,
       so you suppose that I enter extinction.
       When I look at living beings
       I see them drowned in a sea of suffering;
       therefore I do not show myself,
       causing them to thirst for me.
       Then when their minds are filled with yearning,
       at last I appear and preach the Law for them." (p. 339)

(33) "Such are my transcendental powers.
       For asamkhya kalpas
       constantly I have dwelled on Holy Eagle Peak
       and in various other places.
       When living beings witness the end of a kalpa
       and all is consumed in a great fire,
       this, my land, remains safe and tranquil,
       constantly filled with heavenly and human beings.
       The halls and pavilions in its gardens and groves
       are adorned with various kinds of gems.
       Jeweled trees abound in flowers and fruit
       where living beings enjoy themselves at ease.
       The gods strike heavenly drums,
       constantly making many kinds of music.

Mandarava blossoms rain down,
scattering over the Buddha and the great assembly." (**p. 343**)

(34) "My pure land is not destroyed,
yet the multitude sees it as consumed in fire,
with anxiety, fear, and other sufferings
filling it everywhere.
These living beings with their various offenses,
through causes arising from their evil actions,
spend asamkhya kalpas
without hearing the name of the three treasures." (**p. 355**)

(35) "But those who practice meritorious ways,
who are gentle, peaceful, honest, and upright,
all of them will see me
here in person, preaching the Law.
At times for this multitude
I describe the Buddha's life span as immeasurable,
and to those who see the Buddha only after a long time
I explain how difficult it is to meet a Buddha." (**p. 361**)

(36) "Such is the power of my wisdom
that its sagacious beams shine without measure.
This life span of countless kalpas
I gained as the result of lengthy practice.
You who are possessed of wisdom,
entertain no doubts on this point!
Cast them off, end them forever,
for the Buddha's words are true, not false." (**p. 367**)

(37) "He is like a skilled physician
who uses an expedient means to cure his deranged sons.

Though in fact alive, he gives out word he is dead,
yet no one can say he speaks falsely.
I am the father of this world,
saving those who suffer and are afflicted." (p. 371)

(38) "Because of the befuddlement of ordinary people,
though I live, I give out word I have entered extinction.
For if they see me constantly,
arrogance and selfishness arise in their minds.
Abandoning restraint, they give themselves up to the five
   desires
and fall into the evil paths of existence.
Always I am aware of which living beings
practice the way, and which do not,
and in response to their need for salvation
I preach various doctrines for them." (p. 375)

(39) "At all times I think to myself:
How can I cause living beings
to gain entry into the unsurpassed way
and quickly acquire the body of a Buddha?" (p. 379)

Notes

The "Expedient Means" Chapter

1. In July 1943, Josei Toda was detained and imprisoned on charges of violating the Peace Preservation Law, a key tool for the suppression of dissent in wartime Japan, and showing disrespect to the Japanese emperor. Alone in his prison cell, he began to chant Nam-myoho-renge-kyo and to intensely study the Lotus Sutra. Over time, he came to two major realizations. First, after repeated contemplation and prayer about a difficult passage in the sutra that referred to the Buddha, he came to a revolutionary insight: The Buddha is life itself. It exists within one's life and throughout the universe. It is the entity of cosmic life. Second, as the weeks and months passed, he came to realize that it was his mission as a Bodhisattva of the Earth to spread the Lotus Sutra as widely as possible to lead all people to happiness, and he resolved to dedicate the remainder of his life to do so.

2. For more details on Nichiren Shoshu's deviations from Nichiren's teachings, please go to www.sokaspirit.org.

3. Nichiren Daishonin advises specific followers slightly differently in this regard in other writings. For instance, in "Reply to the Lay Priest Soya," he writes: "I have written out the prose section of the 'Expedient Means' chapter for you. You should recite it together with the verse portion of the 'Life Span' chapter, which I sent you earlier" (WND-1, 486). In 2002, the Soka Gakkai adopted the practice of reciting the key prose section from the "Expedient Means" chapter and the verse section of the "Life Span" chapter, to be carried out once every morning and evening together with the chanting of Nam-myoho-renge-kyo. See the Editor's Note on p. ix for more information.

4. Johann Wolfgang von Goethe, *Herman and Dorothea*, trans. Ellen Frothingham, vol. XIX, Part 4, The Harvard Classics (New York: P.F. Collier & Son, 1909–14); Bartleby.com, 2001. www.bartleby.com/19/4/5.

5. In 1995, when this lecture first appeared, SGI ha spread to 115 countries and territories. As of this edition, the number has increased to 192.

6. Translated from Japanese. Leo Tolstoy, *Torusutoi no kotoba* (Words of Tolstoy), trans. Fumihiko Konuma (Tokyo: Yoyoi Shobo, 1970), 94.
7. www.worldofquotes.com/author/Thomas+Carlyle/1/index.html.
8. Comte de Lautréamont, *Maldoror and Poems*, trans. Paul Knight (London: Penguin Books, 1978), 277.
9. D.H. Lawrence, *Apocalypse* (New York: Penguin Books, 1976), 126.
10. Ibid.

The "Life Span" Chapter Prose Section

1. At the time these lectures were originally published, this section was a part of SGI members' daily gongyo. In 2002, the SGI adopted a new format, which no includes the prose section of the "Life Span" chapter. See the Editor's Note on p. ix for more information.
2. See "Samannaphala Sutta," *Dialogues of the Buddha*, vol. 1, ed. F. Max Muller (Oxford: Pali Text Society, 1995), 16–19, 79.
3. Romain Rolland, *Jean-Christope*, trans. Gilbert Cannan (New York: Henry Holt and Company, 1910), 352.
4. This reference to *The Human Revolution* is the book by second Soka Gakkai president, Josei Toda, and is different from President Ikeda's *The Human Revolution*.
5. See "Connected Discourses with Devatas," *The Connected Discourses of the Buddha*, vol. 1, trans. Bhikku Bodhi (Oxford: The Pali Text Society, 2000), 122–23.
6. Ralph Waldo Emerson, *Society and Solitude* (Boston and New York: Houghton, Mifflin and Company, 1904), 183.
7. See "Discourse of the Ariyan Quest," *The Collection of The Middle Length Sayings*, vol. 1, trans. I. B. Horner, M.A. (Oxford: The Pali Text Society, 2000), 213.
8. "Discourse on the Auspicious," *Middle Length Sayings*, vol. 3, trans. I.B. Horner (Oxford: Pali Text Society, 1996), 233.
9. Norman Cousins, *Anatomy of an Illness* (New York: W.W. Norton and Company, 1979), 148.
10. Aristotle, *The Basic Works of Aristotle*, ed. Richard McKeon (New York: Random House, 1941), 1479.
11. On March 16, 1958, Josei Toda organized a meeting at which six thousand youth gathered at Taiseki-ji. He encouraged them with all his might, bequeathing his spirit and responsibility for the achievement of kosen-rufu to the youth in general and to Daisaku Ikeda specifically. March 16, or Kosen-

rufu Day, has since been one of the most solemn and profound anniversaries within the Soka Gakkai.

12. Reward and punishment here refers to the idea that if one lives in accord with the fundamental Law or principle of life and the universe, one will experience gain, benefit, progress and increasing happiness. But if one should live or act counter or in opposition to that Law, one will experience loss and decline.

In Nichiren Buddhism, "reward" and "punishment" are not considered to be doled out by a higher power or authority. In that respect, it is different from the idea of reward and punishment in the secular society or in many religions. Rather, it is purely a function of one's own actions and the workings of the unbiased law of causality inherent in life and the universe.

As an example, if one obeys traffic laws and the principles of safe driving, one is likely to arrive at one's destination without mishap. But if one flouts those laws and drives recklessly, one is more likely to be involved in an accident. Practicing Buddhism correctly is said to set one's life in accord with the universal Law, thus bringing one good fortune and happiness.

13. Victor Hugo, *Les Miserables* (Fairfield, IA: 1st World Library, 2007), 17.

14. The phrase "Some are completely out of their minds (*waku shitsu honshin*)" that appears earlier can more literally be translated as "some have lost their true minds." The word *honshin* in this phrase can be translated as "original mind" or "true mind." Also, the phrase "Because the poison has penetrated so deeply and their minds no longer function as before (*ship ponshin ko*)" in the above passage can be translated as "Because the poison has penetrated so deeply and they have lost their original (or true) minds."

15. Karl Jaspers, *The Origin and Goal of History*, trans. Michael Bullock (London: Rutledge & Kegan Paul Ltd., 1953), 167.

The "Life Span" Chapter Verse Section

1. Percy Bysshe Shelley, *Shelley's Defence of Poetry*, ed. H.F.B. Brett-Smith (Oxford: Basil Blackwell, 1923), 48.

2. Walt Whitman, *Leaves of Grass* (London: Everyman's Library, 1947), 1.

3. Ibid., 41.

4. Translated from Japanese. *Aisurukoto ikirukoto—Roman Roran no kotoba* (To Love and To Live—Words from Romain Rolland), trans. and ed. Yuzura Ninagawa (Tokyo: Shakaishisosha, 1984), 81.

5. Nichiren discusses this phrase in the *The Record of the Orally Transmitted Teaching*, pp. 133–34. The phrase is retranslated in the this book as "[Ever] since I attained Buddhahood" and has a footnote explaining the literal

translation, which we reprint here for further clarification: "The passage consists of five Chinese characters: *ji go toku butsu rai*. It means 'Since I attained Buddhahood.' Literally, however, these five characters mean, respectively, since or ego, I or self, attain or gain, Buddhahood or Buddha, and 'ever' or come. Nichiren combined these characters in two ways in order to clarify that all living beings inherently possess the Ten Worlds and the three bodies: First, the 'Buddha' that 'has attained' both the 'since' ('ego' or the nine worlds) and the 'I' ('self' or Buddhahood) 'has come'; second, 'I' (the Dharma body), 'Buddhahood' (the reward body) and 'ever' ('come' or the manifested body) are 'self-attained.'"

6. Aleksandr Pushkin, *Pushkin Threefold: Narrative, Lyric, Polemic, and Ribald Verse*, trans. Walter Arndt (New York: E. P. Dutton & Co., Inc., 1972), 20.

7. *Bausteine: Aphorismen und Zitate aus alter und neuerer Zeit* (Building Stones: Aphorisms and Quotations from Past and Present), compiled by Carl Hilty (Leipzag: Walter Leopthien Verlag).

8. Whitman, *Leaves of Grass*, 125.

Glossary

amrita   A legendary, ambrosia-like liquid. In ancient India, it was regarded as the sweet-tasting beverage of the gods. In China, it was thought to rain down from heaven when the world became peaceful. Amrita is said to remove sufferings and give immortality. The word "amrita" means immortality and is often translated as "sweet dew."

asamkhya   Innumerable. A numerical unit of ancient India used to indicate an exceedingly large number. One source has it equal to 10^{59}, while another describes it as 10^{51}.

Atsuhara Persecution   A series of threats and acts of violence against followers of Nichiren in Atsuhara Village, in Fuji District of Suruga Province, Japan, over a period of three years, beginning in earnest in 1278. In 1279, twenty farmers, all practitioners of Nichiren's teachings, were arrested on false charges. They were interrogated by the deputy chief of the Office of Military and Police Affairs, Hei no Saemon, who demanded that they renounce their faith. Not one of them yielded, however, and Hei no Saemon eventually had three of them executed. This event opened the way to Buddhism in which ordinary people are not mere believers but active players.

beginningless time   See *kuon-ganjo.*

Bodhisattva Never Disparaging   A bodhisattva described in "Bodhisattva Never Disparaging," the twentieth chapter of the Lotus

Sutra. This bodhisattva, Shakyamuni in a previous lifetime, deeply respected everyone, and his practice consisted of addressing all he met with the words: "I have profound reverence for you, I would never dare treat you with disparagement or arrogance. Why? Because you are all practicing the bodhisattva way and are certain to attain Buddhahood" (LSOC, 308). The people ridiculed him and attacked him with staves and stones. The sutra explains that his practice of respecting others' Buddha nature became the cause for him to attain Buddhahood and that those who attacked him also would attain Buddhahood eventually through the "reverse relationship" they had formed with the Law.

boy Snow Mountains   The name of Shakyamuni Buddha in a previous lifetime when he was practicing austerities. Deciding to test Snow Mountain's resolve, the god Shakra appeared before him in the form of a hungry demon and recited half a verse from a Buddhist teaching. The boy begged the demon to tell him the second half of the verse. The demon agreed but demanded flesh and blood in payment. Snow Mountains gladly promised to offer his own body to the demon, which in turn gave him the latter half of the teaching. When, resolved to fulfill his promise, the boy jumped from a tall tree into the demon's mouth, the demon changed back into Shakra and caught him. He praised Snow Mountains for his willingness to give his life for the Law.

Brahma and Shakra   Two deities of ancient Indian mythology. In Buddhism, they are said to protect and watch over the world as leaders of the heavenly deities, the protective forces of the universe.

Buddha Burning Torch   Also known as Fixed Light. A Buddha to whom Shakyamuni, when practicing as a bodhisattva named Learned Youth in a previous existence, once offered flowers. It is recorded that, when Learned Youth tossed five lotus blossoms toward the Buddha

Burning Torch as an offering, they remained afloat in the air. When Bodhisattva Learned Youth spread his cloak and his own hair over marshy ground for the Buddha to walk upon, Burning Torch predicted that Learned Youth would become a Buddha in the future.

Buddhahood The state of awakening a Buddha has attained. The ultimate goal of Buddhist practice and the highest of the Ten Worlds. The word "enlightenment" is often used synonymously with Buddhahood. Buddhahood is regarded as a state of perfect freedom, in which one is awakened to the eternal and ultimate truth that is the reality of all things. This supreme state of life is characterized by boundless wisdom and infinite compassion. The Lotus Sutra reveals that Buddhahood is a potential in the lives of all beings.

Buddha of beginningless time Also, eternal Buddha, original Buddha, or true Buddha. The Buddha who has been eternally endowed with the three bodies—the Dharma body, the reward body and the manifested body, thereby embodying the eternal Law or the ultimate truth of life and the universe.

This term appears in Nichiren's writing given to his successor Nikko and signed by Nichiren. Titled *On the Mystic Principle of the True Cause,* it refers to "the Mystic Law, uncreated and eternal, of the Buddha of beginningless time" and states that the Mystic Law lies in the depths of the "Life Span" chapter of the essential teaching of the Lotus Sutra. Nichikan, the twenty-sixth chief priest of Taiseki-ji temple, identified Nichiren as that Buddha, based on the fact that Nichiren was the first to spread the Mystic Law.

Buddhism of sowing The Buddhism that plants the seeds of Buddhahood, or the cause for attaining Buddhahood, in people's lives. In Nichiren's teachings, the Buddhism of sowing indicates the Buddhism of Nichiren in contrast with that of Shakyamuni, which is called the

Buddhism of the harvest. The Buddhism of the harvest is that which can lead to enlightenment only those who received the seeds of Buddhahood by practicing the Buddha's teaching in previous lifetimes. In contrast, the Buddhism of sowing implants the seeds of Buddhahood, or Nam-myoho-renge-kyo, in the lives of those who had no connection with the Buddha's teaching in their past existences, that is, the people of the Latter Day of the Law.

Buddhist deities Also, heavenly gods and benevolent deities. The gods that protect the correct Buddhist teaching and its practitioners. Gods who function to protect the people and their land and bring good fortune to both. Rather than primary objects of belief or devotion, Buddhism tends to view them as functioning to support and protect the Buddha, the Law, or Buddhist teachings, and practitioners. They can be viewed as manifestations of the Buddha nature in one's life and as the inherent functions of nature and society that protect those who uphold that Law.

cause-awakened ones Also known as *pratyekabuddhas*. Those who perceive the twelve-linked chain of causation, or the truth of causal relationship. Together with voice-hearers, they constitute the persons of the two vehicles. Unlike bodhisattvas, they seek their own emancipation without thought of preaching for and instructing others. The realm of caused-awakened ones constitutes the eighth of the Ten Worlds and is sometimes referred to as the world of realization.

Ceremony in the Air The second of the three assemblies described in the Lotus Sutra, in which the entire gathering is suspended in space above the ground. The two other assemblies take place on Eagle Peak. The Ceremony in the Air is depicted from the latter half of "Treasure Tower," the eleventh chapter, through "Entrustment," the twenty-second chapter. In the "Treasure Tower" chapter, the treasure tower of the Buddha Many Treasures emerges from beneath the earth and is suspended in midair. Shakyamuni, after summoning the Buddhas who are his emanations from the ten directions, stations himself in midair, opens the treasure tower, and enters it, taking a seat beside the Buddha Many Treasures. Then, using his transcendental powers, he lifts the entire assembly into space so that they are at the same level. This begins the Ceremony in the Air. The heart of this ceremony consists of the revelation of Shakyamuni Buddha's original enlightenment and the transfer of the essence of the sutra to the Bodhisattvas of the Earth. Nichiren states that the object of devotion he revealed as the Gohonzon is the perfect embodiment of the Law, which is the essence of the Lotus Sutra, and that it is also a representation of the Ceremony in the Air.

Dharma-realm The phenomenal world or the world of all phenomena.

Eagle Peak Also known as Vulture Peak, Holy Eagle Peak or Sacred Eagle Peak, and simply Holy Mountain, Sacred Mountain or Holy Peak. A small mountain located northeast of Rajagriha, the capital of Magadha in ancient India. Eagle Peak is known as a place frequented by Shakyamuni, where he is said to have expounded the Lotus Sutra and other teachings. Eagle Peak also symbolizes the Buddha land or the state of Buddhahood, as in the expression "the pure land of Eagle Peak."

essential teaching of the Lotus Sutra The teaching expounded by Shakyamuni from the perspective of his true identity as the Buddha who attained enlightenment countless kalpas ago. It consists of the latter fourteen chapters of the Lotus Sutra, from the "Emerging from the Earth," the fifteenth chapter, through the "Universal Worthy," the twenty-eighth chapter. The core of the essential teaching is the "Life Span," the sixteenth chapter, which reveals Shakyamuni's enlightenment in the distant past.

five desires   (1) The desires that arise from the contact of the five sense organs (eyes, ears, nose, tongue and body) with their respective objects (color and form, sound, smell, taste and texture). (2) The desires for food and drink, wealth, sexual love, fame and sleep.

five senior priests   Five of the six senior priests, excluding Nikko, designated by Nichiren Daishonin as his principal disciples. He formally designated Nikko as his successor, but after Nichiren's death, the other five refused to follow Nikko. They gradually departed from Nichiren's teachings, compromising with schools their teacher had refuted as erroneous and misleading.

Former, Middle or Latter Day of the Law   Three consecutive periods or stages into which the time following a Buddha's death is divided. During the Former Day, the spirit of Buddhism prevails and people can attain enlightenment through its practice. During the Middle Day, although Buddhism becomes firmly established in society, it grows increasingly formalized, and fewer people benefit from it. In the Latter Day, people are tainted by the three poisons—greed, anger and foolishness—and lose their aspiration for enlightenment; Buddhism itself loses the power to lead them to Buddhahood. See also *Latter Day of the Law.*

four inverted views   Also, four wrong-headed views or four topsy-turvy views. They are called "inverted" because one takes an opposite view of the truth. Mistaking impermanence for permanence, suffering for happiness, non-self for self and impurity for purity. This indicates the inverted views of ordinary people who do not recognize the world of delusion for what it is.

four virtues   Four noble qualities of a Buddha's life—eternity, happiness, true self and purity. These describe the true nature of a Buddha's life, which is pure and eternal, and which manifests the true self and enjoys absolute happiness. Because ordinary people possess the Buddha nature, they too can develop the four virtues when they attain Buddhahood by fulfilling the Buddha's teachings.

fundamental darkness   Also, fundamental ignorance or primal ignorance. The most deeply rooted illusion inherent in life, said to give rise to all other illusions. "Darkness" in this sense means inability to see or recognize the truth, particularly, the true nature of one's life. Nichiren interprets fundamental darkness as ignorance of the ultimate Law, or ignorance of the fact that one's life is essentially a manifestation of that Law, which he identifies as Nam-myoho-renge-kyo.

good roots   Also, root of goodness, root of merit, good act, good cause or act of merit. A cause, or action, that produces a good effect or reward. Good acts are compared to the roots that nourish the plants and trees so that they bear flowers and fruit. In Buddhism, "good roots" are necessary for the attainment of Buddhahood. Greed, anger and foolishness are called the three bad roots or the three poisons. In contrast, "no greed, no anger and no foolishness" are called the three good roots.

great pure Law   In Nichiren's teaching, the Law of Nam-myoho-renge-kyo. Nichiren uses this term in his writings to indicate the ultimate Law implied in the "Life Span" chapter of the Lotus Sutra, in contrast with the pure Law, or Shakyamuni's teachings.

heavenly eye   One of the five types of vision or five kinds of perceptive faculty. The heavenly eye, or divine eye, can perceive things in the darkness, at a distance or beyond the physical limits of obstruction.

heavenly gods and benevolent deities   See *Buddhist deities.*

Hei no Saemon (d. 1293)   A leading official in the Hojo regency, the de facto ruling body of Japan during the Kamakura period. He collaborated with Ryokan and other leading priests to persecute Nichiren and his followers.

Hinayana   Literally "Small Vehicle" or "Lesser Vehicle." One of two major streams of Buddhism, the other being Mahayana, meaning "Great Vehicle." The term Hinayana originated with Mahayanists to refer to early Buddhist schools they criticized as inaccessible to many people due to their focus on monastic discipline. They referred to their own teaching, which emphasized the bodhissatva ideal to work for the salvation of others, as a "great vehicle" able to convey many people to the destination of enlightenment. The designation "Hinayana" was derogatory, and the early Buddhist schools naturally did not apply the name to themselves.

Mahayana schools in China and Japan used Hinayana to refer to a category of Buddhist teachings in Chinese translation. In T'ien-t'ai's system of classification, Hinayana corresponds to the twelve-year period in which Shakyamuni was held to have preached the Agama sutras and to the class of teachings known as the Tripitaka (Three Baskets), which includes early sutras, monastic rules and commentaries. It was in this sense that Nichiren employed the term. Today, its use should be avoided when referring to any present or historical Buddhist school or tradition.

Holy Eagle Peak   See *Eagle Peak.*

immediate attainment of enlightenment   Literally "immediate arrival at correct perception." Similar to the principle of "attaining Buddhahood in one's present form," the idea of immediate attainment of enlightenment describes the power of the Lotus Sutra to enable one to tap one's innate Buddha nature and immediately manifest the life state of a Buddha. It is taught in contrast to the idea, prevalent in the pre-Lotus Sutra teachings, that Buddhahood can only be attained after carrying out intensive practice over vast expanses of time and countless lifetimes.

kalpa   In ancient Indian cosmology, an extremely long period of time. There are various views on its length. In Buddhist cosmology, a kalpa is described as being 16 million years.

karma   Potentials in the inner, unconscious realm of life created through one's actions in the past or present that manifest themselves as various results in the present or future. Karma is a variation of the Sanskrit *karman,* which means act, action or a former act leading to a future result. Buddhism interprets karma in two ways: as indicating three categories of action, i.e., mental, verbal and physical, and as indicating a dormant force thereby produced. That is, one's thought, speech and behavior, both good and bad, imprint themselves as a latent force or potential in one's life.

One's actions in the past have shaped one's present reality, and one's actions in the present will in turn influence one's future. This law of karmic causality operates in perpetuity, carrying over from one lifetime to the next and remaining with one in the latent state between death and rebirth.

The Buddhist doctrine of karma is not fatalistic. Rather, karma is viewed not only as a means to explain the present but also as the potential force through which to influence one's future. Buddhism therefore encourages people to create the best possible karma in the present in order to ensure the best possible outcome in the future.

King Shibi The name of Shakyamuni in a past existence when he was the ruler of a great kingdom, according to *The Garland of Birth Stories*. That work compares King Shibi's love for the people to a mother's love for her children. He was seeking the teachings of a Buddha, and one day the god Vishvakarman and the god Shakra decided to test him. They disguised themselves respectively as a dove and a hawk, the hawk relentlessly pursuing the dove, which flew into King Shibi's robes for protection. The hungry hawk demanded the dove as food, and Shibi decided that to save the dove he would offer the hawk an amount of his own flesh equal to the weight of the dove. He sliced off a piece of his flesh, placed it on one side of a balance and placed the dove on the other. Strangely enough, although he continued slicing off his flesh and placing it on the scale, he could not equal the weight of the dove. Finally he placed himself on the scale, demonstrating his willingness to offer his entire body, and felt such delight and satisfaction as he had never experienced. At that time, Vishvakarman and Shakra reverted to their original forms as Buddhist gods and praised his practice of almsgiving.

kosen-rufu Wide propagation, or wide proclamation and propagation. A term from the Lotus Sutra that literally means "to declare and spread widely." Nichiren Daishonin defines Nam-myoho-renge-kyo as the Law to be widely declared and spread throughout the world. Kosen-rufu refers to the process of securing lasting peace and happiness for all humankind by establishing the humanistic ideals of Nichiren Buddhism in society.

kuon-ganjo   Literally *kuon* means the remote past, and *ganjo*, beginning or foundation. Nichiren interprets *kuon-ganjo* on two different levels: (1) In the context of the "Life Span" chapter, *kuon* refers to the remote past when Shakyamuni originally attained enlightenment, and *ganjo*, to the foundation of his original enlightenment. (2) *The Record of the Orally Transmitted Teachings* states: "*Kuon* means something that was not worked for, that was not improved upon, but that exists just as it always has. Because we are speaking here of the Buddha eternally endowed with the three bodies, it is not a question of something attained for the first time at a certain time, or of something that was worked for. This is not the kind of Buddhahood that is adorned with the thirty-two features and eighty characteristics, or that needs to be improved on in any way. Because this is the eternally abiding Buddha in his original state, he exists just as he always has. This is what is meant by *kuon*. *Kuon* is Nam-myoho-renge-kyo, and 'true attainment' means awakening to the fact that one is eternally endowed with the three bodies" (pp. 141–42). In essence, for Nichiren, *kuon*, or *kuon-ganjo*, means the eternal Law of Nam-myoho-renge-kyo and the original state of life that embodies Buddhahood.

Land of Eternally Tranquil Light   Also, Land of Tranquil Light. The Buddha land, which is free from impermanence and impurity. In many sutras, the actual saha world in which human beings dwell is described as an impure land filled with delusions and sufferings, while the Buddha land is described as a pure land free from these and far removed from this saha world. In contrast, the Lotus Sutra reveals the saha world to be the Buddha land, or the Land of Eternally Tranquil Light, and explains that the nature of a land is determined by the minds of its inhabitants.

Latter Day of the Law   The last of the three periods—the Former, Middle and Latter Day of the Law—following Shakyamuni Buddha's death, when his teachings are said to fall into confusion and lose the power to lead people to enlightenment. The Latter Day of the Law is said to last for ten thousand years. The fifth of five five-hundred-year periods following Shakyamuni's death described in the Great Collection Sutra corresponds to the beginning of the Latter Day of the Law. The sutra predicts that it will be an "age of quarrels and disputes," when monks will disregard the precepts and feud constantly among themselves, when erroneous views will prevail, and when Shakyamuni's teachings will "be obscured and lost."

In contrast, the Lotus Sutra views the Latter Day of the Law as the time when the teaching it contains will be propagated.

Mahayana   Buddhism of the Great Vehicle. The Sanskrit *maha* means great, and *yana*, vehicle. One of the two major divisions of the Buddhist teachings, Mahayana and Hinayana. Mahayana emphasizes altruistic practice—called the bodhisattva practice—as a means to attain enlightenment for oneself and to help others attain it as well. Around the end of the first century BCE or the beginning of the first century CE, a new Buddhist movement began to emerge among those who were dissatisfied with what they perceived as the sterile academicism and rigidity of the existing schools. Feeling it was important to model their behavior after that of the Buddha himself, they advocated bodhisattva practice, or practice to benefit others, and engaged themselves in instructing laypersons while practicing among them. These practitioners called themselves bodhisattvas and their teachings Mahayana (Great Vehicle), indicating that their teaching was the vehicle to transport a great many people to enlightenment.

Mandarava   Also mandara. A flower said to bloom in heaven. It is fragrant, and its beauty delights those who see it. In Buddhist sutras, mandaras and other heavenly flowers rain down from the heavens when a Buddha preaches or when other wonderful events occur.

Miao-lo (711–82)   Also known as Chan-jan and the Great Teacher Miao-lo. A patriarch of the T'ien-t'ai school in China. He produced a number of important commentaries on T'ien-t'ai's works and is revered as the school's restorer.

Mount Minobu   A mountain in what is today Yamanashi Prefecture, Japan. Nichiren lived there during the later years of his life, from the fifth month of 1274 through the ninth month of 1282 just prior to his death.

mutual possession of the Ten Worlds   One of the component principles of T'ien-t'ai's doctrine of three thousand realms in a single moment of life. "Mutual possession" means that life is not fixed in one or another of the Ten Worlds but can manifest any of the ten, from hell to the state of Buddhahood, at any given moment. While one of the ten is manifest, the other nine remain latent. The important point of this principle is that all beings in any of the nine worlds possess the Buddha nature. This means that every person has the potential to manifest Buddhahood, while a Buddha also possesses the nine worlds and in this sense is not separate or different from ordinary people.

Mystic Law   (Jpn *myoho*) The ultimate Law, principle or truth of life and the universe in Nichiren's teachings; the Law of Nam-myoho-renge-kyo. This term derives from Kumarajiva's Chinese translation of the Sanskrit word *saddharma,* from the title of the *Saddharma-*

pundarika-sutra, or the Lotus Sutra. It has been translated into English also as Wonderful Law, Wonderful Dharma, Fine Dharma, etc.

mystic principle of the true cause   See *true cause.*

Nam-myoho-renge-kyo   The ultimate Law or truth of the universe, according to Nichiren's teaching. Nichiren first taught the invocation of Nam-myoho-renge-kyo on April 28, 1253. Nichiren Daishonin teaches that this phrase encompasses all laws and teachings within itself and that the benefit of chanting Nam-myoho-renge-kyo includes the benefit of conducting all virtuous practices. *Nam* means "devotion to"; *myoho* means "Mystic Law"; *renge* refers to the lotus flower, which simultaneously blooms and seeds, indicating the simultaneity of cause and effect; *kyo* means sutra, the teaching of a Buddha, and also indicates the power of the human voice to express the innate Buddha nature.

Nagarjuna   A Mahayana scholar of southern India, thought to have lived between the years of 150 and 250. Born to a Brahman family, he first studied early Buddhist teachings but later converted to Mahayana. He wrote many important treatises on a great number of Mahayana sutras and organized the theoretical foundation of Mahayana thought, thus making an inestimable contribution to its development.

nayuta   An ancient Indian numerical unit. Explanations of its magnitude differ. *The Dharma Analysis Treasury* defines it as one hundred billion. Other sources define it as ten million.

Nichikan (1665–1726)   The twenty-sixth chief priest of Taiseki-ji, the head temple of the Nikko school or what today is called Nichiren

Shoshu. He is revered as a restorer of Nichiren's teachings because he worked to clarify their true meaning and to correct misinterpretations.

Nichiren (1222–82) The founder of the Buddhist tradition that is based on the Lotus Sutra and urges chanting the phrase Nammyoho-renge-kyo as a daily practice. Nichiren revealed that Nam-myoho-renge-kyo (Myoho-renge-kyo being the title of the Lotus Sutra) represents the essence of the Lotus's teaching. He embodied it in a mandala called the Gohonzon and taught that chanting that phrase with faith in the Gohonzon is the practice that enables people in the present age, the Latter Day of the Law, to attain Buddhahood.

nirvana Enlightenment, the ultimate goal of Buddhist practice. The Sanskrit word *nirvana* means "blown out" and is variously translated as extinction, emancipation, cessation, quiescence or non-rebirth. Nirvana was originally regarded as the state in which all illusions and desires as well as the cycle of birth and death are extinguished. In Mahayana Buddhism, nirvana came to mean not so much an exit from the phenomenal world as an awakening to the true nature of phenomena, or the attainment of Buddha wisdom. Even in Mahayana sutras, however, this attainment is regarded as requiring the elimination of earthly desires in the same manner as expounded in the Hinayana teachings. Therefore, it is taught that nirvana requires an immeasurably long period to achieve.

In contrast, the Lotus Sutra teaches that, by awakening to one's innate Buddha nature, one can reach the state of nirvana in his or her present form as an ordinary person who possesses earthly desires and undergoes the sufferings of birth and death. It reveals the principle that the sufferings of birth and death are none other than nirvana. From the standpoint of the Lotus Sutra, birth and death are two integral phases of eternal life. Nirvana, therefore, is not the cessation of birth and death but a state of enlightenment experienced as one repeats the cycle of birth and death. The sufferings of birth and death and nirvana, or enlightenment, are inseparable: it is not necessary to extinguish one in order to attain the other. These sufferings belong to the nine worlds, and nirvana, to the world of Buddhahood. The nine worlds and the world of Buddhahood are mutually inclusive. By manifesting the state of Buddhahood, one enjoys nirvana while repeating the cycle of birth and death.

observing one's own mind Or observation of the mind. To perceive or awaken to the ultimate reality inherent in one's life. Also, the method of practice that makes this possible. In contrast with doctrinal study of the Buddhist sutras, observation of the mind means to perceive in the depths of one's being the truth that is beyond verbal explanation. In Nichiren's teaching, the observation of the mind means to believe in the Gohonzon, the embodiment of three thousand realms in a single moment of life, chant Nam-myoho-renge-kyo, and thereby awaken to and manifest the state of Buddhahood inherent in one's life. This is the teaching that embracing the Gohonzon is in itself observing one's own mind, i.e., attaining enlightenment.

Observation of the mind also means to interpret the sutras from the viewpoint of the truth one realizes in one's life. In Nichiren's teaching, it means to read the sutras from the viewpoint of the principle of Nam-myoho-renge-kyo.

original Buddha See *Buddha of beginningless time.*

paramita Practices that Mahayana bodhisattvas must undertake to attain enlightenment. Generally, *paramita* is interpreted as "perfection" or "having reached the opposite shore." These practices were so called because by perfecting them one was said to cross from the shore of delusion and suffering to the shore of enlightenment.

pratyekabuddhas   See *cause-awakened ones.*

provisional Buddha   Also, transient Buddha. A Buddha who does not reveal his true identity but assumes a transient status or role in order to save the people. The term is used in contrast with "true Buddha," a Buddha who has revealed his true identity. A true Buddha can be compared to the moon in the sky and a provisional Buddha to its reflection on the surface of water. A provisional Buddha does not expound the truth in its entirety but only partial aspects of the truth.

Ryokan (1217–1303)   A priest of the True Word Precepts school in Japan. With the patronage of the ruling Hojo clan, Ryokan became chief priest of Gokuraku-ji, a temple in Kamakura. He undertook numerous social welfare projects, including building hospitals and roads, and commanded enormous influence both among government officials and the general populace. He was hostile to the Daishonin and contrived to have accusations brought against Nichiren, which eventually led to the Tatsunokuchi Persecution.

saha world   This world, a world in which people must endure suffering. It is also defined as an impure land, a land defiled by earthly desires and illusion, in contrast with a pure land. The saha world describes the land where Shakyamuni Buddha makes his appearance and instructs living beings. In Buddhist scriptures, the saha world indicates either Jambudvipa, which is one of the four continents of ancient Indian cosmology, or the entire world containing all four continents. It also indicates the major world system, considered to be the realm of Shakyamuni's instruction. In some Buddhist scriptures, including the Lotus and Vimalakirti sutras, it is held that the saha world is in itself a pure land, the Land of Eternally Tranquil Light. In the "Life Span" chapter, Shakyamuni states, "Ever since then [i.e., since attaining enlightenment in the remote past] I have been constantly in this saha world, preaching the Law, teaching, and converting" (LSOC, 266), indicating that the place where the Buddha dwells, the Buddha land, is in fact the saha world.

samadhi A state of intense concentration of mind, or meditation, said to produce inner serenity. The term "samadhi" is translated as meditation, contemplation or concentration.

Shakyamuni Also known as Gautama Buddha. The founder of Buddhism. "Shakyamuni" means "sage of the Shakyas," Shakya being the name of the tribe or clan to which his family belonged.

Shariputra One of Shakyamuni Buddha's ten major disciples, known as foremost in wisdom.

simultaneity of cause and effect The principle that both cause and effect exist together simultaneously in a single moment of life. Cause (the nine worlds) and effect (Buddhahood) simultaneously exist in one's life. Nichiren writes "Anyone who practices this Law will obtain both the cause and the effect of Buddhahood simultaneously" (WND-I, 421). Specifically, Nichiren is referring here to the practice of chanting Nam-myoho-renge-kyo and its function to instantaneously tap and bring forth one's innate Buddhahood.

stage of non-regression One of the stages of bodhisattva practice. One who reaches this stage never backslides, always advancing in Buddhist practice toward attaining Buddhahood.

Taiseki-ji The head temple of Nichiren Shoshu, located in Japan.

Tatsunokuchi Persecution An unsuccessful attempt to execute Nichiren at Tatsunokuchi on the western outskirts of Kamakura in Japan. A month later, he was sent into exile on the desolate Sado Island.

Tendai school   Also known as the Tendai Lotus school or the Tendai Hokke school. The Japanese counterpart of the Chinese T'ien-t'ai school. It was founded in the early ninth century by Dengyo, also known as Saicho. Its head temple is Enryaku-ji on Mount Hiei, near Kyoto.

ten directions   The entire universe, all physical space. Specifically, the ten directions are the eight directions of the compass, plus up and down. Buddhist scriptures refer to the existence of Buddha lands in all directions throughout the universe, each with its own Buddha. The expression "the Buddhas of the ten directions" in the sutras indicates these Buddhas.

ten honorable titles   Ten epithets for a Buddha, expressing such qualities as power, wisdom, virtue and compassion. Several versions exist. One lists the ten as (1) Thus Come One; (2) Worthy of Offerings; (3) Right and Universal Knowledge; (4) Perfect Clarity and Conduct; (5) Well Attained; (6) Understanding the World; (7) Unexcelled Worthy; (8) Trainer of the People; (9) Teacher of Heavenly and Human Beings; (10) Buddha, the World-Honored One.

ten powers   Ten powers that a Buddha possesses described in *The Great Commentary on the Abhidharma* and other treatises. They are (1) the power of knowing what is true and what is not; (2) the power of knowing karmic causality at work in the lives of all beings throughout past, present and future; (3) the power of knowing all stages of concentration, emancipation and meditation; (4) the power of knowing the states of life of all people; (5) the power of judging all people's levels of understanding; (6) the power of discerning the superiority or inferiority of all people's capacity; (7) the power of knowing the effects of all people's actions; (8) the power of remembering past lifetimes; (9) the power of knowing when each person will be born and die, and in what realm that person will be reborn; and (10) the power of eradicating all illusions. Some explanations of the ten powers give a different order or differ slightly in content.

Ten Worlds   Ten distinct realms or categories of beings referred to in Buddhist scriptures. From the lowest to the highest, the realms of (1) hell, (2) hungry spirits, (3) animals, (4) *asuras*, (5) human beings, (6) heavenly beings, (7) voice-hearers, (8) cause-awakened ones, (9) bodhisattvas and (10) Buddhas. The Ten Worlds were viewed originally as distinct physical locations, each with its own particular inhabitants. The Lotus Sutra, however, teaches that each of the Ten Worlds contains all ten within it, making it possible to interpret them as potential states of life inherent in each individual being. In other words, from the standpoint of the Lotus Sutra, the Ten Worlds indicates ten potential states or conditions that a person can manifest or experience.

theoretical teaching of the Lotus Sutra   The first half of the twenty-eight-chapter Lotus Sutra, from "Introduction," the first chapter, through "Peaceful Practices," the fourteenth chapter. The latter fourteen chapters are identified as the essential teaching. The theoretical teaching takes the form of preaching by a "provisional Buddha," the historical Shakyamuni Buddha depicted as having first attained enlightenment during his lifetime in India. "Expedient Means," the second chapter, is the core of the theoretical teaching, which reveals the true aspect of all phenomena and that the ten factors endow all life. This chapter also states that the Buddha's sole purpose is to lead all people to Buddhahood. See also *essential teaching of the Lotus Sutra.*

thirty-two features   Remarkable physical characteristics attributed to Buddhas, bodhisattvas, Brahma, Shakra and wheel-turning kings, symbolizing their superiority over ordinary people. The descriptions and order of these features differ slightly among the Buddhist scriptures.

three bodies of a Buddha Three kinds of body a Buddha may possess. A concept set forth in Mahayana Buddhism to organize different views of the Buddha appearing in the sutras. The three bodies are as follows: (1) The Dharma body, or Law, to which a Buddha is enlightened; (2) the reward body, obtained as the reward of completing bodhisattva practices and acquiring the Buddha wisdom; (3) the manifested body, or the physical form that a Buddha assumes in this world in order to save the people. On the basis of the Lotus Sutra and the principle of three thousand realms in a single moment of life derived from it, T'ien-t'ai (538–97) maintained that the three bodies are not separate entities but three integral aspects of a single Buddha.

three evil paths The worlds of hell, hunger and animality, the lowest of the ten states of life known as the Ten Worlds.

three existences Past existence, present existence and future existence. Used to indicate all of time, from the eternal past, through the present, through the eternal future. In Buddhism, they are the three aspects of the eternity of life, linked inseparably by the law of cause and effect. In the sutras, expressions such as "the Buddhas of the three existences" and "the Buddhas of the three existences and ten directions" indicate all Buddhas throughout eternity and boundless space.

threefold world The world of unenlightened beings who transmigrate within the six paths (from hell through the realm of heavenly beings). The threefold world consists of, in ascending order, the world of desire, the world of form and the world of formlessness. In a general sense, it refers to the world in which we dwell.

Three Great Secret Laws The core principles of Nichiren Daishonin's teaching. They are the object of devotion of the essential teaching (the Gohonzon), the daimoku of the essential teaching (Nam-myoho-renge-kyo) and the sanctuary of the essential teaching (where we enshrine the Gohonzon). Here, "essential teaching" refers to the teaching of Nam-myoho-renge-kyo and not to the essential teaching, or the latter fourteen chapters, of the Lotus Sutra. They are called secret because they are implicit in the text of the Lotus Sutra and remained hidden until Nichiren revealed them. The Three Great Secret Laws represent Nichiren's embodiment of the Mystic Law, to which he was enlightened, in a form that all people can practice and thereby gain access to that Law within their own lives.

three powerful enemies Three types of arrogant people who persecute those who propagate the Lotus Sutra in the evil age after Shakyamuni Buddha's death, described in the twenty-line verse section of "Encouraging Devotion," the thirteenth chapter of the Lotus Sutra. Miao-lo summarizes them as arrogant lay people, arrogant priests and arrogant false sages.

three thousand realms in a single moment of life "A single moment of life" (*ichinen*) is also translated as one mind, one thought or one thought-moment. A philosophical system established by T'ien-t'ai in his *Great Concentration and Insight* on the basis of the phrase the "true aspect of all phenomena" from the "Expedient Means" chapter of the Lotus Sutra. The three thousand realms, or the entire phenomenal world, exist in a single moment of life. The number three thousand here comes from the following calculation: 10 (Ten Worlds) x 10 (Ten Worlds) x 10 (ten factors) x 3 (three realms of existence). Life at any moment manifests one of the Ten Worlds. Each of these worlds possesses the potential for all ten within itself, and this "mutual possession," or mutual inclusion, of the Ten Worlds is represented as 10^2, or a hundred, possible worlds. Each of these hundred worlds possesses the ten factors, making one thousand factors or potentials, and these operate within each of the three realms of existence, thus making three thousand realms.

three treasures   The three things that all Buddhists should revere. They are the Buddha, the Law (the Buddha's teachings) and the Buddhist Order (community of believers). In Sanskrit, they are known as Buddha, Dharma and *Samgha*. The Buddha is one who is awakened to the truth of life and the universe. The Dharma, or Law, means the teachings that the Buddha expounds in order to lead all people to enlightenment. The *Samgha*, or Buddhist Order, is the group of persons who practice the Buddha's teachings, preserve the Law, spread it and transmit it to future generations.

three truths   The truth of non-substantiality, the truth of temporary existence and the truth of the Middle Way. The truth of non-substantiality means that phenomena have no existence of their own; their true nature is non-substantial, indefinable in terms of existence or nonexistence. The truth of temporary existence means that, although non-substantial, all things possess a temporary reality that is in constant flux. The truth of the Middle Way means that the true nature of phenomena is that they are neither non-substantial nor temporary, though they display attributes of both. The Middle Way is the essence of things that continues either in a manifest or a latent state.

three vehicles   A classification in Mahayana Buddhism of three kinds of teachings, each tailored to the capacity of a specific set of practitioners and enabling them to attain a state of awakening suited to that capacity. "Vehicle" means that which carries one to a state of awakening. The three vehicles are the teachings expounded for voice-hearers, for cause-awakened ones and for bodhisattvas. The Lotus Sutra, however, declares that the sole purpose of a Buddha's advent in the world is to enable all people to become Buddhas, and that the three vehicles are accordingly not ends in themselves but means to lead people to the one Buddha vehicle.

three virtues The Dharma body, wisdom and emancipation; three attributes of a Buddha. The Dharma body means the truth that the Buddha has realized, or the true aspect of all phenomena; wisdom is the capacity to realize this truth; and emancipation means the state of being free from the sufferings of birth and death.

Thus Come One One of the ten honorable titles of a Buddha, meaning one who has come from the realm of truth. This title indicates that a Buddha embodies the fundamental truth of all phenomena and has grasped the law of causality spanning past, present and future.

T'ien-t'ai (538–97) Also known as Chih-i. The founder of the T'ien-t'ai school in China. He classified all of Shakyamuni's sutras into "five periods and eight teachings" and through this classification demonstrated the superiority of the Lotus Sutra. His major works, compiled by his disciple Chang-an, are *The Profound Meaning of the Lotus Sutra*, *The Words and Phrases of the Lotus Sutra* and *Great Concentration and Insight*, all of which Nichiren cited frequently. In the latter work, based on his insight into the Lotus Sutra, T'ien-t'ai describes the principle of three thousand realms in a single moment of life. Nichiren employed this as a philosophical framework for explaining his teaching of Nam-myoho-renge-kyo.

time without beginning See *kuon-ganjo*.

treasure tower Any of a variety of jeweled stupas depicted in Buddhist sutras. The best known is the treasure tower of Many Treasures Buddha appears in the "Treasure Tower" chapter of the Lotus Sutra. According to the sutra, this massive tower [thousands of miles high and wide] emerges from below the earth and is adorned with the seven kinds of treasures: gold, silver, lapis lazuli, seashell, agate, pearl and carnelian. Nichiren viewed the treasure tower as an allegory for human life in its enlightened state achieved through the chanting of

Nam-myoho-renge-kyo. He also refers to the Gohonzon, the object of devotion in his teaching, as "the treasure tower."

true Buddha   From the perspective of the content of the Lotus Sutra, the true Buddha corresponds to the Shakyamuni depicted in the latter half (essential teaching) of the Lotus Sutra, while the Buddha in his transient identity is the Shakyamuni of the first half (theoretical teaching) of the sutra. Nichiren is regarded as the teacher of the true cause and Shakyamuni as the teacher of the true effect. This is because in the Lotus Sutra Shakyamuni revealed his eternal Buddhahood, the effect of his original bodhisattva practice. He did not, however, reveal the true cause or the nature of the specific practice by which he attained it. Nichiren, on the other hand, revealed the teaching and practice of Nam-myoho-renge-kyo, which he identified as the true cause for attaining Buddhahood, i.e., as the cause that enables all people to attain Buddhahood. This viewpoint identifies Nichiren as the true Buddha.

true cause   Refers to the practice Shakyamuni carried out countless kalpas in the past in order to attain his original enlightenment. The term contrasts with the true effect, or the original enlightenment Shakyamuni achieved as a result of the true cause countless kalpas before his enlightenment in India. Nichiren identified the true cause, or fundamental Law, that enables all Buddhas to attain their enlightenment, as the Law of Nam-myoho-renge-kyo.

two vehicles   The vehicles, or teachings, that lead voice-hearers and cause-awakened ones to their respective levels of enlightenment. The provisional Mahayana teachings condemn persons of the two vehicles for seeking their own enlightenment without working for the enlightenment of others and assert that they can never attain Buddhahood. According to the Lotus Sutra, however, even those of the two vehicles can become Buddhas.

Vimalakirti Sutra   A Mahayana sutra about the wealthy layman Vimalakirti of the city of Vaishali at the time of Shakyamuni. He is sick in bed, and Bodhisattva Manjushri inquires about the nature of his illness. Vimalakirti replies that because all living beings are ill, he is ill; if all living beings are relieved of sickness, then his sickness will likewise be relieved. The sutra thus sets forth the ideal of the Mahayana bodhisattva, which is to draw no distinction between self and others.

voice-hearers   Shakyamuni Buddha's disciples who heard his preaching and strove to attain enlightenment. Voice-hearers and cause-awakened ones are called persons of the two vehicles. The realm of voice-hearers constitutes the seventh of the Ten Worlds and is sometimes referred to as the world of learning.

World-Honored One   One of the ten honorable titles of a Buddha. The Sanskrit *bhagavat* is usually translated into English as "blessed one." In the Chinese Buddhist scriptures, *bhagavat* was rendered as World-Honored One. A Buddha is so called because he is widely revered in the world.

Index

14, 363, 373

The Six-Volume Writings (Nichikan), 43

"The True Aspect of All Phenomena,"
103, 110

T'ien-t'ai, 6, 34, 48–49, 59, 113–14, 119,
137–38, 193, 198, 200, 215, 217, 230,
232, 262–63, 269–70, 287, 299, 371;
Buddhism of, 115; Lotus Sutra of, 4

three bodies, 116, 138–39, 215–20, 310,
312–13, 318, 383

Three Great Secret Laws, 270, 328

three poisons, 268, 272

three powerful enemies, 53

three thousand realms in a single
moment of life, 26, 111–13, 116,
214, 218, 233–35, 242, 270, 335, 346,
349–50, 358–59, 363

three treasures, 357–358

three truths, 116

three types of learning, 269

three vehicles, 20

three vehicles being replaced by the one
vehicle, 199

three virtues, 116, 372–73

threefold contemplation in single mind,
114

threefold world, 208–10, 212, 214, 221

"Thus Come One," 139; Nichiren Daishonin on, 129

Toda, Josei, 23, 32, 46, 50–51, 54, 62,
64–65, 67, 69, 72, 79, 81–82, 92,
94–95, 99, 101, 106, 112, 119–20,
136, 139, 154–56, 171, 181, 184, 192,
195, 205, 208, 212, 218, 235, 249,
256, 264, 309, 311–12, 327, 330–32,
344–45, 347–48, 350, 352, 364–65,
369, 381, 384–85; as a great common
mortal, 377; and common mortal of
beginningless time, 241; and death,
321; declaration of, 170; disciples of,
248; on enlightenment, 41; guidance
sessions of, 74–75; on joy, 341; life
state of, 165; Lotus Sutra lectures of,
1–4, 333; on Nichiren Daishonin, 8;
proclamation of, 271; realization of,
154, 336; spirit of, 7, 120–21, 226,
265, 272, 382–84; on T'ien-t'ai, 8; on
the saha world, 187; on the verse sec-

tion of "Life Span" chapter (Lotus
Sutra), 302

Tokuro Moritsuna (Sennichi's son), 83

Tolstoy, Leo, 95

"transitory as a dream," viewing sufferings as, 357

tranquillity, 326

treasures of the heart, 348–49

true aspect of all phenomena, the, 21,
103–04, 109, 111, 114, 117–18,
121–24

truth, 148, 150–51, 192

two vehicles, 20, 35, 37, 48, 52, 99

"Treasure Tower" chapter (Lotus Sutra),
6, 49

understanding, providing heartfelt,
67–68

unity, 272

unity of three mystic principles, 358–59

universe, 178, 326; and Gohonzon, 184;
Nam-myoho-renge-kyo and, 184;
and self, 168; unlocking the benefits
of, 332

"unlimited [eloquence]," meaning of,
82–84, 86

unsurpassed way, advancing along the,
383

value creation, 117, 266

victory, 28, 53, 211, 213–14, 264, 363;
basis for, 85

Vimalakirti Sutra, 27

voice-hearers, 20–21, 31–35, 52, 89, 175

votary of the Lotus Sutra, actions of, 6–7

vow, lives dedicated to, 150

Whitman, Walt, 378; spirit of, 302

wisdom, 24, 28, 45, 74, 78, 171, 192, 208,
219, 246, 297–98, 313, 315, 318, 351,
363, 367–69; Nichiren Daishonin
on, 35

Words and Phrases of the Lotus Sutra, 230,
299

world peace, 137, 304, 326, 356

youth division, 249